INDUSTRIAL RELATIONS RESEARCH

ASSOCIATION SERIES

The Future of the Safety Net
Social Insurance and Employee Benefits

EDITED BY

Sheldon Friedman and David C. Jacobs

First Edition

ISBN 0–913447–81–1

INDUSTRIAL RELATIONS RESEARCH ASSOCIATION SERIES:
Proceedings of the Annual Meeting
Annual Research Volume
Membership Directory (every fourth year)
IRRA Newsletter (published quarterly)
Perspectives on Work (published biannually)

Inquiries and other communications regarding membership, meetings, publications, and general affairs of the Association, as well as notice of address changes should be addressed to the IRRA National Office.

INDUSTRIAL RELATIONS RESEARCH ASSOCIATION
University of Illinois at Urbana-Champaign
121 Labor and Industrial Relations Building,
504 E. Armory Avenue
Champaign, IL 61820 USA
Phone: 217/333-0072
Fax: 217/265-5130
Email: irra@uiuc.edu   Internet: www.irra.uiuc.edu

CONTENTS

CHAPTER 1

Introduction and Overview

SHELDON FRIEDMAN
AFL-CIO

DAVID C. JACOBS
American University

Social insurance and employee benefits are important instruments of economic security and social inclusion in the United States and other nations. They constitute the so-called safety net, which provides citizens and employees with insurance against impoverishment as a result of old age, disability, costly medical treatment, unemployment, or other conditions that limit their ability to earn income from work. Thus, the safety net insulates vulnerable or afflicted members of society or employees of an organization in the case of employee benefits against shortfalls in personal or family resources or the stigma and uncertainty of private charity. It is a mutual, reciprocal obligation that all or nearly all members of society finance when they are able and upon which certain members of society draw when eligible or in need. In a society in which the market has become the dominant mechanism for distributing income, social insurance has emerged as a vital exception to market distribution.

This Industrial Relations Research Association research volume, *The Future of the Safety Net: Social Insurance and Employee Benefits,* assembles original studies by scholars and practitioners on several important dimensions of benefits, public and private. It is by no means exhaustive, as there are many important topics, such as unemployment insurance, welfare, childcare, and long-term care, that we were unable to consider. Another important issue, workplace disability policy, is largely omitted here because it was addressed at length in another recent IRRA research volume (Thomason, Burton, and Hyatt 1998). The present volume focuses on the performance and future development of Social Security, Medicare, and selected employee benefits. As with any IRRA undertaking, this volume presents a variety of viewpoints. While the views are those of the chapter authors alone and are not always shared by the editors or our organizations, all of them deserve to be part of the public dialog and debate.

Social Insurance

The United States has evolved institutions of social insurance that are unique in the industrialized world. On the one hand, the United States remains the only major industrialized democracy without some form of national medical insurance that covers all or most of the population. More than 110 years after Germany pioneered national medical insurance under Bismarck, the United States still lacks national health insurance and spends a higher proportion of its gross domestic product on medical care than any other nation. Despite this huge and rapidly growing expenditure of resources, the United States has 42 million people who are completely uninsured and achieves mediocre results as measured by public health (World Health Organization 2000).

Yet when we've established comprehensive public safety net programs, such as Social Security, the results have been tremendously successful. Social Security provides middle quintile retirees with roughly two thirds of their total income, taking a huge burden off their adult children and enabling many millions to retire with dignity. Without Social Security, the incidence of poverty among retirees would be nearly 50%; with Social Security, retiree poverty is reduced to around 10%. Before Social Security, most workers worked until they died or ended up in poorhouses or as wards of their families if they could no longer work.

Of course, Social Security is much more than a retirement program. It also provides vital income support to disabled workers and their families and to the surviving spouses and young children of workers who die. It is a remarkably efficient program with administrative overhead of only 1%, compared with 12% to 14% for most private insurers.

Despite its popularity and success, Social Security in the last few years has come under attack as at no other time in its 65-year history. In the wealthiest nation the world has ever seen and after nearly a decade of uninterrupted economic expansion, questions have been raised about our ability to afford Social Security in the future and whether its key social insurance features should be sacrificed in favor of a privatized system of individual accounts, as President George W. Bush and others advocate. Social Security privatization has emerged as a top domestic policy priority of the Heritage Foundation and other influential think tanks of the right (Butler and Holmes 2001).

As we write this introduction, President Bush has appointed a high-level panel to consider options for the privatization of Social Security. This is an astonishing development in that among those who are widely regarded as social insurance experts, many of whom worked for or advised the Social Security Administration in years past, the consensus has long been for expanded benefits and expanded financing rather than for privatization. President Bush has looked beyond this constituency to appoint to his panel only individuals known to favor Social Security privatization.

Social Security has endured over the decades and has been expanded because of wide popular support. Critics have called it the "third rail" of American politics, complaining that it was politically untouchable. Wide majorities of the American population have accepted the notion that Social Security represents a sacred contract between the individual and society and have opposed cuts. In accord with this contract, benefits are provided as a matter of right. Voters have resisted the idea that this right is negotiable. While welfare and other means-tested programs have been ravaged by cuts, Social Security has remained largely intact.

The Chamber of Commerce, the National Association of Manufacturers, and other business lobbies opposed Social Security when it was introduced in 1935. Business critics regarded it as totalitarian because it was a robust exercise of government power, requiring contributions and redistributing income. Conservatives soon grew frustrated by its success (Jacobs 1999). Spending and benefits grew, uncontrollably, from the perspective of opponents. Conservatives began to fear that the welfare state could never be rolled back because of a "corrupt" alliance between Social Security administrators and allies in the labor movement and social welfare professions.

Critic Martha Derthick (1979:416–17) wrote:

> [The executives of the Social Security Administration] have sought to foreclose the options of future generations by committing them irrevocably to a program that promises benefits by right as well as those particular benefits that have been incorporated in an ever-expanding law. In that sense, they designed Social Security to be uncontrollable.

The large budget deficits of the Reagan years seemed to provide an opportunity for the opponents of Social Security to rein in spending. President Reagan argued that rising Social Security expenditures contributed to the deficit, even though Social Security is funded primarily by dedicated payroll taxes rather than by general revenues. Certain cuts in the program were legislated during his administration: the minimum benefit was eliminated, the age of full eligibility for old-age insurance was increased on a phased-in basis by two years to age 67, and Medicaid and disability benefits were reduced. Reagan initially proposed far deeper cuts, but he was deterred by Republican losses in the 1982 elections.

Since then, critics of Social Security have found another angle of attack to be more effective. They began to charge that the system is approaching bankruptcy, in large part because of the increasing proportion of the population who are elderly or who are otherwise beneficiaries. More recently, until the bursting of the NASDAQ bubble last year, a booming stock market led some to assert that privatization of the system is a sure route to greater return and prosperity for senior citizens. Assertions that Social Security faces a financial crisis and that individual accounts would be superior have achieved unprecedented political salience despite powerful evidence to the contrary (Baker and Weisbrot 1999).

All of these critiques have ideological foundations and are rooted in the rejection of the very concept of social insurance. First, the solvency of Social Security is not merely a function of an actuarial relationship between projected expenditures and revenues from payroll taxes. It rests ultimately on the government's ability to adjust taxes and raise revenues to sustain a widely appreciated "sacred" contract. Second, Social Security is not a vehicle for individual profit maximizing. It is a means to economic security. The security it provides (e.g., an inflation-adjusted pension for life) cannot be guaranteed by any private investment vehicle. Economist Daniel J. B. Mitchell (2000:128) notes that the pay-as-you-go nature of Social Security is "merely a government version of extended family networks in traditional societies through which the young take care of their elderly parents and relatives."

Indeed, Social Security represents that enduring element of solidarity in human institutions. The ideas of the "commons," land left fallow, national parks, and social insurance reflect the varied ways in which human societies elevate community above narrow and short-term economic interests.

Private Employer Benefits

Another unique feature of the U.S. safety net is the degree to which it relies on private, job-related coverage. Since the 1800s, employers have used fringe benefits as a means to enhance employee commitment.

"Paternalist" employers sought to build loyal communities of workers from the diverse ethnic groups who worked side by side in ever larger factories, sometimes even building company towns to house them. For example, the Pullman company town offered housing and other services to employees, but the inevitable cuts in these benefits led to the bitter Pullman strike of 1894. Company towns usually combined desirable benefits (however limited and insecure) with a system of control (Jacoby 1997).

Trade unions struggled against arbitrary employer power and to secure a more favorable array of benefits. Where unions were strong, labor and employers used collective bargaining to fashion an elaborate private welfare state from such elements as medical insurance, life insurance, and pensions (programs more commonly provided by governments in other industrialized countries). While employers tended to resist the elaboration of government programs of benefits, they were much more willing to improve their private benefit structures. Employers expected to reap commitment and performance advantages from this choice.

Unfortunately, the decline of unionization and collective bargaining coverage in the private sector, the rise of corporate strategies that rely on domestic and foreign subcontracting and contingent labor rather than a committed U.S. workforce, and the growing cost of major employee benefits including pensions and medical care, are eroding the edifice of the private welfare state. The pervasive suppression of U.S. workers' freedom of association, meticulously documented by Human Rights Watch, presently makes it unlikely that employers who deny needed benefit coverage to nonunion workers will be called to account (Human Rights Watch 2000).

These factors have led many employers, union and nonunion alike, to cut benefits and shift costs and risks to workers. The net result is that private employee benefits have been reduced at the very time that the public safety net has also come under challenge. One important but largely unexplored question is the extent to which U.S. unions will be able to convert adversity into opportunity: against a backdrop of retrenchment of the public safety net and cutbacks in private employer coverage, is there a greater role for unions in the future in providing high-quality, portable benefits for their members? More broadly, what does the future hold for social insurance and employee benefits in the 21st century? Who will, and who should, bear the economic risks of the exigencies of life, and in what proportions: workers, employers, or society (Kuttner 2001)?

Summary of the Volume

To address several key aspects of these crucial questions, we have assembled a distinguished group of contributors. Christian Weller provides a detailed comparative analysis of public and private pension systems in the United States, Japan, and five European countries. Despite substantial institutional, economic, and demographic differences among these countries, a remarkably consistent pattern emerges from the analysis.

In each of the seven advanced industrialized countries, Weller finds that the public pension system forms the bedrock of retirement income security for the nation's pensioners. The proportion of total retiree household income provided by the national public pension system ranges from a low of 58% in Italy to a high of 83% in Germany; the proportion in the United States is 67%. Absent public pensions, a large majority of retirees would fall into poverty in each of the seven countries, with the retiree poverty rate reaching as high as 92% in Sweden's case. When public pensions are factored in, the incidence of retiree poverty drops to single digits in most of the seven countries and falls below 5% in two European countries.

The heavy reliance of retirees on public pensions and the tremendous success of these programs in alleviating elderly poverty come at a price. In all but one of the seven countries, public pensions represent the largest single category of public spending on any social program. As the population ages, public pension expenditures have risen as a proportion of GDP since 1980 in each of the seven countries. Interestingly, the increase for the United States has been at the low end of the range, a mere 0.3% of GDP. Looking ahead, in each country, demographic changes will continue to boost the ratio of retirees to active workers, which raises long-term concerns about the financial viability of current public pension systems.

While numbers vary from country to country, Weller finds in all cases that rising worker productivity will likely offset much of the impact of graying populations and longer life expectancies. He concludes that the modest tax increases on tomorrow's workers that may be needed to finance public pensions would still leave those workers far better off, as measured by real after-tax income, than workers are today, given the likelihood of continued productivity improvements.

Dean Baker provides additional international and comparative perspective. He considers macroeconomic and demographic projections for

19 OECD countries and evaluates the impact on after-tax living standards of workers in 2030 that may result from the following four factors: productivity growth, wage inequality, rising health care costs, and tax increases needed to support an aging population.

Baker finds, especially for the United States, that tax increases to support an aging population are by far the smallest of the four major factors affecting future active workers' living standards. Policy changes that boost productivity growth, reduce inequality, or keep skyrocketing health care costs in check all hold far more promise for raising workers' future living standards than failing to adopt the tax increases that may be required to maintain Social Security benefits for future retirees. Even this overstates the impact of higher taxes on future active workers' living standards if one makes the reasonable assumption that inadequate Social Security benefits would trigger an increase in financial contributions by active workers to assist their aging parents.

Baker also evaluates one of the leading rationales for Social Security privatization: the notion that stock market investment returns will boost the resources generated by payroll tax revenues, thereby increasing resources available to support retirees. An aging retiree population will require a larger transfer of resources from the economically active population to retirees, whether or not Social Security is privatized. Privatization, Baker explains, does nothing to alter either the total of society's resources or their division between the economically active and retiree populations.

Valerie Rawlston and William Spriggs explore another dimension of Social Security. They document its role as a family insurance program that keeps nearly one million children under the age of 18 above the poverty line. Social Security achieves this primarily through its survivors and disability insurance provisions that bolster the incomes of several million families with minor children. These families, who have suffered the misfortune of disability or untimely death of their principal breadwinners, are disproportionately nonwhite. As a result of Social Security's family insurance features, 26% of African American and 20% of Hispanic recipients are children, as are 10% of white recipients.

Proposals to replace Social Security in whole or in part with a system of private accounts, Rawlston and Spriggs note, would destroy these family insurance aspects of the program. Low-wage workers who die or become disabled at an early age would be unable to accumulate enough in their private accounts to keep surviving family members out of poverty. The unique features of current Social Security—the progressive benefits structure, protection against inflation through indexation of benefits, and the lifetime benefits guarantee—would all be lost under a privatized system. It is therefore meaningless, Rawlston and Spriggs conclude, to compare returns on investment of current Social Security with those of a hypothetical system of private accounts. Given their vulnerability to life's major misfortunes of disability and premature death, African Americans and other minorities have an especially heavy stake in the current debate about the future of Social Security.

Peter Diamond's contribution to the volume is a thoughtful and provocative essay about the design of public retirement income security systems. His chapter focuses on crucial questions such as whether social security systems should be defined benefit (DB) or defined contribution (DC), should be prefunded or pay-as-you-go, or should feature collective investment versus individual accounts. He also addresses transition issues that arise when social security systems are redesigned or newly introduced.

While noting that DB systems generally have lower administrative costs and impose less risk on individual workers than DC systems, Diamond believes that the choice between DC and DB can matter less than whether the overall system is designed well or poorly. Key features of the DB Social Security system in the United States include low administrative costs, inflation protection, lifetime guarantee of benefits, and implicit redistribution of benefits from higher-wage to lower-wage workers.

Diamond asserts that with the exception of low administrative costs, DC systems could in theory be designed to accomplish these positive objectives. He acknowledges, however, that no real-world examples of DC systems with these desirable attributes presently exist. Moreover, administrative costs are no small matter. As Diamond notes, the cumulative impact of annual charges will typically trim DC account balances by about 30% by the end of a 40-year working career. Even worse, absent strict regulation, owners of individual DC accounts may fall victim to misrepresentation, fraud, and other abuse, which Diamond reminds us has been the sad experience in the United Kingdom.

Diamond closes with suggestions for Social Security reform in the United States, most notably the need to increase benefits for elderly widows. This change, he argues, would lower the high poverty rate for elderly widows, which is far above the rate for elderly married couples.

Dallas Salisbury provides an extensive overview of private pensions. He describes the Employee Retirement Income Security Act (ERISA), which was passed in response to widespread concerns about the loss of pension benefits when an employer goes bankrupt, as happened to thousands of Studebaker workers and retirees. Salisbury traces the history of private pensions in North America all the way back to 1636. He notes, however, that rapid growth in pension coverage beyond top executives began in the late 1940s, as a result of collective bargaining.

Salisbury documents and explains the shift in more recent years away from defined-benefit pension plans toward defined-contribution plans, a trend he regards as inexorable. In DB plans, workers and in most cases their surviving spouses are guaranteed a lifetime benefit, and plan sponsors bear investment risks. In DC plans, investment risks are shifted to workers, and lifetime benefits are not guaranteed. The risks borne by workers would, of course, be magnified if proposals supported by President Bush and others to privatize Social Security are adopted.

Even more significant than the shift from DB to DC plans is the fact that many U.S. workers are not covered by pension plans of any kind on their jobs, and few who are covered receive adequate benefits. Given the modest level of Social Security benefits, inadequate private pension coverage and benefits are serious national problems that can only get worse as the population ages. To address these problems, Salisbury proposes a major campaign to educate the public about the importance of personal saving for retirement. Whether savings education can offset declines in DB pension coverage and benefits from levels that were inadequate to begin with is a major question.

Teresa Ghilarducci examines retirement income security for women. Three fourths of the elderly poor are women, who experience poverty at twice the rate of older men. Ghilarducci analyzes the factors contributing to the high poverty rate of older women and proposes solutions.

Although the gender gap in pension coverage has been closing slightly in recent years, Ghilarducci finds that the main reason is declining coverage for men rather than rising coverage for women. Even when women are covered by a pension plan at their place of employment, they are less likely to participate in it than men. When they do participate, their pension benefit is likely to be smaller; women's private pension benefits average just $3,000 per year, only half as large as men's.

The switch from DB to contributory DC plans is worsening the pension situation for women. With lower earnings than men, women generally cannot afford to contribute as much as men do to their DC plans.

One important factor that could close the gender pension gap, Ghilarducci finds, is unionization. Unions tend to equalize pension benefits between women and men, and a higher proportion of collectively bargained pensions are DB plans that do not depend on worker contributions to finance benefits.

Not surprisingly, given the inadequacy of their private pensions, older women are especially dependent on Social Security for their retirement income. Social Security provides a far higher percentage of older unmarried women's total income than of older married couples'.

Ghilarducci closes with several important policy recommendations to alleviate elderly women's poverty and close the retirement income security gender gap.

David Jacobs introduces the issue of medical benefits with an assessment of the prospects for national health insurance (NHI) in the United States. Well over a century after its introduction in Germany, the United States remains today the only major industrialized nation without NHI. Jacobs analyzes the historical reasons for American exceptionalism in this regard, tracing the positions of labor, business, the insurance industry, and the medical profession.

Despite the compelling case for NHI on public health and economic grounds and strong public support for it, Jacobs shows how elements of the business community and the insurance industry have been able to thwart this urgently needed social reform for more than 65 years. As a result, the United States devotes a far higher proportion of GDP to health care expenditures than any other country, yet achieves only mediocre outcomes as measured by major public health indicators such as life expectancy and infant mortality. Meanwhile, the number of Americans with no medical insurance of any kind has reached 42 million, and many who nominally have insurance face serious and growing gaps in their coverage.

The last major attempt at reform was the Clinton health plan of 1994, the failure of which Jacobs analyzes. At this writing, the proposals of George W. Bush's administration for addressing the nation's medical care crisis have not yet been revealed but will likely focus on a program of tax credits along lines advocated by the Heritage Foundation and other conservative think tanks (Butler and Holmes 2001). Even under the most optimistic of assumptions, it is difficult to see how tax credits could avoid leaving millions of Americans un- or underinsured. Nor would tax credits reap the huge administrative cost savings that could be achieved under NHI.

Edith Rasell addresses the past, present, and future of the Medicare program. Medicare, established in 1965, provides health insurance to 39 million beneficiaries. Most beneficiaries are older Americans age 65 and up, but five million of them are disabled persons under 65. The program is one of the nation's largest and most important, accounting for 12% of the federal budget.

Skyrocketing costs led to a focus on cost containment within Medicare starting in the 1980s. Rasell notes that this effort has been relatively successful. The program is run quite efficiently, with overhead and administrative expenses below 2% of benefit payments, far lower than the 12% to 14% that is typical for private insurers.

Much attention has been paid recently to the fact that Medicare lacks a prescription drug benefit, but as Rasell makes clear, the Medicare benefit package should be improved in other ways as well. As the proportion of firms offering supplemental health benefits to retirees continues to decline, Medicare increasingly has become the sole or main source of coverage for older Americans.

Despite the enormous demands on Medicare, Rasell finds that the financial outlook for the program is much less dire than is commonly supposed. As with Social Security, the Medicare trustees base their long-term forecasts on extremely pessimistic economic assumptions. Furthermore, the 75-year Medicare forecasts that current law requires are subject to such a wide margin of error as to be of dubious policy-making value.

Rasell cogently evaluates proposals to "voucherize" Medicare, as advocated by think tanks such as the Heritage Foundation and supported by the Bush administration (Butler and Holmes 2001). She also examines proposals to cut costs by raising the age of Medicare eligibility. She offers several alternative means to improve Medicare and strengthen its financing in the years ahead.

Helene Jorgensen and Robert McGarrah address the important topic of access by temporary and other nonstandard workers to job-related benefits, especially medical insurance and pensions. Nonstandard work arrangements such as temporary and leased employees and independent contractors have grown by leaps and bounds, far outstripping the growth in traditional employment since the 1970s. According to Jorgensen and McGarrah, the number of temp jobs alone has doubled to 3.5 million just since 1993. Such jobs symbolize for many the rising insecurity that is a defining feature of the new economy. Indeed, nonstandard work arrangements constituted the entire focus of last year's IRRA research volume (Carré et al. 2000).

Jorgensen and McGarrah cite survey evidence that one important reason prompting employers to substitute nonstandard for traditional work arrangements is employers' desire to reduce costs for employee medical insurance and pensions. Not surprisingly, therefore, temporary agency employees rarely receive medical insurance or pension coverage through their jobs. Less than 9% of temps receive medical insurance through their jobs, versus 58% of workers in regular jobs. Nor is this gap in coverage made up from other sources, such as a spouse's coverage or the purchase of individual insurance. A shocking three fifths of temps are without medical insurance from any source, compared with 17% of workers in regular jobs.

The disparity in pension coverage is similar. Fewer than 6% of temps have pension coverage through their jobs, compared with almost half of workers in regular jobs. More than four fifths of temps are without pension coverage from any source, versus 46% of workers in regular jobs.

Clearly, as employers have shifted jobs from standard to nonstandard, the private safety net has frayed, causing growing numbers of workers to fall between the cracks without medical insurance or pension coverage. The trend toward nonstandard employment poses a serious challenge to the future of the safety net. This challenge must be met through public policy, collective bargaining, and socially responsible business practice in the years ahead.

The volume ends with a chapter by Nancy Sedmak on job-related benefits for same-sex partners. Gay and lesbian workers are confronted with a Catch-22 when it comes to job-related benefits: in the United States, they are prohibited by law from marrying domestic partners with whom they share a committed, long-term relationship, but their partners are denied eligibility for health insurance, pension, and other benefit coverage because they are not married. Sedmak contends that this widespread practice is a serious form of workplace discrimination against gays and lesbians and is a violation of the basic principle of equal compensation for equal work.

As larger numbers of gays and lesbians have come out of the closet and become more assertive and organized in defense of their rights, access to job-related benefits for same-sex partners has emerged as an important employment policy and collective bargaining issue. Sedmak traces the history and evolution of benefits for same-sex partners, starting with the 1982 collective bargaining agreement between the UAW and *The Village Voice*. As a result of that pioneering agreement, *The Village Voice* became the first U.S. employer to cover domestic partners of its gay and lesbian workers under the company's medical insurance plan.

Today, access to same-sex domestic partner benefits is more common but still not widespread. In some cases, employers adopting such policies have found themselves the targets of a gay-bashing backlash. As Sedmak explains, there remains a large unfinished agenda with regard to the fundamental human rights issue of equal access to job-related benefits for gay and lesbian workers.

Conclusion

The future of social insurance and employee benefits hinges on a set of fundamental questions about the relationship of the citizen to society and among the employee, his or her union, and the employer. The trends that emerge will reveal a great deal about the state of the social contract among the economic actors in the United States and other nations. It remains to be seen whether Social Security will be defended successfully as an important bulwark against economic insecurity and whether new challenges for the safety net, such as the need for national health insurance and improved childcare and long-term care, will be met. Also to be determined are whether private benefits will reflect the new concerns and enduring interests of employees and whether unions and collective bargaining will be able (or, indeed, allowed) to fill widening gaps in workers' economic security against a backdrop of increasingly challenged public and private safety nets. The editors hope that this research volume will provide grist for the public debate and illuminate some of the key choices we face.

References

Baker, Dean, and Mark Weisbrot. 1999. *Social Security: The Phony Crisis.* Chicago: University of Chicago Press.

Butler, Stuart M., and Kim R. Holmes, eds. 2001. *Priorities for the President.* Washington, DC: Heritage Foundation.

Carré, Françoise, Marianne A. Ferber, Lonnie Golden, and Stephen A. Herzenberg, eds. 2000. *Nonstandard Work: The Nature and Challenges of Changing Employment Arrangements.* Champaign, IL: Industrial Relations Research Association.

Derthick, Martha. 1979. *Policy-Making for Social Security.* Washington, DC: Brookings Institution.

Human Rights Watch. 2000. *Unfair Advantage: Workers' Freedom of Association in the United States under International Human Rights Standards.* Washington, DC: Human Rights Watch. <http://www.hrw.org/reports/2000/uslabor/>.

Jacobs, David. 1999. *Business Lobbies and the Power Structure in America.* Westport, CT: Quorum Books.

Jacoby, Sanford. 1997. *Modern Manors: Welfare Capitalism Since the New Deal.* Princeton, NJ: Princeton University Press.

Kuttner, Robert. 2001. "Pensions: How Much Risk Should Workers Have to Bear?" *Business Week*, April 16, p. 23.

Mitchell, Daniel J. B. 2000. "The Retirement of the Baby Boomers: Will They Get Their Ham and Eggs?" *WorkingUSA*, Vol. 4, pp. 112–32.

Thomason, Terry, John F. Burton, Jr., and Douglas E. Hyatt, eds. 1998. *New Approaches to Disability in the Workplace*. Madison, WI: Industrial Relations Research Association.

World Health Organization. 2000. *World Health Report 2000, Health Systems: Improving Performance*. <http://www.who.int/whr/2000/en/report.htm>.

Chapter 2

Programs without Alternative: Public Pensions in the OECD

Christian E. Weller
Economic Policy Institute

Introduction

Life expectancies in industrialized economies have grown, and birth rates have fallen. The number of those who pay for public pensions is shrinking, while the number of beneficiaries is growing, which supposedly puts public pensions in crisis. The question thus is whether we can still afford to pay for public pension programs in industrialized countries.

Most industrialized countries introduced public pensions to avert old-age poverty. Because lifetime earnings and savings are unpredictable, public pensions offer retirees a guarantee of sufficient income for life out of poverty. Without Social Security in the United States, an additional 39% of Americans over 65 would have lived in poverty in 1998.

Even though countries are still committed to providing public support for workers to reduce old-age poverty, this promise seems to have hit a stumbling block. The argument is that because of demographic changes—more old people and fewer young people—governments have to scale back their promises of public pensions or raise taxes to unrealistic levels.

The impediments to paying for public pensions, however, are caused more by political decisions than by economic realities in seven Organisation for Economic Co-operation and Development (OECD) countries. By and large, public pensions may encounter a willingness-to-pay crisis but not an ability-to-pay crisis.

Expenditures for old-age income programs are already the largest social expenditure. In most cases, expenditures can be expected to increase with the aging of each country's population. However, whether growing expenditures can still be financed depends on the expected economic trends, on the structure of each country's public pension system, and on the willingness of policy makers to increase revenues for public pensions if needed.

The growing financial needs of public pensions, mirrored in rising tax rates, are attributable to economic changes and to the structure of public pension systems. Slow or declining employment growth, low productivity and wage growth, and increasing income inequality have resulted in increasing demands on workers to finance public pensions.

As far as the future is concerned, most projections are overly pessimistic in their economic assumptions. Yet even with pessimistic assumptions, tax rates may decline and living standards may increase over the next decades. If better-than-expected economic trends materialize, each country's ability to pay for public pensions should also grow.

Because of a growing sense of crisis regarding the future of public pensions, though, more attention has been focused on private-market investments as a substitute for public pensions. But opponents of privatization point to its higher risks and costs, which make private pensions a poor substitute for public pensions. However, because people's life expectancies are increasing, long-term financial needs are likely to increase, too. Some of these additional needs may not be met by public pensions. Hence, private pensions may serve as a supplement to public pensions.

Background

The Antipoverty Success of Public Pensions

Public pensions are designed to keep most, if not all, of the elderly out of poverty. The evidence suggests that public pensions are an important income source for pensioners (Hauser 1998). Public pensions in 1989 ranged from 58% of total gross household income in Italy to 83% in West Germany. Also, pensions provided more than two thirds of gross household income in France (81%) in 1989, in the United Kingdom (68%) in 1991, and in the United States (67%) in 1991.[1]

Consequently, old-age poverty is significantly reduced through government transfers, mainly in the form of pensions (Smeeding 1997). Germany and Sweden have high market-income poverty rates, 65.8% in 1989 and 91.6% in 1992, respectively. Thanks largely to public pensions, the German rates dropped to 7.5%, and the Swedish to 6.4%. Similarly, in France and Italy, old-age poverty is reduced through a variety of programs, of which public pensions are the largest. In France, old-age poverty declined from 79.9% in 1984 to 4.8%, and in Italy from 55.7% to 4.4%. Finally, in the United Kingdom and the United States, public pensions are also an important tool to lower old-age poverty. Due to low benefit levels, the reductions were from 68.5% to 23.9% in the United Kingdom in 1991 and from 58.7% to 19.6% in the United States in 1994 (Smeeding 1997).[2]

Using different poverty thresholds for the United States, the success of public pensions shows the same order of magnitude. According to the Social Security Administration (SSA 2000b), public pensions lowered old-age poverty by 39% to 10.4% of pensioner households in 1998.

Crisis? What Crisis?

Public pension expenditures are the largest social expenditure in six of the seven OECD countries—with Japan, where medical expenses are slightly larger, as the exception.

The fact that public pension expenditures relative to GDP have grown between 1980 and 1995 seems important for the growing sense that there is a public pension crisis in OECD countries (table 1). The smallest increases appear in Germany (+0.3%) and in the United States (+0.3%). In comparison, the increases are most pronounced in Japan (+2.0%), France (+2.6%), and Italy (+3.6%), leaving Sweden (+1.3%) and the United Kingdom (+1.4%) with more moderate changes.

TABLE 1
Old-Age Cash Benefits as Share of GDP

	France	Germany	Italy	Japan	Sweden	U.K.	U.S.
1980	7.79	9.99	7.36	3.50	6.83	5.07	5.05
1985	8.81	10.11	9.04	4.29	7.35	5.57	5.21
1990	9.32	9.52	9.63	4.42	7.50	6.37	5.05
1995	10.36	10.29	10.99	5.49	8.17	6.46	5.36

Notes: All figures are percentages. Old-age cash benefits include old-age pensions, old-age civil servant pensions, old-age veteran's pensions, early retirement pensions, and other old-age cash benefits.
Source: OECD Social Expenditure Database (SOCX).

Even where expenditures have increased, expenditures relative to GDP are still manageable. France and Italy surpassed Germany in their spending on old-age cash assistance only in the 1990s. By 1995, Italy's expenditures were 0.7% higher than Germany's, and France's were

0.07% larger than Germany's. Furthermore, if Japan's expenditures relative to GDP continue to grow at the same rate as they had between 1980 and 1995, it would take more than 30 years for them to exceed 10% of GDP. Incidentally, this is the level that was sustained by Germany between 1980 and 1995. The expenditure levels do not leave the impression that public pensions are in a state of crisis.

The tax burden for workers, not expenditures, seems to be more at the heart of the asserted public pension crisis, however. Most funding for public pensions stems from payroll taxes, with some additional support from general revenues.

Table 2 provides data on tax rates in the seven OECD countries since 1961. Tax rates have continuously increased only in the United States, which is also one of the two countries where expenditures relative to GDP have been relatively stable. In France and Italy, tax rates have increased since the 1970s. However, while the largest increases in French tax rates occurred in the 1970s, the largest jumps in Italian tax rates came in the 1990s. Furthermore, Swedish tax rates increased sharply in the 1960s but declined in the 1970s and again in the 1990s after remaining stable in the 1980s. Also, Japanese tax rates dropped slightly in the 1980s before increasing again in the 1990s. Finally, British tax rates increased sharply in the 1970s before declining in the 1980s and increasing in the 1990s.

TABLE 2
Combined Tax Rates as Share of Average Wage, 1961–1999

	France	Germany	Italy	Japan	Sweden	U.K	U.S.
1961	19.50	19.05	21.10	N/A	17.67	N/A	6.00
1971	8.75	20.00	19.00	N/A	25.55	N/A	9.20
1981	13.00	21.51	24.31	13.74	22.62	26.16	10.70
1991	15.02	20.73	26.28	15.32	22.85	13.92	12.40
1999	16.45	24.38	32.70	18.72	19.56	17.41	12.40
Average annual rate of change							
1961–99	−0.08	0.14	0.31	N/A	0.05	N/A	0.17
1961–69	−1.28	0.34	−0.75	N/A	0.74	N/A	0.14
1969–79	0.43	0.14	0.46	N/A	−0.08	2.45	0.10
1979–89	0.29	0.05	0.09	−0.08	0.00	−1.07	0.14
1989–99	0.14	0.36	0.64	0.34	−0.33	0.35	0.00

Notes: All figures are percentages. All combined tax rates are based on author's own calculations based on SSA, *Social Security Programs throughout the World*, various years. See the appendix for assumptions made in calculations.

However, the tax rate increases in five countries in the 1990s hardly support the argument that public pensions are already in a crisis. First, in France, combined tax rates in 1999 are still below their 1961 levels.

Similarly, the combined British tax rates in 1999 were only 0.37 percentage points higher than the ones in 1975. Moreover, average tax increases in France in the 1990s were the smallest ever. Also, American rates have remained flat in the 1990s, and Swedish rates have declined over the course of the 1990s. Finally, German tax rates have increased, despite the fact that expenditures have remained stable. Thus, only two out of seven countries, Italy and Japan, have both rapid tax increases and rising expenditure levels.

For the outlook on public pension finances, forecasts of economic trends become crucial. The crisis scenario is often predicated on the notion that life expectancies increase, fertility rates decline, and the demographic slowdown leads to less economic growth.[3]

Table 3 shows the relevant demographic forecasts. The share of people 65 years old and over relative to the total population is expected to increase dramatically. By 2000, the share of the elderly is expected to be somewhere between 13% (United States) and 18% (Italy) and is expected to increase to between 20% (United States) and 36% (Italy) by 2050.

TABLE 3

65-Year-Olds as Share of Total Population, 1990–2050

	France	Germany	Italy	Japan	Sweden	U.K.	U.S.
1990	14.02	—	—	11.96	17.79	—	12.50
2000	16.00	16.25	18.09	17.01	17.29	15.67	12.64
2010	16.79	19.70	20.55	21.76	19.18	16.69	13.23
2020	20.61	21.41	23.55	26.83	22.69	19.59	16.52
2030	23.98	25.75	28.15	28.31	25.08	23.50	20.02
2040	26.45	28.43	34.24	31.85	27.11	26.35	20.44
2050	27.25	28.55	36.10	33.86	27.23	26.83	20.30

Note: All figures are percentages.
Source: U.S. Bureau of the Census International Database.

While the share of the elderly is projected to rise dramatically, these forecasts are rather meaningless. What matters to future generations is their standard of living, which depends only partially on the number of retirees they have to support. Gains in labor productivity make it easier for future workers to support more retirees. Also, unemployment may decline and employment may grow, making it even easier for all workers to support all the elderly.

The OECD's estimates also highlight some of the problems with long-range forecasts. Most forecasts are sensitive to the underlying assumptions, especially with respect to labor force participation and productivity growth. Labor force participation often receives only scant attention despite its importance in determining future projections (Turner et al. 1998; Herbertsson, Orszag, and Orszag 2000). Without any changes in labor force participation rates, GNP per capita will be 95% higher in the EU in 2050 than in 1995 (Turner et al. 1998). Allowing for higher labor force participation and lower unemployment, GDP per capita could be 138% higher than in 1995. In the OECD's calculation, changes in labor force participation have a greater impact on living standards in the EU than any other change. Furthermore, productivity growth is one of the most important determinants of future living standards (Baker, this volume). But, the OECD study does not even consider the impact of faster-rising productivity. Instead, historically low levels of productivity growth, 1.4%, are extrapolated over 50 years. Historically, productivity growth has never been this low for extended periods of time (see table 6).

Other model calculations that focus on tax rates rely on pessimistic economic assumptions, too. Sinn (1999) argued that German tax rates will rise from 20% to over 30% by 2030. Also, Prognos AG (1998) estimated that German tax rates will increase merely to 24% by 2040, but it put a significantly higher burden on general revenues, thereby increasing the overall tax burden (Sinn and Thum 1999). Both studies assume constant or low labor force participation rates of the working-age population and constantly high or even increasing unemployment rates (Sinn and Thum 1999). Both model calculations also assume low productivity and wage growth.

Forecasts of rising tax rates and lower than otherwise expected living standards are based on overly pessimistic assumptions. Furthermore, even where tax rates are expected to increase, living standards, as measured by after-tax wages, are still projected to rise (Baker, this volume).

Economic and Demographic Factors Influencing Public Pensions in Theory

The following schematic discussion may be helpful to understand how economic factors could affect public pension finances. In general, public pension finances can be affected by employment and productivity growth and by changes in income distribution. Declining employment and lower wages both result in a smaller tax base. Furthermore, a redistribution of income from labor to capital shrinks the tax base because wages are not rising as fast as productivity, and a rise in income inequality raises benefit payments disproportionately because public pensions are income insurance programs designed to keep people out of poverty.

Public pensions receive income either from payroll taxes or from general revenues. Generally speaking, public pension income is the product of the tax rate and covered income. The tax rate is the combined tax rate levied on employers and employees and the implicit tax rate charged to general revenue. Covered income is the sum of all covered incomes:

$$\text{Contribution}_T = t_T Y(N_T, \Sigma\, y_{wT}) \tag{1}$$

where t_T is the combined tax rate in period T, Y is total covered income, N_T is the number of covered employees in period T, and y_{wT} is an individual worker's income in period T.

Increasing financial needs can arise as contributions decline relative to benefit payments. The share of the population that contributes to public pensions declines or grows more slowly than the number of beneficiaries because of lower employment growth or higher unemployment. Furthermore, covered income either declines or grows more slowly than the benefits because real wages decline or grow at a slower pace. Slower wage growth may be the result of sluggish productivity growth, a redistribution of income toward profits, or both. Also, where countries have implemented a cap on income above which taxes are not applicable, greater income inequality means that an increasing amount of total income lies above the cap, leaving a smaller taxable base. Finally, tax rates can be lowered by legislative act to reduce the revenue stream to public pensions.

Greater financing needs can also arise from faster growth of benefits (relative to contributions). Benefits are a function of eligibility criteria, individual earnings histories, indexation of past earnings and benefits, a redistributive factor, and a demographic factor:

$$\text{Benefits}_T(N_{BT}) = \Sigma\, b_{iT} \tag{2}$$

$$b_{iT} = \rho \delta \gamma I_{BT} [EI_w w_{BT} / \text{Time(NRA, pensionable earnings years)}] \tag{3}$$

Total benefits payable in period T are the sum of all individual benefits, b_{iT}, over all beneficiaries in period T, N_{BT}. Individual benefits are determined by individual earnings histories indexed by earnings indexation factor, I_B, and divided by the number of eligible years, which is again a function of the normal retirement age, NRA, and the number of years of pensionable earnings an individual has had. The average wage is then multiplied by a replacement rate, ρ, by a redistributive factor, δ, by a demographic factor, γ, and by a benefits indexation factor, I_{BT}.

Benefit increases result both from economic and demographic factors. Since public pensions are an insurance against old-age poverty, they redistribute income toward lower lifetime earners. If the number of low lifetime earners rises, benefits grow disproportionately. Also, to maintain relative benefit levels, benefits are indexed to inflation, wages, productivity, or GDP growth. Faster growth of any of these factors leads to higher benefit payments. Finally, if benefit payments are not adjusted to demographic changes, the fact that people live longer should raise the total amount of benefits. Greater life expectancy is an automatic benefit increase.

Changes in the benefits formula can result in growing financial needs. For instance, the number of beneficiaries may increase as more categories of people become eligible or as the retirement age is lowered. Furthermore, indexation and redistribution factors can be changed to make the system more generous.

Economic and Demographic Changes in Reality

In theory, a number of economic factors can affect the financing needs of public pensions. To see which factors could have had an impact on public pension finances in the OECD, I present evidence on employment, productivity and wage growth, and inequality.

Employment. Table 3 showed the rising share of those over 65 years old. This graying of the population is due to low birth rates and improving life expectancies. From 1992 to 1997, population growth was below that of the early 1970s. In particular, fertility rates—births per woman— declined everywhere from the 1970s to the 1990s (table 4), with the largest drop in Japan. Also, life expectancies have increased by six years in France, Germany, Italy, and Japan; by five years in Sweden; by four years in the United Kingdom; and by three years in the United States.

Demographic changes, though, only set the limits for employment growth. If employment declines, those who bear the financial burden for public pensions may face greater demands. Employment relative to the working-age population has declined steadily since the 1960s in France and Italy and dropped sharply in Sweden from the 1980s to the 1990s (table 5). In comparison, employment relative to the working-age population has grown in the United States since the 1960s, in Japan since the 1970s, and in the United Kingdom and Germany since the 1980s.

TABLE 4
Population Growth, Fertility Rates, and Life Expectancy for OECD Countries

	Population growth			Fertility rate			Life expectancy		
	1970–75	1980–85	1992–97	1970–75	1980–85	1992–97	1970–75	1980–85	1992–97
France	0.4	0.5	0.4	1.9	1.8	1.7	72	75	78
Germany	0.2	–0.2	0.2	1.5	1.4	1.4	71	73	77
Italy	0.6	0.1	0.2	2.2	1.4	1.2	72	75	78
Sweden	0.4	0.1	0.3	1.8	1.7	1.7	75	76	79
U.K.	0.2	0.1	0.3	1.8	1.8	1.7	72	74	77
Japan	1.4	0.7	0.2	1.9	1.8	1.4	74	78	80
U.S.	1.0	0.9	0.8	1.8	1.8	2.0	73	75	76

Notes: Population growth and fertility rates are percentages; life expectancy is in years.
Source: World Bank Poverty Monitoring Database.

TABLE 5
Employment as Share of Total Population and as Share of Population between 15 and 64, 1960–2000

	France	Germany	Italy	Japan	Sweden	U.K.	U.S.
Average employment as share of total population							
1960–1999	40.07	44.22	36.50	48.83	48.61	45.05	42.43
1960–1973	41.02	44.74	37.30	48.34	47.74	45.68	37.43
1973–1979	40.96	42.56	35.91	46.96	49.61	44.66	41.65
1979–1999	39.38	44.26	35.95	49.79	48.90	44.63	46.21
Average employment as share of working age population (15 to 64 years)							
1960–1999	62.52	66.21	55.33	71.62	75.12	70.00	66.10
1960–1973	65.85	68.99	57.86	71.26	72.52	71.59	61.38
1973–1979	65.14	65.85	55.98	69.53	77.44	70.83	64.00
1979–1999	60.24	64.36	53.12	72.40	76.22	68.57	70.06

Notes: All figures are percentages.
Sources: OECD Economic Outlook, various years, and the U.S. Bureau of the Census International Database.

Also, employment levels vary across countries. Japan, Sweden, and the United States all had ratios of average employment to working-age population above 70% in the 1990s. In comparison, the United Kingdom had slightly less than 70%, Germany 65%, France below 60%, and Italy 52%.

The divergence in employment rates suggests that the low levels observed in some countries toward the end of the 1990s could possibly improve again—contrary to what is often assumed in projections for public pension systems (Turner et al. 1998; Sinn 1999; SSA 2000a). First, employment levels are low by historical standards in France,

Germany, and Italy. In countries where employment levels were high, such as the United States, the United Kingdom, and Japan, they nevertheless continued to grow. Once high employment levels are reached, they may remain high, as they did in Sweden (table 5). Thus, Italy's employment could increase by 30 percentage points relative to the working-age population and France's and Germany's by about 20 percentage points before reaching 80%, which was the highest level in any country over the past 40 years.

Growing employment could also result from declining unemployment, from rising female labor force participation rates, or from fewer early retirees. In 1998, German women had an employment rate of 54%, whereas men had an employment rate of 69%. In France, the employment rate for women was 54% and for men 68%; in Italy, 37% for women and 68% for men; in the United Kingdom, 64% for women and 79% for men; and in Sweden, 67% for women and 73% for men (European Commission 1999).

Low labor force participation rates may be a result of a broadened application of early retirement options. Occasionally, public pensions have substituted for unemployment benefits (Herbertsson et al. 2000; Sinn 1999; Blanchet and Pelé 1997). For the EU as a whole, early retirement may have meant a loss in potential output of more than 10%. In the United States, 19.8 million out of 27.5 million retirees received reduced retirement benefits because they chose early retirement (SSA 1999). Also, in Germany, about 2.3 million out of 5.9 million retirees received retirement pensions outside the regular schedule. German women, for example, are entitled to full retirement benefits at age 60, while the normal retirement age for men is 65. Furthermore, long-term unemployed workers have the option to retire early (Bundesversicherungsanstalt fuer Angestellte [BfA] 2000). Under the Italian system, workers can retire before the normal retirement age with full benefits after 35 years of service. Thus, early retirement is widespread, despite low expenditures on separate programs (Brugiavini 1997).

Productivity. Faster increases in productivity should ease the burden of paying for the elderly. A future dependency ratio the same as today's may put less demand on current income if productivity and wages have grown faster than overall benefits.

There is little evidence to suggest that productivity growth will remain at low levels for extended periods. Between 1979 and 1999, productivity growth in Germany, Italy, Japan, and Sweden was lower than during the period from 1973 to 1979, but it accelerated in France, the United Kingdom, and the United States at the same time. Thus, no clear long-term trends toward lower productivity growth are emerging in the OECD, and there is no evidence that countries will suffer low productivity growth rates for extended periods as has been assumed in some projections for future public pension finances (Turner et al. 1998; SSA 2000a).

In the long run, wage growth should equal productivity growth. Wage growth has slowed in the past 20 years from its previous levels everywhere, except in the United States, where wages have recovered some ground lost in the late 1970s. Also, in most countries, wage growth has been below productivity growth. Thus, there has been a gradual shift in national income from labor to capital. Slower wage growth and a shift from labor income to capital income reduced the size of the tax base relative to GDP and relative to promised benefits.

Inequality. Rising or falling earnings inequality matters for public pension finances. In particular, most systems redistribute funds to ensure that low lifetime earners receive an income that is close to or above the national poverty threshold.

Technically, rising inequality should lead to growing demands for financing of public pensions if benefits are related to average earnings or if taxable earnings are capped. Benefits are generally directly connected to a worker's earnings history. In addition, individual earnings histories are often set in relation to average earnings. If earnings inequality increases, either the number of people or their aggregate earnings below the average will fall. An indexation of benefits to average earnings would thus result in an increase in benefits that is disproportionate to contributions. On the contribution side, earnings above a certain level are often not subject to public pension taxes. Higher earnings inequality may also mean that a growing share of aggregate earnings comes to lie above the earnings cap, thereby reducing contributions. In either case, the financing demands on those who are contributing to public pensions grow.[4]

Both earnings and income inequality appear to have grown in the 1980s and 1990s in most of the seven OECD countries. For instance, Gottschalk and Smeeding (1997:636) found that "[a]lmost all industrial economies experienced some increase in wage inequality among prime aged males." They also found that inequality grew fastest in the United Kingdom and in the United States and the least in the Nordic countries.

Other studies support some of these findings. The exceptions with respect to earnings inequality appear to be Germany and possibly Italy. In comparison, the exception with respect to rising income inequality appears to be France in the 1990s.[5] Elsewhere, both earnings and income inequality appear to have grown.

In general, earnings inequality will be the more relevant aspect to consider since most contributions come in the form of payroll taxes and most benefits are related to earnings histories. Whether and how much inequality can adversely affect public pension finances depends on the exact benefit formula of each country's pension system.

Earnings inequality in France appears to have increased in the 1980s. For the years between 1976 and 1987, several studies suggest rising earnings inequality (Katz, Loveman, and Blanchflower 1995).

There also appears to be little evidence of growing earnings inequality in Germany in the 1980s. Wage inequality was found to remain stable throughout the 1980s (Freeman and Katz 1995). Also, earnings inequality stayed the same in Germany in the 1980s (Abraham and Houseman 1995; Katz, Loveman, and Blanchflower 1995).

The evidence for Italy on earnings inequality appears to be mixed. Freeman and Katz (1995) reported signs of expanding wage differentials by occupation and education in the late 1980s in Italy. In comparison, others have found that earnings inequality remained the same for Italy in the 1980s (Abraham and Houseman 1995; Katz, Loveman, and Blanchflower 1995).

Japan's earnings inequality appears to have grown, too. According to one study, Japanese earnings inequality grew between 1974 and 1990 (Katz, Loveman, and Blanchflower 1995).

Sweden is yet another country with rising earnings inequality. Earnings inequality seems to have grown in Sweden in the 1980s, with the stronger growth of inequality in the second half of the 1980s than before (Edin and Holmlund 1995).

The United Kingdom appears to be the European country with the fastest-growing earnings inequality. Wage inequality rose at double-digit rates in the United Kingdom between 1979 and 1990 (Freeman and Katz 1995; Katz, Loveman, and Blanchflower 1995).

Finally, the United States appears to be another country where earnings inequality grew sharply. According to Freeman and Katz (1995), wage inequality in the United States rose at double-digit rates—similar to the United Kingdom—between 1979 and 1990.

Predicting the Future

While demographic and economic changes can affect the finances of public pension systems, future trends may not warrant dire scenarios for public pension finances.

The idea that public pensions will incur a crisis depends largely on demographic projections that are often superimposed on recent adverse economic trends. For instance, Turner et al. (1998) assumed no improvements in employment shares and continuously low productivity growth for the United States, Japan, and the EU. Similarly, U.S. Social Security's trustees continue to forecast productivity growth rates at 1.5% annually and real wage growth at 1% each year. Given historical and international experiences, these figures appear unduly pessimistic (table 6).

TABLE 6
Productivity and Wage Growth Rates, 1960–1999

	France	Germany	Italy	Japan	Sweden	U.K.	U.S.
Productivity growth rates
1960–1999	2.36	2.31	2.99	3.92	2.16	2.13	1.54
1960–1973	2.24	7.67	3.97	4.25	5.37	3.08	3.48
1973–1979	0.29	2.73	2.65	2.35	2.34	1.24	0.53
1979–1999	1.36	1.88	1.01	1.64	1.62	1.74	1.81
Wage rate growth (in business sector)
1960–1999	1.42	2.20	2.82	2.32	1.70	1.86	0.53
1960–1973	N/A	5.11	6.11	8.08	N/A	3.58	1.48
1973–1979	2.73	2.25	4.26	1.65	N/A	0.99	−1.13
1979–1999	0.61	0.40	0.38	0.50	1.79	1.87	0.43

Notes: All figures are percentages. Hourly earnings for Germany are from 1963, for the United Kingdom from 1964, for Italy and France from 1969, and for Sweden from 1971. Wage rates are available for Japan only from 1966, for France from 1970, for the United Kingdom from 1969, and for Sweden from 1980.
Source: OECD Economic Outlook Database.

Assumptions that labor force participation rates will remain constant at their low levels for the next 50 years (Turner et al. 1998) appear unduly pessimistic. Considering the labor market situation in the OECD countries, there seems to be room for employment to grow. First, employment levels are low by historical standards in France, Germany, and Italy. Second, employment levels continued to grow in the United States, the United Kingdom, and Japan even after relatively high levels at or above 65% of the working-age population had been reached. Similarly, employment levels remained high in Sweden (see table 5). If we assume that the rate of workers to the working-age population reaches its maximum around 80%—the highest level for any country during the past 40 years—Italy's employment could increase by 30 percentage points relative to the working-age population, and France's and Germany's by about 20 percentage points.

To illustrate the impact of different assumptions on projections for public pensions, I calculated a ratio of the elderly to current workers that is adjusted for employment and productivity growth[6]—the Care for the Aged and Retired by Employees Ratio (CARER). I calculated CARER to gain a tool for a cross-country comparison of each country's ability to pay for its public pension system. To facilitate cross-country comparisons, I indexed CARER to 2000 and treated each public pension system as if it were a pay-as-you-go (PAYG) system.[7]

For ease of comparison of each country's ability to pay, I made a few simplifying assumptions. First, I assumed that everybody over the age of 65 is a beneficiary. Because all countries offer retirement, disability, and survivorship benefits in addition to a minimum or poverty pension, few people over the normal retirement age are not covered by public pensions. Second, differences in the normal retirement age are therefore ignored. Since rapid changes in the normal retirement age are rare, this assumption may understate the level of the dependency ratio but not the changes in it. Third, I ignored the redistributive characteristics of public pension systems. Since income inequality has increased in almost every country, this assumption is likely to understate the burden of caring for future retirees. However, this is partially offset by calculating benefit increases on the basis of average wage growth. Increasing income inequality suggests below-average earnings growth for low-income earners, who benefit the most from public pension redistribution. Thus, including average wage growth—equal to productivity growth—as a measure of benefit increases means that I am likely overstating benefit increases.[8]

One characteristic of each country's public pension system that is included in the calculations is the indexation method. Most countries index their benefits to price increases after retirement (France, Italy, Sweden, the United Kingdom, and the United States). In comparison, Germany and Japan index their benefits to after-tax wages.

The changes in CARER are subsequently used to calculate after-tax wage increases over the next 50 years as a measure of future living standards. Both the expected burden to care for the elderly and the changes in future living standards help us to answer two questions. First, both measures can be used to discover how sensitive future projections are to the underlying assumptions, and second, they can be employed to analyze whether each country can afford a PAYG public pension system.

Table 7 calculates the burden of caring for the elderly and the resulting after-tax wages on the basis of each country's experience during the past 20 years. After adjusting for changes in employment and productivity gains, the burden of caring for the elderly increases in three countries and declines in the other four. The decline in the burden of caring for the elderly falls between 20% (France) and 52% (Sweden and the United States). In comparison, increases in the burden of caring for the elderly range from 25% in Japan to 40% in Germany.

TABLE 7
Burden of Caring for the Elderly for Current Workers (CARER), Short-Range Assumptions, 2000–2050

	France	Germany	Italy	Japan	Sweden	U.K.	U.S.
Productivity growth %	1.36	1.88	1.01	1.64	1.62	1.74	1.81
Δ(employment/ population) %	–0.22	–0.10	–0.19	0.22	–0.35	–0.01	0.38
CARER							
2000	100.00	100.00	100.00	100.00	100.00	100.00	100.00
2010	90.05	108.89	102.07	118.75	91.30	91.13	83.61
2020	90.05	114.34	100.84	132.64	86.15	87.19	74.94
2030	89.42	128.05	102.21	134.67	74.29	84.61	68.28
2040	86.68	137.11	106.94	135.23	62.46	75.35	57.71
2050	79.90	139.71	92.09	125.25	47.94	60.51	48.17
After-tax wage							
2000	100.00	100.00	100.00	100.00	100.00	100.00	100.00
2010	116.18	117.95	109.72	113.89	119.41	120.54	121.86
2020	133.14	140.52	121.76	130.48	141.33	144.19	147.49
2030	152.54	164.17	134.56	152.86	169.80	172.12	177.84
2040	175.23	192.73	146.12	179.59	203.87	207.43	215.47
2050	202.78	230.93	168.42	214.71	246.24	252.87	260.90

Notes: See appendix for methodology, assumptions, and sources. An increase in CARER indicates a growing burden for workers; a decline in the index indicates a shrinking burden for workers. Both CARER and net wages are indexed to 2000 as the base year.

Even where the burden of caring for the elderly is expected to increase, living standards are likely to grow. After-tax wages will be more than twice as high in six out of seven countries in 2050 than in 2000, and two thirds higher in Italy.

The experience of the past 20 years, however, appears rather poor and may hence underestimate the future economic performance of the seven OECD economies. With the exception of the United States, the average productivity growth rate for the past 40 years has been higher than for the past 20 years. Furthermore, the rate of change of the ratio of employment to the working-age population for the past 20 years is rather similar to that of the past 40 years, with the exception of Japan (table 8).

TABLE 8

Burden of Caring for the Elderly for Current Workers (CARER), Long-Range Assumptions, 2000–2050

	France	Germany	Italy	Japan	Sweden	U.K.	U.S.
Productivity growth (%)	2.36	2.31	2.99	3.92	2.16	2.13	1.54
Δ (employment/ population) (%)	–0.15	–0.13	–0.26	0.03	–0.03	–0.05	0.34
CARER							
2000	100.00	100.00	100.00	100.00	100.00	100.00	100.00
2010	81.39	108.94	84.35	119.89	86.10	87.93	85.96
2020	73.61	114.72	67.37	136.69	77.69	81.25	79.06
2030	66.06	128.98	51.44	133.39	64.33	75.99	73.88
2040	57.78	138.66	35.94	116.83	52.47	64.50	64.10
2050	48.01	141.83	18.43	89.13	39.14	48.76	54.94
After-tax wage							
2000	100.00	100.00	100.00	100.00	100.00	100.00	100.00
2010	129.78	123.02	140.22	142.09	127.05	125.85	118.36
2020	166.13	152.77	198.66	202.13	159.61	157.16	139.17
2030	212.35	185.95	281.04	297.89	202.76	195.79	163.14
2040	271.60	227.37	395.81	449.87	256.81	246.14	192.29
2050	348.44	283.78	562.23	693.59	326.30	312.26	226.62

Notes: See appendix for methodology, assumptions, and sources. An increase in CARER indicates a growing burden for workers; a decline in the index indicates a shrinking burden for workers. Both CARER and net wages are indexed to 2000 as the base year.

Given the different set of assumptions based on long-term historical experiences, the forecasts for the burden of caring for the elderly and for after-tax wages become more optimistic. The burden of caring for the elderly is still expected to increase in two countries: Germany and Japan. However, CARER actually decreases between 2040 and 2050 in Japan. Only in Germany does CARER seem to be unaffected by the different set of assumptions. However, because of the largely more optimistic outlook on the economy, the forecasts in table 8 suggest more than a tripling of after-tax wages in France, Italy, Japan, Sweden, and the United Kingdom after 50 years. After-tax wages in Germany are expected to increase by 184%, and in the United States by 130%.

Table 9 summarizes the changes, which indicate that, with the exception of Germany and the United States, the long-range assumptions lead to lower forecasted burdens of caring for the elderly than the short-range assumptions. In Germany, a change in the underlying assumptions appears to have little effect on the burden of caring for the elderly, while the less optimistic assumptions lead to a higher burden in the U.S. case, as one would expect.

TABLE 9

Comparison of CARER and After-Tax Wages Based on Short-Range and Long-Range Assumptions, 2000–2050

	France	Germany	Italy	Japan	Sweden	U.K.	U.S.
CARER							
2010	–9.6	0.1	–17.4	1.0	–5.7	–3.5	2.8
2020	–18.3	0.3	–33.2	3.1	–9.8	–6.8	5.5
2030	–26.1	0.7	–49.7	–0.9	–13.4	–10.2	8.2
2040	–33.3	1.1	–66.4	–13.6	–16.0	–14.4	11.1
2050	–39.9	1.5	–80.0	–28.8	–18.4	–19.4	14.1
After-tax wage							
2010	11.7	4.3	15.5	24.8	6.4	4.4	–2.9
2020	24.8	8.7	30.3	54.9	12.9	9.0	–5.6
2030	39.2	13.3	49.6	94.9	19.4	13.8	–8.3
2040	55.0	18.0	79.8	150.5	26.0	18.7	–10.8
2050	71.8	22.9	135.0	223.0	32.5	23.5	–13.1

Notes: All figures are percentages representing the difference between the results based on the long-range assumptions and the results based on the short-range assumptions. See the appendix for methodology, assumptions, and sources. An increase in CARER indicates a growing burden for workers; a decline indicates a shrinking burden for workers. Both CARER and net wages are indexed to 2000 as the base year.

The calculations have so far combined changes in two underlying assumptions at the same time: productivity growth and growth in the ratio of employment to the working-age population. Table 10 records the impact of alternative assumptions about productivity growth and employment growth separately. As a baseline scenario, I assumed—similar to the OECD studies—that each economy's productivity grows initially at 1.4% annually and that the ratio of employment to working-age population remains unchanged. First, I increased annual productivity growth to 2%, then I raised employment growth relative to the working-age population by 0.4% annually, and finally, I changed both assumptions at the same time.

Faster productivity growth translates into a lower burden of caring for the elderly in six countries. The only exception here is Germany, where faster productivity growth has no effect on caring for the elderly. In countries where benefits are indexed to inflation, an increase in annual productivity growth from 1.4% to 2.0% results in a 25% to 34% decline of the burden of caring for the elderly over 50 years.

The impact of faster employment growth is ambiguous. In three countries—France, Germany, and the United States—the burden of caring for the elderly declines, whereas it increases in the other four

TABLE 10

Changes in CARER under Different Economic Assumptions, 2000–2050

	France	Germany	Italy	Japan	Sweden	U.K.	U.S.
Faster productivity growth							
2010	−5.6	−0.1	−5.6	0.1	−5.3	−5.4	−5.7
2020	−10.8	0.0	−11.0	0.6	−10.5	−10.1	−11.1
2030	−15.6	0.2	−17.2	−0.2	−16.4	−14.6	−16.1
2040	−20.2	0.4	−24.8	−3.5	−21.8	−19.8	−20.8
2050	−24.6	0.6	−33.5	−8.1	−27.9	−25.8	−25.3
Faster employment growth							
2010	−2.3	−1.7	−0.3	−1.0	−1.1	−0.5	−1.2
2020	−5.2	−3.7	1.4	−0.5	0.2	0.5	−2.7
2030	−8.2	−6.1	3.4	0.7	3.3	3.9	−3.2
2040	−11.1	−8.3	6.2	2.1	6.1	8.0	−3.2
2050	−12.9	−9.0	11.2	3.0	8.3	11.4	−3.2
Faster productivity growth and faster employment growth							
2010	−7.8	−1.8	−5.8	−0.8	−6.3	−5.8	−6.9
2020	−15.4	−3.7	−9.0	0.5	−9.7	−9.2	−13.4
2030	−22.6	−5.9	−12.1	1.4	−12.0	−9.7	−18.7
2040	−29.1	−7.9	−15.2	0.1	−14.5	−10.5	−23.4
2050	−34.3	−8.2	−18.4	−3.4	−18.8	−13.4	−27.7

Notes: All figures are percentages. Baseline assumptions are 1.4% productivity growth and 0% employment growth relative to working-age population. Alternative assumptions are 2% productivity growth and 0.4% annual increase in employment relative to working-age population up to a maximum of 80%. See the appendix for methodology, assumptions, and sources. An increase in CARER indicates a growing burden for workers; a decline indicates a shrinking burden for workers. Both CARER and net wages are indexed to 2000 as the base year.

countries. The ambiguity in the effect of increasing employment can be explained by the fact that higher employment also leads to increases in future benefit payments.

The combined effects of faster productivity growth and faster employment growth are a declining CARER for all countries. The combined gains in CARER from faster productivity and employment growth are smallest in Japan (3.4%) and Germany (8.2%), where benefits are indexed to after-tax wage increases.

The effects of different economic assumptions vary with the indexation of benefits. Table 11 thus shows the changes resulting from a switch in the indexation method given 1.4% productivity growth and no change in the ratio of employment to the working-age population. Switching from a price indexation to an after-tax wage indexation means a benefit increase and therefore increases CARER by about 80% to 90% in all five countries (France, Italy, Sweden, the United Kingdom, and the United States) after 50 years. In comparison, switching from an after-tax wage or GDP indexation to a price indexation in Germany and Japan lowers CARER by 46% over 50 years.

Another change in the level of benefits that has entered the debate in some OECD countries is a decrease in the retirement age.[9] Several

TABLE 11

Changes in CARER and After-Tax Wages under Different Policy Assumptions, 2000–2050

	France	Germany	Italy	Japan	Sweden	U.K.	U.S.
CARER with changed indexation (% change from baseline)							
2010	14.7	–11.2	11.8	–9.0	14.1	13.7	13.4
2020	29.7	–22.0	24.7	–18.5	28.4	28.1	27.3
2030	46.6	–30.2	38.7	–28.8	46.5	43.7	44.0
2040	66.1	–37.9	52.2	–38.1	67.4	62.9	65.1
2050	90.0	–45.8	76.3	–46.8	93.9	88.4	89.8
CARER with lower retirement age (% change from baseline)							
2010	9.3	5.9	11.3	7.6	8.2	7.5	4.1
2020	20.3	16.1	26.3	11.7	15.9	16.1	10.5
2030	27.4	23.6	47.9	18.1	23.4	25.0	11.3
2040	25.1	17.4	44.0	19.6	20.0	19.7	10.0
2050	26.9	20.7	37.7	16.4	24.2	23.3	11.0
After-tax wages with changed indexation (index levels)							
2010	114.7	115.6	111.77	113.1	114.1	113.7	115.0
2020	129.7	135.7	124.73	129.7	128.4	128.1	131.2
2030	146.6	156.4	138.66	152.7	146.5	143.7	149.2
2040	166.1	181.3	152.22	179.5	167.4	162.9	171.1
2050	190.0	213.5	176.35	212.4	193.9	188.4	196.7
After-tax wages with lower retirement age (index levels)							
2010	115.6	111.1	111.89	109.6	115.2	114.8	116.0
2020	131.4	123.2	125.01	120.9	131.1	130.5	133.4
2030	150.1	133.2	136.36	136.4	151.4	147.6	153.7
2040	174.7	152.4	158.13	155.6	178.4	173.2	179.2
2050	203.7	172.8	200.29	183.4	210.2	203.9	208.3

Notes: Productivity growth is assumed to be 1.4% per year, and employment growth is assumed to be 0.4% annually relative to working-age population. Baseline indexation is actual indexation (see table 12). Indexation is subsequently changed from net wages and GDP to prices for Germany, Italy, and Japan and from prices to after-tax wage growth for all other countries. The assumed retirement age is lowered from 65 to 60 in a linear progression at a rate of 0.2 year per year. See the appendix for methodology, assumptions, and sources. An increase in CARER indicates a growing burden for workers; a decline indicates a shrinking burden for workers. Both CARER and net wages are indexed to 2000 as the base year.

countries, such as France and Germany, already use de facto lower retirement ages to combat persistently high unemployment levels. What would happen to public pension finances if the hypothetical retirement age were lowered? To illustrate the impact of a lower retirement age, I reduced the retirement age in a linear fashion by 0.2 year each year for the next 25 years, increased the number of retirees, and lowered the number of people in the working-age population.

By definition, a lower retirement age increases the burden for current workers to care for the elderly. The increase is largest in Italy, with its most rapidly changing demographics, and smallest in the United States, which is also the country with the highest population growth rate and the youngest population among the seven OECD countries. The impact of a lower retirement age is a CARER that is between 11% and 38% higher than with a normal retirement age of 65.

By looking at two possible benefit increases, higher indexation and lower retirement age, and connecting these to the resulting after-tax wages, we can not only gauge whether benefit increases are affordable but also demonstrate that there is little to worry about. If a public pension system can afford benefit increases—when so desired by policy makers—there is little basis to assert that its future is in jeopardy. In the five countries where the indexation is changed from prices to after-tax wages, after-tax wages of workers are still about twice as high in 2050 as they are in 2000. Furthermore, with a lower retirement age, after-tax wages are 73% to 110% higher in 2050 than in 2000. Benefit increases are possible if policy makers are willing to increase tax rates, which should result in slower growth of after-tax wages than otherwise, but growth of after-tax wages nevertheless.

My simulations are merely indications of broad trends. They illustrate the sensitivity of future projections to what often appears to be marginal differences in the underlying assumptions. Furthermore, the scenarios speak directly to the claim that public pension systems in the OECD are going to be in a crisis. Even if we use the most pessimistic assumptions, the simulations do not spiral out of control. Quite the contrary, even with pessimistic assumptions, benefit increases appear affordable, if policy makers are willing to introduce them. The apparent exception appears to be Italy due to its very generous indexation of benefits.

My projections take the characteristics of each country's system into account only to a limited degree. Nevertheless, my simulations provide a sense of each country's ability to pay for the elderly. This ability to pay should not be confused with the willingness of policy makers to implement the necessary changes. Despite an improving ability to pay for the elderly, tax increases may be necessary. Some factors that require higher tax rates may be connected not to economic trends but to policy decisions. The following section therefore provides a description of the designs of public pension systems.

Country Experiences with Public and Private Pensions

The discussion over the future of public pension systems has helped to generate a sense of crisis among policy makers and increasingly among the public. It seems that the greater the sense of crisis becomes, the less willing policy makers are to consider changing the structures of public pension systems so that they can take advantage of the possibly greater ability to pay for public pensions in the future. Thus, privatization appears to be a viable solution to perceived problems of public pensions. We consider existing private pension systems in each country in the following discussion. Tables 12 and 13 summarize the changes to and characteristics of each system.

The French Experience with Public and Private Pensions

The French public retirement system offers a variety of coexisting schemes, all on a pay-as-you-go (PAYG) basis. For private-sector

TABLE 12
Changes to Retirement Benefits in Public Pension Systems, 1960–1998

Year	Variables affected	Nature of change	Change
France			
1971	W_{BT}	Benefit cut	Years of required coverage extended to 34 from 30
	N_B	Benefit increase	Pre-retirement benefit for unemployment
	Δ	Benefit increase	Increase in replacement ratio beginning in 1975
	N_B	Benefit increase	Voluntary affiliation for nonworking homemakers
1975	W_{BT}	Benefit cut	Years of required coverage extended to 37.5 from 34
1980	N_B	Benefit increase	Compulsory old-age pension affiliation for women receiving family supplement
	N_B	Benefit increase	Surviving spouse's allowance
1993	W_{BT}	Benefit cut	Years of required coverage extended to 40 starting in 2003
	W_{BT}	Benefit cut	Benefit calculation based on best 25 years in 2008, up from best 10, with gradual increases in between
Germany			
1972	N_B	Benefit increase	Introduction of early retirement benefits
	I_B	Benefit increase	Shifting of benefits indexation from inflation to average gross wage growth
1992	I_B	Benefit cut	Indexation shifted from gross wage to net wage growth
	N_B	Benefit cut	Gradual increase in the retirement age of women from 60 to 65 in 2004
	EI_w	Benefit cut	Replacement ratio lowered from 70% to 64%
1999	I_B	Benefit cut	Benefits indexed to inflation for two years (2000 and 2001) and to net wages thereafter
	W_{BT}	Benefit cut	Contributions for the unemployed based on unemployment benefits and not on last income
Italy			
1965	NRA	Benefit increase	Pension payable after 35 years of service at any age

TABLE 12 (*Continued*)
Changes to Retirement Benefits in Public Pension Systems, 1960–1998

Year	Variables affected	Nature of change	Change
1969	$t_T Y$, Benefits$_T$	—	Funding switched to PAYG
	w_{BT}	Benefit increase	Benefit computation based on "final salary"
	Δ	Benefit increase	Introduction of means-tested minimum pension
	I_B	Benefit increase	Inflation indexation of benefits
	w_{BT}	Benefit increase	Introduction of early retirement benefits
1976	I_B	Benefit increase	Real wage growth indexation
1982	NRA	Benefit increase	Age for pre-retirement benefits lowered to 55 (men) and 50 (women)
1989	γ	Benefit cut	Redistributive benefits formula weakened
1992	NRA	Benefit cut	As of 1993, NRA raised to 60 (men) and 55 (women)
	NRA	Benefit cut	As of 1994, NRA raised by 1 year every 2 years to age 65 (men) and 60 (women)
	Time	Benefit cut	Reference period for average wages lengthened and minimum requirement of years raised
1995	w_{BT}	Benefit increase	Cap on earnings for purposes of benefit calculation eliminated
Sweden			
1976	NRA	Benefit increase	Mandatory retirement age lowered from 67 to 65
1998	w_{BT}	Benefit cut	Pensions based on lifetime income
	I_B	—	Benefits from PAYG system indexed to real income growth
	δ	Benefit cut	Benefits from PAYG system adjusted for life expectancy
	w_{BT}	Benefit increase	Guaranteed minimum pension
United Kingdom			
1966	w_{BT}	Benefit increase	Means-tested allowance introduced
1971	w_{BT}	Benefit increase	Old person's pension for retirees age 80 and above introduced
1978	w_{BT}	Benefit increase	Introduction of earnings-related pension (SERPS)
Japan			
1973	I_B	Benefit increase	Inflation indexation of benefits for both programs
1994	ρ	Benefit cut	Target replacement ratio reduced to 30% of monthly wages—down from 60%—by 2025
	—		Benefit indexation changed to net wage growth from inflation
United States			
1973	I_B	Benefit increase	Inflation indexation of benefits introduced
1983	N_B	Benefit increase	Federal employees hired after December 31, 1983, included
	NRA	Benefit cut	NRA gradually increased to 67 by 2022 for workers who attain age 62 in 2000 and thereafter

Notes: Only changes to old-age retirement benefits are included.
Source: Social Security Administration, *Social Security Programs throughout the World,* various years.

TABLE 13
Summary of Public Pension System Characteristics

	France	Germany	Italy	Sweden	U.K.	Japan	U.S.
Funded	Partial	PAYG	PAYG	PAYG (basic), full (complementary)	Partial	Partial	Partial
Earned benefit Replacement ratio	Yes 50% of best 11 to 25 years (depending on year of birth)	Yes 70% of net average wages in economy	Yes 80% of average lifetime earnings	No 96% of basic amount (basic) plus 60% of covered earnings (complementary)	Yes 16% of average male earnings (basic) plus 25% of average lifetime earnings (supplement)	Yes Target of 30% of monthly wages in 2025	Yes 39.6% of average earnings in economy
Indexation of benefits	Prices	Net wages	Prices	Government discretion	Prices	Net wages	Prices
Income cap on contributions	Yes	Yes	No	No	No	No	Yes
Impact of lower ratio of workers to retirees	→	→	→	→	→	→	→
Effects of growing inequality	→	→	→	→	→	→	→
Effects of lower productivity and real wage gains	→	→	→	→	→	→	→

Source: Social Security Administration, *Social Security Programs throughout the World*, various years.

employees, there are two public pensions: the general regime and com-plementary schemes.

Changes to the French retirement system have been implemented on occasion since the early 1970s. Most notable are increased replace-ment ratios and the affiliation of homemakers. On the other hand, bene-fit cuts have come in the form of extensions of the years required for maximum benefits and the years over which average earnings are calcu-lated.

Approximately 65% of all workers are eligible for the defined bene-fits of the general scheme, which was created in 1945. In addition, there are roughly 180 complementary schemes, based on occupation, that belong to one of two federations. AGIRC manages pensions for workers in executive and managerial positions for the portion of their income that is above the income cap of the general scheme. ARRCO handles pensions for all other workers and for the part of managerial and execu-tive wages that are below the cap. Even though complementary schemes were created between 1946 and the mid-1960s, participation did not become mandatory until 1972 (Blanchet and Pelé 1997). There are also approximately 120 specialized systems (Blanchet and Pelé 1997). These are pensions for the self-employed and for public-sector employees, and they remain outside the public pension system. Finally, 1 million retirees in 1997 received means-tested minimum pensions, down from 2.55 million in 1959 (Commissariat Général du Plan 1995).

Public pension contributions are collected mainly as payroll taxes. Taxes for the general system amount to an employee contribution of 6.55% of pensionable earnings and 0.1% of total earnings for surviving spouse's benefits. The employer pays an additional 8.2% of covered wages plus 1.6% of total wages (Blanchet and Pelé 1997; SSA 1999). For the complementary schemes, payroll taxes are 2% on income up to three times the income ceiling for nonmanagerial workers. Managerial workers pay 2% for the income below the income ceiling and 4.68% on income above the income ceiling as long as it is below four times the ceiling. In 1994, the actual contribution rates for complementary schemes were calculated by multiplying the tax rates by a factor of 1.25 (Blanchet and Pelé 1997).

All benefits are defined benefits based on an individual's earnings history. General benefits are based on the 11 to 25 highest income years—depending on the year of birth—up to a maximum of 37.5 years of contribution and on age at retirement. The replacement ratio amounts to 50% of average wages of the 25 best years as of January 1,

2008 (SSA 1999). For each quarter that a retiree is shy of the maximum of 37.5 years, the replacement rate of a worker's highest 10-year average is reduced by 1.25% in addition to a penalty for contributing for fewer than the maximum years. Similarly, for each quarter that a worker is shy of age 65, the replacement rate is reduced by 1.25%. In cases where workers are younger than 65 and have contributed for fewer than 37.5 years, the higher retirement income is chosen. Benefits are indexed to prices or average wages on a discretionary basis (Blanchet and Pelé 1997). In the complementary system, workers earn "points" toward their pension benefit, which are accumulated relative to contributions. The pension is ultimately equal to the total number of points collected multiplied by a variable coefficient. There is no preset replacement rate for the complementary system.

Since 1963, French workers have the option to retire early. Between 1963 and 1972, early retirement was used as an income support for older workers who had been affected by mass layoffs (Blanchet and Pelé 1997). Since 1972, this system was replaced with a more general program that was intended to provide 60% to 70% of income to workers who had lost their jobs at age 60 or older. Lowering the normal retirement age to 60 in 1983 had a small impact as most workers had already taken early retirement (Blanchet and Pelé 1997).

Workers have other early retirement options. First, benefits under the National Fund for Employment can be negotiated between the employer and the government. Second, unemployment benefits for workers 58 years old or over help them make the transition to retirement (Blanchet and Pelé 1997).

The French public pension system also offers means-tested spousal benefits, disability pensions for workers under the age of 60, and survivorship benefits if the surviving spouse is over 55 or for children of the deceased.

Since public pensions offer relatively generous benefits, as indicated by comparatively high replacement ratios, private pensions are rare in France[10] (Davis 1994). Only a small number of firms offer group-insured plans for executives, referred to as top-hat plans. These can be either defined-benefit or defined-contribution plans.

The German Experience with Public and Private Pensions

The German public pension system is separate from but subsidized by the government. Originally designed as fully funded disability insurance in 1889, it eventually turned into a PAYG system when the Great Depression and World War II affected its finances.

Over the decades, there have been several reforms. In 1972, the government expanded benefits by introducing early retirement benefits and indexation by average before-tax wage instead of inflation. The 1992 pension reform introduced benefit cuts by changing indexation to after-tax wages by raising the normal retirement age for women from 60 to 65 in 2004 and by lowering the replacement rate from 70% to 64% over time (Sinn 1999). Finally, in 1999, it was proposed to index benefits to inflation for two years and to after-tax wages thereafter.

Payroll taxes cover 80% of benefits, while the government covers the rest out of general revenues (Börsch-Supan and Schnabel 1997; BfA 2000). Since 1973, combined tax rates—split evenly between employer and employee—have been between 18% and 20% on earnings below an income cap. Because the income ceiling is indexed to average wage growth, the tax base has become wider over time.

Pension benefits are generous. They offer an average replacement rate of 71% of average after-tax wages, based on a worker's earnings. After-retirement benefits are indexed to average after-tax wages. To calculate benefits, a worker's contributions are indexed to annual average contributions, which are then averaged over the full working life. In 1972, a floor of 75% of average contributions for benefit calculations was introduced, thereby lifting the averages for low lifetime earners. The 1993 reform eliminated the floor. For workers whose contributions are below 50% of average contributions, contributions below 75% of average contributions are multiplied by a factor of 1.5, up to a ceiling of 75%. Furthermore, benefits are based on years of service, which include years of no contributions, such as unemployment, military service, or years spent in school. To combat high unemployment, the eligibility for benefits has been widened, especially by expanding early retirement (Börsch-Supan and Schnabel 1997).

Early retirement has become a popular option. Following the 1973 reform, which made it possible to retire early with full benefits, the average retirement age declined from age 63 to 58.5 (Börsch-Supan and Schnabel 1997). Early retirement incentives also led to a sharp drop in labor force participation rates in East Germany immediately following unification. In particular, labor force participation rates in East Germany declined from 56.9% in 1990 to 37.4% in 1992, which is attributed largely to generous early retirement benefits (Börsch-Supan and Schnabel 1997).

German workers have different options for retiring early. Out of 5.9 million retirees in 1999, 1.1 million were women, who were entitled to full retirement benefits earlier than men. A little over half a million retirees received retirement benefits because of unemployment (BfA 2000). Furthermore, Börsch-Supan and Schnabel (1997) report that at age 59, about 45% of men consider themselves retired, half of whom have taken advantage of early retirement options and the other half of whom qualify for disability benefits. In addition to regular retirement options, workers can also use unemployment benefits as early retirement income after age 56 or as subsidized support from their employers after age 58 (Börsch-Supan and Schnabel 1997).

In addition to retirement pensions, Germany's system also offers disability benefits of at least two thirds of the applicable old-age pension. Furthermore, survivorship benefits are paid at 60% of the spouse's applicable old-age pension if children are present and 25% if not.

Even though a large share of employees receive private pensions, these pensions are relatively small. Only 5% of a typical household's retirement income comes from employment-based private sources (Börsch-Supan et al. 2000). German workers receive few pension benefits from their employers as a result of the generosity of public pensions on the one hand and of provisions of private pensions that keep the associated risks largely with the employer on the other hand. Most private pensions offer defined benefits, and companies are legally mandated to index benefits. Pension coverage has declined from 70% to 66% in the 1980s (Davis 1994).

There are four types of private pensions (Deutsche Bundesbank 1984; Ahrend 1996; Davis 1994). Direct commitments, which appear on the balance sheets of companies, are the largest type. In 1991, direct commitments—valued at 240 billion deutsche marks—were 60% of pension liabilities. They are insured in case a firm goes bankrupt, and since 1987, provisions for otherwise unfunded liabilities have been mandatory. Contributions are tax free; they earn 6% nominally and can be invested only within the firm. Second, external pensions exist, and about 10% of pensions are in the form of direct insurance, where a firm contracts with a life insurer on behalf of its employees (Davis 1994). Investment risks are borne by the insurer, and investments are governed by insurance regulations. Third, a company can set up a separate pension fund or a support fund. In 1991, pension funds held 20% of all pension liabilities, and support funds held an additional 10% (Davis 1994). While pension funds are similar to those elsewhere, support funds are set up as mutual insurances to handle a company's pension scheme. The portfolio choices of pension funds are limited (see table 16), while those of support funds are not. Finally, special security funds have become increasingly relevant. These are funds managed by investment companies that allow highly liquid companies with direct commitments on their balance sheets to invest part of their pension provisions in the capital markets (Davis 1994).

The Italian Experience with Public and Private Pensions

Italy's public pensions date back to 1889, when pensions for members of the army were introduced. By the 1960s, a variety of public pension schemes existed. For instance, the National Institute for Social Security (INPS) collected mandatory contributions from a large portion of private-sector employees and from some self-employed people. Subsequently, the INPS and the Public Sector Employees Fund became the main branches of Italy's public pension system. Also, several occupations set up their own funds, guided by their own rules.

Italy's system has been changed several times in the past (Brugiavini 1997). In 1969, funding was switched to a PAYG system, benefits were based on "final salary," a means-tested minimum pension for uncovered workers was introduced, benefits became indexed to inflation, and early retirement for private-sector employees with at least 35 years of service was offered. In 1976, pensions became indexed to real wage growth. In 1982, the pre-retirement age was lowered to 55 for men and 50 for women. In 1984, requirements for disability benefits were tightened. In 1989, the redistributive aspects of the benefits formula were weakened. In 1992, the amount that a worker could earn without loss of retirement benefits was lowered, the reference period for average wages was lengthened, the minimum requirement of years was raised, and the retirement age for men and women increased. Also, a reform in 1995 eliminated the earnings cap on benefits; benefits were indexed to inflation. Finally, in 1997 the harmonization of public-sector pensions to private-sector pensions was accelerated, and the harmonization of special schemes to private-sector pensions was introduced (OECD 2000).

Revenues are mainly payroll taxes. In 1998, the employee contribution amounted to 8.89% of earnings up to an income threshold and 9.9% of earnings beyond that threshold, while the employer contribution was at 23.81% of payroll. The government covered any shortfall of contributions in the form of lump-sum subsidies for the past decades.

Benefits are computed on the basis of age, years of service, and earnings. Workers who entered the workforce after 1996 become eligible at 57 with at least five years of contributions. With less than 19 years of coverage, men are eligible at 65 and women at 60 (SSA 1999). Private-sector employees can collect full benefits at age 55 with 35 years of service. Under current law, there are three benefits calculations. For new entrants after 1996, pensions are based on accumulated contributions multiplied by an age-varying coefficient ranging from 4.72 at age 57 to 6.136 at age 65. Second, if a worker has fewer than 19 years of contributions, benefits are based on a progressive percentage between 0.9% and 2% of salary times years of contributions, while years after 1995 are calculated in the same way as they are for new entrants. Third, for workers with more than 19 years of contributions in 2000, benefit calculations are based on a progressive percentage ranging from 0.9% to 2% of salary times years of contributions (SSA 1999).

There are other benefits. Since 1977, survivorship benefits are available for surviving spouse, children, and other dependents. Workers who have contributed for at least five years are also eligible for disability benefits.

Italy is another country where private pensions have played a relatively small role. Private pensions are mostly supplements to public pensions and can take different forms, as there is no law on private pensions. There are book entries similar to Germany's direct commitments, separate pension funds, or pension funds within a firm. Additionally, companies can set up tax-free severance funds that are book reserves (Davis 1994). However, if the firm goes bankrupt, the worker bears the risk of loss of retirement income.

The Swedish Experience with Public and Private Pensions

Sweden implemented its first compulsory, fully funded, old-age pension system in 1913. It consisted of a means-tested basic pension and a supplementary pension relative to a worker's earnings and covered everybody, not just workers. In 1935, the system switched to a PAYG system, funding switched to employers' contributions, and benefit levels increased (Palme and Svensson 1997). The minimum pension increased from about 11.3% of earnings of an industrial worker in 1913 to 29.4% in 1941. The minimum pension was replaced with the basic pension in 1946. Based on a referendum in 1959, compulsory supplementary pensions were introduced. In 1976, the mandatory retirement age was lowered from 67 to 65. A survivor's benefit was introduced in 1990 to replace the widow's pension.

Sweden changed its system in 1998 (Ministry of Health and Social Affairs 1998). Now, pensions are based on lifetime income, and the combined tax rate is 18.5% of a worker's lifetime average income, split between employer and employee, of which 16% pays for benefits and 2.5% goes into an individual retirement account. Benefits from the PAYG system are indexed to real income growth and adjusted for life expectancy. In addition to the new pension system, there is a guaranteed pension as a supplement for low lifetime earners.

Employer contributions and government subsidies finance most of the old system. In 1999, the contribution rate for the national basic pension amounted to 5.86% of payroll for employers and 1% of assessable income for employees. The government covered 25% of the costs. There is no income ceiling for contributions.

For workers covered under the old system, benefits are based on the basic amount (BA). Everybody is entitled to a full basic pension if they have lived in Sweden for 40 years or worked there for 30 years. The basic pension is 96% of the BA for a single pensioner and 78.5% for a married worker. Pensioners who are not covered by the supplementary scheme are also entitled to a special supplement, equal to 55.5% of the BA. The share of income that exceeds the BA determines supplementary pension benefits. Three years of income greater than the BA are required to qualify for supplementary benefits. Income that exceeds 7.5 times the BA is not counted for benefit calculations. For income that is equal to or above the BA, a worker earns one pension point, up to a maximum of 6.5 points per year. The average points of the best 15 years are taken and multiplied by a factor of 0.6, by the BA, and by the number of service years up to a maximum of 30 years. If a worker has earned 30 years of service, she receives a replacement ratio of 60% of her best 15 years (below the income cap). Benefits nowadays are indexed to inflation (Palme and Svensson 1997). Everybody receives the basic pension, and there are no benefits for dependents under the supplementary scheme.

Early retirement is an option for workers between the ages of 61 and 65. Under the new system, early retirement benefits are actuarially fair reductions of full benefits at the normal retirement age (Herbertsson et al. 2000). Labor force participation rates for men between the ages of 60 and 64 have continuously declined from a high of about 85% in 1964 to close to 60% in 1996 (Palme and Svensson 1997). In contrast, labor force participation rates for women between the ages of 60 and 64 have increased from about 35% to 45% in the early 1990s, before dropping to about 40% in the wake of the Swedish recession.

The old system offers also survivorship, disability, and early retirement benefits. The basic pension offers survivorship benefits of 90% of the BA for women born before 1945. For everybody born after 1945, survivorship benefits replace the old system's widow's pensions. Under the supplementary scheme, widow's benefits for women born before 1945 offer 35% or 40% of a deceased worker's pension until the normal retirement age of 65. Since 1997, all survivors receive 20% of the deceased spouse's pension if there are children entitled to a children's pension, and 40% otherwise. Furthermore, disability benefits consist of the basic and the supplementary pension. Calculation of disability benefits is the same as for pension benefits at full retirement age. Finally, both basic and supplementary pensions can be claimed as early as age 60. The monthly benefit is reduced by 0.5% for each month of early retirement.

In addition to its complementary fully funded pensions, Sweden also has numerous private pensions, which are arranged through collective bargaining. Every worker is covered by one of the plans. White-collar workers are covered by the so-called ITP plan, and blue-collar workers are covered by the STP plan. Funding for the ITP comes from book reserves, insurance contracts, or contracts with a special pension company, whereas the STP is offered only through a mutual insurance organization (Davis 1994).

The private pensions offer only a small addition in retirement income with a replacement ratio of roughly 10% to 15% of the final wage. Up to 1998, investments were limited to insurance companies, mainly in the life insurer Säker Pensions Partner (SPP) for the ITP and the AMF System for blue-collar workers. Both SPP and ITP are now allowed to invest in domestic shares. Since 1998, workers can decide where to allocate their pension assets and who will manage the funds.

The U.K. Experience with Public and Private Pensions

Retirees in the United Kingdom only receive a small fraction of their retirement income from public pensions. The basic state pension amounted to 16% of male average earnings in 1996 (Blundell and Johnson 1997). Introduced in 1906, the basic pension offers a flat-rate benefit, which is an earned benefit paid for by payroll taxes. In 1978, a supplementary scheme, the State Earnings Related Pension Scheme (SERPS), was introduced. It had originally a target benefit level equal to 25% of average wage-indexed lifetime earnings. Changes introduced to

SERPS in 1986 and 1995 reduced the benefits payable under the supplementary program from 25% to 20% of wages, which was supposed to result in lower tax rates (Congressional Budget Office 1999).

Contributions for the basic pension and the SERPS amounted to a maximum marginal rate of 21.6% in 1999 (SSA 1999), with employees contributing 10% up to the upper earnings limit and employers contributing 12.2%, depending on a worker's earnings. Employers can opt out of the SERPS by providing similar private market alternatives, thereby lowering their contribution rates to between 9.6% and 11.6%.

"Perhaps the most important feature of the basic pension system is its low level" (Blundell and Johnson 1997:19). In 1996, it represented 16% of average male earnings, down from about 20% in the 1970s. Since it is indexed to the Retail Price Index, it is expected to continue to fall to 7% or 8% of average male earnings by 2030. To receive the full basic pension, only past contributions and age matter. Forty four years of contributions are required for men and 39 years of contributions (rising to 44 years when the normal retirement age becomes the same in 2020) for women at the normal retirement age, which is 65 for men and 60 for women. The basic pension also offers spousal benefits and survivorship benefits, but there is no early retirement provision. There is, however, the option of deferral for up to five years, with each year of deferral earning a 7.5% increase. Furthermore, there is also a means-tested supplementary income support that offers a higher pension benefit than the basic pension for low-income pensioners. In 1997, 1.5 million out of 10 million pensioners relied on this minimum pension (Blundell and Johnson 1997).

Early retirement is not an option in the United Kingdom. However, about 43% of men between the ages of 60 and 64 receive some form of benefits. The highest incidence rate of benefits before the normal retirement age comes from invalidity benefits, which 25% of males received in 1994–95, followed by income support, or poverty pensions, which went to 17% of males; 10% of males received other health-related benefits (Blundell and Johnson 1997).

The SERPS benefits are relative to a worker's earnings. Earnings above a lower limit and below an upper limit are counted; all other earnings are not counted. Both upper and lower limits are indexed to inflation. Relevant earnings are indexed by average earnings in each year up to the year when the beneficiary reaches pensionable age. The lower earnings limit is subtracted from the average of the indexed earnings. The resulting difference is then multiplied by an accrual factor and by the contribution years. Similar to the basic pension, SERPS offers survivorship benefits equal to 50% of the worker's pension and a disability pension, but no early retirement option.

If a worker is covered under an employment-related scheme with certain benefits, the worker can give up rights to SERPS. Since 1988, traditional occupational schemes and personal pension schemes could contract out of SERPS. Seventy-five percent of eligible workers are not covered by SERPS, two thirds of which are in occupational schemes and one third in personal pension schemes.

There is a heavy reliance on private pensions. Only 44% of retirement income comes from the basic pension, which is expected to decline to 28% in 2025 (Office of Fair Trading [OFT] 1997). An additional 4% of benefits came from SERPS in 1994, which is expected to grow to 16% in 2025 (OFT 1997). More than half of an average worker's retirement benefit comes from occupational schemes (with employer contributions) and personal pension savings (without employer contributions).[11] Fifty percent of all workers are covered by an occupational scheme, and 20% by personal pension plans. While 60% of male workers are covered by an occupational scheme, only 35% of female workers are covered. Furthermore, all public-sector employees but only 59% of private-sector employees are covered by occupational schemes (Davis 1994). While the pension coverage is unequally distributed, the coverage level has been constant since 1967 (Davis 1994).

All public-sector employees and most private-sector workers receive a defined benefit, sometimes even with indexation provisions. Defined-benefit plans became less attractive for employers due to high inflation and low returns in the mid-1970s. From 1971 to 1981, employers' contributions to private pensions grew from 1.75% to 3.23% of GDP to cover shortfalls in defined-benefit plans. Their finances improved so that employers' contributions dropped to 2% of GDP in 1987 and to 1.22% in 1992 (Davis 1994).

In the early 1990s, defined-contribution plans and individual retirement savings schemes became more popular. A survey of employers found a clear preference for them when employers were establishing a new plan (Confederation of British Industry 1994). Reasons for this preference are that the risks are borne by the employee, that—at least for smaller employers—there is a cost advantage in setting up defined-contribution plans over defined-benefit plans, and that more employment contracts are contingent and short-term (OFT 1997). In 1993, 3%

of all workers were covered by an occupational defined-contribution plan, but 19% of workers working for small firms were covered by such plans (Davis 1994). Also, OFT (1997) reported that survey evidence suggests that there is a steady increase in defined-contribution plans, especially in smaller firms.

The Japanese Experience with Public and Private Pensions

The Japanese public pension system dates back to 1942, when a pension insurance was established. The current system with two pillars for pensions was created in 1961. One pillar covers self-employed workers and unpaid workers; the other covers both public- and private-sector employees. The employee pension consists of a basic pension that is also offered to the self-employed and to unpaid workers and an earnings-related pension (Oshio and Yashiro 1997).

Basic pensions offer the main public retirement benefit to the self-employed. Benefits paid are a flat amount and are unrelated to a worker's earnings. Each worker contributes a flat yen amount per month. The basic pension does not offer spousal or survivorship benefits, but it does offer a disability pension.

The earnings-related system is managed by eight plans covering different occupations, with the largest one, the Kosei Nenkin Hoken (KNH), covering roughly 85% of all employees. Contributions to KNH are split evenly between employers and employees for a combined tax rate of 16.5% in 1995. The Japanese public pension schemes are partially funded systems because they hold government securities. Hence, additional funds come from interest on government debt on top of government transfers equal to one third of benefits and expenses.

Benefits are based on earnings and on the age of the worker. At retirement age, normally 65, the worker's wages are converted into standard average monthly earnings using a scale of currently 30 brackets. After conversion, a worker's earnings are averaged over the entire career because there is no minimum or maximum of years. The target replacement ratio was revised in 1994 to become slightly lower than 30% of monthly wages by 2025, down from 60%. Also, indexation was changed from price indexation to net wage indexation in 1994.

Additionally, the KNH offers benefits at flat rates for spouses and children under the age of 18. Dependent spouses are entitled to their own basic benefits in addition to spousal benefits under the supplementary earnings-related plan.

The supplementary system also offers early retirement, survivorship, and disability benefits. Workers between the ages of 60 and 65 can retire early, and their pensions are subject to an earnings test. Furthermore, surviving spouses and other dependents receive 75% of the deceased worker's full benefit beginning at age 60. Finally, after the age of 20, workers can receive disability benefits, which are calculated similarly to pension benefits, with an additional 25% available for severe disabilities. Alternatively, a disabled worker can choose to collect a flat amount.

Early retirement is an option at age 60. Early retirement benefits depend on the worker's meeting certain earnings criteria. Even a minimal amount of earnings reduces early retirement benefits by 20%. A fair number of people, though, opt to leave the labor force at age 60. In 1990, labor force participation rates for women declined with age from a high of 70% for 45-year-old women to a little over 40% for 60-year-olds. Similarly, labor force participation rates for men dropped from close to 100% for 45-year-olds to about 85% for 60-year-olds and to about 65% for 65-year-olds (Oshio and Yashiro 1997).

Public pensions offer a small basic benefit, yet private pension schemes are still rare. There are three private pension systems, which are all defined-benefit plans. First, tax-qualified pension plans (TQPP) have been allowed for firms with 15 or more employees since 1962. By 1989, TQPPs covered 28% of private-sector employees and held $76 billion in assets (Davis 1994). Second, employees' pension funds (EPFs) were introduced in 1966 for firms with 500 or more employees. The advantage of EPFs to employers results from the option to contract out of the earnings-related public pension portion, though benefits from EPFs exceed 30% of public pensions. By 1989, EPFs covered 26% of the workforce and held assets to the tune of $143 billion. Trust banks or life insurance companies manage funds of private pensions in Japan. Trust banks control 60% of all pension assets, and life insurers the remaining 40%. Third, Japanese firms carry unfunded retirement bonuses as liabilities on their books.

The American Experience with Public and Private Pensions

U.S. Social Security was established in 1935. Originally, all workers in commerce and industry, with the exception of railroads, were covered. Its coverage has gradually grown. Only some state and local employees may not be included (Diamond and Gruber 1997).

Social Security's structure has changed over the years. Early retirement benefits for women between the ages of 62 and 65 were offered in

1956 and for men in 1961. Benefits for dependents and widows were introduced in 1939 and for widowers and dependent husbands in 1950. In 1973, Social Security's benefits were indexed to inflation, and average lifetime wages were indexed by average wages. Finally, in 1983, a gradual increase in the normal retirement age from 65 to 67 for workers reaching age 62 in 2022 or later was implemented.

Contributions to Social Security come from combined payroll taxes amounting to 12.4%, which are evenly split between employers and employees, up to an income ceiling. Also, Social Security earns interest on a portfolio of government securities.

Benefits are based on age and earnings. To calculate benefits, a worker's earnings are indexed by average wages. The earnings of the 35 highest years are subsequently averaged and build the basis for a redistributive replacement formula, whereby a three-piece linear progressive schedule is applied. Thus, there is a declining replacement ratio as average lifetime earnings go up. After-retirement benefits are adjusted each year for price increases. Dependent benefits amount to 50% of the worker's benefits for spouses and children, up to a family maximum of roughly 175% of the worker's benefit.

U.S. workers are eligible for early retirement benefits at the age of 62. Benefits are reduced in an actuarially fair manner by $6^2/_3$% for each year or $5/_9$ of 1% per month that a worker retires early. Thus, a 62-year-old receives 20% less than she would have if she had continued to work to the normal retirement age of 65. Most U.S. workers retire early. In 1998, 19.2 million out of 27.5 million retirees received reduced retirement benefits because they retired before the normal retirement age (SSA 1999).

The system also offers a low-income pension. The Supplemental Security Income program offers income support for low-income elderly and disabled individuals based on their income relative to the rest of the population.

Additional benefits of Social Security include dependent, survivor, and disability benefits. Surviving spouses receive 100% of a worker's benefits beginning at age 60. Disability benefits offer workers full benefits based on their earnings record.

The United States is another country where private pensions have traditionally played an important role in the provision of retirement income. At the end of 1998, financial assets of pension funds amounted to roughly $8 trillion (Board of Governors of the Federal Reserve 1999).

While 39% of all workers had a defined-benefit plan as their primary plan in 1975, only 23% did so in 1995. In contrast, the percentage of full- and part-time private-sector workers who were covered by a defined-contribution plan rose from 6% in 1975 to 23% in 1995 (U.S. Department of Labor 1999). Furthermore, while 91% of full-time private-sector workers at medium and large firms were covered by some form of a retirement plan in 1985, only 79% were in 1997 (Bureau of Labor Statistics 1999). The percentage of workers enrolled in defined-benefit plans declined from 80% in 1985 to 50% in 1997, and coverage by defined-contribution plans grew from 53% to 57% over the same period. Finally, less than half of all full-time workers in small firms are covered by any form of retirement benefit. The portion enrolled in defined-benefit plans declined from 20% in 1990 to 15% in 1996, whereas the portion enrolled in defined-contribution plans grew from 31% to 41%.

Comparison of OECD Experiences with Public and Private Pensions

Public pension systems that have helped to provide income support for the elderly have faced growing financing needs. Both economic and policy changes have resulted in rising expenditures relative to GDP and higher tax rates. In recent years, employment growth has been low or even negative, productivity and wage growth have been sluggish, and inequality has risen.

Assuming that all of these trends will continue or possibly even get worse in the medium to long term seems unrealistic. However, proponents of the theory that public pensions will inevitably end up in crisis base their scenarios on the assumption that all adverse trends we have observed in the recent past will continue over the next 50 years (Turner et al. 1998). If we assume even marginally better economic scenarios, the forecasts of looming crises often become much less pronounced or even disappear (Turner et al. 1998; Baker and Weisbrot 1999).

Due to the design of public pension systems in all seven countries, the adverse economic trends could have given rise to greater financing needs everywhere. Demographic changes could have contributed to more severe financial constraints of public pension systems if they had direct impacts on employment growth. In particular, none of the seven countries had a demographic factor in its benefit formula that linked benefit payments to either demographic or employment changes. Only Sweden introduced a demographic factor into its benefits formula when it reformed its public pension system in 1998.

It is important to keep in mind that demographic changes only set the parameters for employment growth. Demographic trends are not necessarily reflected in the changes in the share of employment relative to the population. In France and Italy, employment relative to the working-age population has declined steadily since the 1960s. In comparison, employment relative to the working-age population has continuously increased in the United States since the 1960s, in Japan since the 1970s, and in the United Kingdom and Germany since the 1980s. Furthermore, levels of employment relative to the working-age population are at or above 70% in Japan, Sweden, the United Kingdom, and the United States but substantially lower in France and Italy.

Early retirement options have helped to lower employment relative to the working-age population. Early retirement exists in all countries except the United Kingdom. In addition to formal early retirement options, some countries (France, Germany) use unemployment insurance provisions to offer de facto early retirement benefits for elderly unemployed workers. In some cases (France, Germany, United Kingdom), disability benefits also serve partially as early retirement benefits. All in all, the share of retirees who have retired under some form of early retirement often exceeds 50% of all retirees, thereby lowering the median retirement age and the labor force participation rates of workers close to the normal retirement age.

Lower productivity and wage growth also may have played a role everywhere. In all countries, benefits are related to past earnings, which means that funding constraints arise because income is growing more slowly than benefits. In contrast, in France, Italy, Sweden, the United Kingdom, and the United States, future benefits are indexed to inflation. Thus, faster real wage growth can help to ease funding constraints because benefits growth is slower than wage growth. Finally, Germany's and Japan's benefits are indexed to after-tax wage growth, which means that slower wage growth has little impact on public pension finances.

Furthermore, increasing income inequality may have affected all systems. In France, Germany, and the United States, there are income ceilings for covered wages. Greater income inequality can cause a smaller share of national income to be covered, thereby lowering the income to public pension systems. Furthermore, all systems have some redistributive aspects, such as minimum pensions; non-earnings-related flat benefits; or explicit redistributive factors in the benefit formula, which means that benefits relative to covered income rise for the relevant income groups. The impact of greater income inequality is larger, however, where the income ceiling is lower or where redistribution is greater: more aggregate income reaches the nontaxable threshold sooner, or more low lifetime earners require larger benefits relative to their earnings.

Funding constraints for public pension systems can result not only from demographic and economic changes but also from policy choices that make the systems more generous. Aside from frequent tax rate changes (see table 2), the seven OECD countries have made infrequent changes to benefits. Out of a total of 43 changes in all seven countries over the course of 28 years, 23 changes have meant benefit increases, 17 have meant benefit cuts, and 3 have had ambiguous benefit effects. The vast majority of benefit increases (21) occurred before the 1990s, whereas the majority of benefit cuts (13) were in the 1990s (table 12). Thus, public pensions became more generous before the 1990s, whereas the likelihood of benefit cuts increased in the 1990s.

Private Pensions as a Solution?

Privatization has been proposed as a means to reduce the financing needs of public pensions. Privatization refers to the investment of public pension assets in private market securities, which can be invested by individuals or the government (or the respective public pension agencies). Since the focus is on investments in private securities, privatization is slightly different from partial or full prefunding. Prefunded public pension systems hold assets, including public securities such as government debt, to cover part or all of their future liabilities.

Rates of Return and Cost Comparisons

Privatization proponents argue that individual accounts will generate higher rates of return, thus reducing financing needs without reducing benefits.

Public pensions promise relatively high rates of return for some workers, especially for low lifetime earners. Most public pensions offer benefits that are also available in the private market but often at higher costs. In particular, public pensions offer indexed lifetime annuities, disability, and life insurance. In an analysis of the U.S. system's implicit rates of return, Baker (1998) estimates that the real rate of return is 5.0% for a couple with one low-wage earner and 3.5% for a couple with two low-wage earners if the insurance value of Social Security is accounted for. In comparison, realistic rates of return for private equity accounts should be around 4% given the long-term projections made by the U.S. public pension trustees (Baker 1997) or around 4% to 4.5% given the current market overvaluation (Diamond 1999).

The two factors that underlie the projections of lower real rates of return in the United States in the future are slower economic growth, and thus also slower profit growth, and the serious overvaluation of the stock market. Both of these trends also hold for the other six countries. Real GDP growth was slower during the 1990s than during the 1970s and—with the exception of Germany—slower than during the 1980s (table 14).

TABLE 14
Real GDP Growth

	France	Germany	Italy	Japan	Sweden	U.K.	U.S.
1990	2.52	5.74	1.97	5.08	1.36	0.64	1.23
1991	0.78	5.01	1.39	3.8	−1.12	−1.49	−0.93
1992	1.16	2.24	0.76	1.02	−1.42	0.05	2.71
1993	−1.33	−1.09	−0.88	0.31	−2.22	2.32	2.32
1994	2.83	2.35	2.21	0.64	3.94	4.39	3.46
1995	2.08	1.75	2.92	1.47	3.71	2.79	2.28
1996	1.55	0.75	0.87	5.05	1.28	2.56	3.45
1997	2.32	1.75	1.48	1.43	1.79	3.51	3.93
1998	3.2	2.25	1.34	−2.83	2.63	2.24	3.88
1999	2.47	1.42	1.23	1.04	3.19	1.14	3.71
Averages							
1970–79	3.73	3.15	3.91	5.21	1.79	2.40	3.19
1980–89	2.27	1.79	2.40	3.78	2.72	2.43	2.76
1990–99	1.76	2.22	1.33	1.70	1.31	1.82	2.60

Source: International Monetary Fund (2000).

In contrast to the real economy, where real economic and productivity growth have been sluggish, equity markets have increased rapidly, particularly during the 1990s. Price–earnings ratios almost doubled in the United Kingdom and in the United States, increased two and a half fold in Sweden, and almost tripled in Germany between 1990 and 1998. Italy's and Japan's price–earnings ratios have fallen precipitously from their heights in the early 1990s, but they still remained significantly higher in the late 1990s than during the early 1990s. Also, dividend yields have fallen everywhere over the course of the 1990s, with the exception of Sweden, despite the fact that in all countries but Japan capital share of business-sector income increased between 1990 and 1998 (OECD 1998c).

The combination of slower economic growth and slower productivity growth with recent rapid growth in stock market valuations increases the chance that future equity rates of return will fall below their past averages. Both lower expected profit growth and overvalued stock markets should result in lower rates of return in the medium to long term.[12]

In comparison, internal rates of return for public pension systems can be largely expected to remain stable. For the United States, the internal rate of return for Social Security has been estimated to be 3.5% for a couple with two low-wage earners (Baker 1998). Rates of return for other public pension systems may be slightly lower than for the United States because of fewer economies of scale (Mitchell 1996). In particular, higher administrative costs elsewhere suggest fewer economies of scale. By and large, administrative costs increase with the size of the funds to be administered or with the number of people to be serviced (Mitchell 1996).[13]

Even though administrative costs for public pension systems appear to differ strongly among countries, they are small compared with the costs of privatized accounts. Fund management alone costs between 1% and 2% of assets annually in the United States. Over a 30-year investment horizon, as administrative costs accumulate, total final savings are over 20% less than they would have been absent administrative costs. Orszag (1999) and Murthi, Orszag, and Orszag (1999) estimated that total administrative costs lower the accumulated savings by 25% over a worker's working life in the United Kingdom. In addition, costs that arise from switching between funds are estimated to amount to 15% of total accumulated savings at the end of a worker's working life.

Privatization of public pensions also requires additional costs that are often ignored. Private pensions require that workers use financial management companies to manage their funds while they work. Once a worker retires, an insurance company needs to provide retirement benefits in the form of lifetime annuities.[14] Mitchell et al. (1997) estimated that annuities on average cost 15% to 20% of annual premiums in the United States. Given current life expectancies at age 65, this translates to 4% to 6% of the total accumulated savings at the end of one's working life. For the United Kingdom, Orszag (1999) and Murthi et al. (1999) estimated annuity costs to be 10% of the account value at retirement. Considering that both the United States and the United Kingdom have well-developed financial markets that are more likely to benefit from economies of scale than financial institutions in other countries, costs in less-developed financial markets can be expected to be at least as high.

Finally, privatization requires transition costs. Workers have already incurred benefit claims against the existing public pension system. To honor these claims, public pension systems require funds even after privatization has ended their revenue stream. In a model calculation for the United States, Olsen et al. (1998) estimated that transition costs under a fully privatized system would amount to 5% over 40 years.

The Risks of Private Accounts

The combination of lower expected rates of returns than in the past and higher costs of private accounts than of public pensions reduces the presumed competitive advantage of private accounts. Even though the higher rates of return that are supposedly associated with private accounts are unlikely to materialize, the higher risks that workers would incur by investing in private accounts remain undiminished. Aside from the obvious financial market risk, workers would face additional economic, regulatory, and political risks.

Private pensions subject workers to more risks than public pensions, such as the risks of bad investment decisions, fraud, or bankruptcy of plan sponsors. While private pensions may be able to match the expected retirement income on average, the variations of retirement income become larger, exposing workers automatically to greater retirement income insecurity. A reliance on private pensions as replacement for public pensions weakens their insurance value.

Private pensions can be defined-benefit or defined-contribution plans. In defined-benefit plans, workers face the risk that the plan sponsor will go bankrupt. Employer bankruptcy poses less of a problem in defined-contribution plans, but workers alone bear financial market risks. Most private pensions in the seven countries are defined-benefit plans (table 15). This is changing in the United Kingdom and the United States, where private pension coverage is most widespread.

Workers cannot rely on private pensions in the same way as they can on public pensions. If permitted by law, employers can change benefit promises; for example, under U.S. law, employers cannot reduce already accrued benefits, but they can change future benefit accruals.

Long vesting periods or restricted portability of pensions reduces the value of private pensions if workers change jobs. How long it takes for workers to become vested depends on the law, the plan type, and the employer. Should the worker leave before she is vested in a plan, no retirement benefits are accrued. Maximum vesting periods range from immediate vesting in Sweden to 30 years in Japan (table 15). If portability of pensions is restricted, workers may keep the benefits, but costs

TABLE 15
Summary of Private Pension Plan Characteristics

	France	Germany	Italy	Sweden	U.K.	Japan	U.S.
Participation	C (partly)	V	V	C (collective agreement)	V	V	V
Plan types	DB, DC	DB mainly	DB	DB	DB mainly	DB mainly	DB, DC
Vesting	—	10 years	—	Immediate	2 years	5–30 years	5 years
Portability	—	—	—	Full	Transfer to other plans	Little transfer value	No transfer of DB; lump-sum payout of DC
Coverage	Top-hat plans for executives	42% (W. Germany 1992)	5% (mainly for executives)	90% (compulsory)	50% (occupational schemes)	37% (funded schemes only)	—
Min. funding requirements	N/A	Yes, up to PBO	Yes, uninsured plans must be fully funded based on 15-year projections	IBO is funded	Only for opted plans	Optional	—
Conversion at retirement	Lump-sum payouts disallowed	Payouts not in interest of firms	Capital-sum payout mandatory under complementary system	Annuity mandatory	Capital-sum payout of ¼ the total possible with max. of 1.5 times annual salary	No mandate	No mandate
Indexation of benefits	—	Mandatory indexation	—	Indexation	Indexation	Rare, except for pensions substituting for public schemes	Discretionary indexation

Notes: C indicates compulsory participation; V denotes voluntary participation in private pension plans. DB indicates defined-benefit plans; DC denotes defined-contribution plans. PBO is projected benefit obligation; IBO is indexed benefit obligation.
Sources: OECD (1998a, 1998b); U.S. Department of Labor (1999); Davis (1994).

and risks cannot be consolidated. Portability is restricted to some degree in all countries except Sweden (table 15).

Accumulated pension wealth can be used for purposes other than retirement income. "Cashing out" account balances requires that workers correctly assess their financial needs over an indeterminate time horizon. Similarly, if pension benefits are not indexed, price increases can erode the value of private pensions over time. Indexation is mandatory only in Germany, but it is possible in Sweden, the United Kingdom, and the United States (table 15).

Regulations may protect workers from investment risks. Permission for individual investors or pension plans to invest in riskier but potentially higher-yielding securities raises the risk of losses. In defined-benefit plans, some risks can be mitigated through diversification, but market risks remain. Most countries impose limits on the asset allocation of pension plans (table 16). The restrictions are loosest in the United States and strictest in Sweden.

Also, large-scale privatization would overwhelm domestic financial markets and local regulators in most countries since private pensions are only a small part of financial market activities. Table 17 shows that in three countries—France, Germany, and Italy—private pension accounts amount to less than 6% of GDP. Furthermore, in all three of these countries, market capitalization is significantly lower than in Sweden, the United Kingdom, and the United States, where private pensions are more widespread (table 18). Privatization would mean the rapid creation of private pension funds. For instance, the German government has proposed to create individual accounts to which workers would contribute 2.5% of payroll in order to replace part of the benefits cut in the 1999 reform of the German public pension system. Given the size of the German public pension system and assuming that the vast majority, say 80%, of private pension funds are invested in equities, German pension funds would increase demand for equities by 2.0% of GDP annually. This additional demand represents more than 4% of Germany's current market capitalization, and this demand would continue indefinitely. Considering that equity markets are already overvalued, additional demand of this magnitude would help to extend a stock market bubble, and workers could face an increasing risk of a market downturn with their retirement assets.

The risks and costs associated with private pensions apply only to those who actually have private pensions. However—as the example of the two countries with the largest private pension systems, the United Kingdom and the United States, indicates—the distribution of those benefits is quite unequal. In the United Kingdom, 65% of full-time workers who earned between £64 and £100 per week had neither an occupational nor a personal pension plan, leaving them with their supplementary SERPS benefits, which are cut from 25% of wages to 20% of wages (Congressional Budget Office 1999). Similarly, while 79% of full-time workers at medium and large U.S. firms were covered by some form of private pension plan in 1997, fewer than half of all full-time workers at small firms were covered by any plan in 1996. Finally, Disney, d'Ercole, and Scherer (1998) reported that in Germany 80% of elderly households (head of household is older than 67) in the bottom quintile had any financial wealth, compared with 98% in the top quintile. Furthermore, the dispersion of families with financial wealth ranges from 84% to 97% in Sweden, from 50% to 80% in the United Kingdom, and from 54% to 97% in the United States (Disney et al. 1998).

TABLE 16

Regulations Governing Pension Fund Investment

Country	Portfolio regulations
France	50% minimum of assets have to be invested in EU public bonds, and 33% maximum in loans to initiators. Insured funds to be at least 34% state bonds, maximum 40% property and 15% treasury deposits. No foreign assets.
Germany	Guidelines: 30% maximum in EU shares, 25% in EU real estate, 6% in non-EU bonds, 20% in foreign assets, 10% self-investment.
Italy	The Decree of Ministry of Finance No. 703 of November 21, 1996, on investments in pension funds in general grants autonomy to the funds to implement their own investment strategies. There are ceilings for investment in some categories: investment in liquid assets is permitted up to 20%, shares in closed funds are permitted up to 20%, and shares and bonds that are not quoted on regulated stock markets in EU countries, the U.S., Canada, or Japan are permitted up to 50% if they are issued by OECD countries.
Sweden	The majority of investments should be made in bonds, loans, and retroverse loans to contributors.
U.K.	5% maximum self-investment; "prudent man rule" concentration limit for defined-contribution plans.
Japan	50% minimum in bonds, 30% maximum in shares, 20% maximum in real estate, 30% maximum in foreign assets, and 10% maximum in the assets of a single company.
U.S.	"Prudent man rule."

Source: OECD (1998b).

The fact that private pensions carry a larger risk than public pensions has put workers in a bind. Also, public pension benefits were reduced in a number of countries (table 12), and there seems to be a

TABLE 17

Pension Fund Assets as Share of GDP, 1987–96

	1987	1990	1992	1994	1995	1996
France	—	3.4	3.2	3.8	4.3	5.6
Germany	3.4	3.3	5.1	5.4	5.2	5.8
Italy	—	—	1.1	2.2	2.6	3.0
Sweden	33.4	31.0	29.6	25.7	30.5	32.6
United Kingdom	62.3	59.7	58.2	69.2	73.2	74.7
Japan	38.0	37.4	37.3	49.4	40.6	41.8
United States	35.7	38.1	48.2	50.6	58.9	58.2

Notes: All figures are percentages. German pension fund assets include company pension fund assets from 1992 onward; figures for Sweden include first pillar assets up to 1992.
Source: OECD (1998b).

TABLE 18

Market Capitalization, Price–Earnings Ratios, and Total Rates of Return for OECD Stock Markets, 1990–1998

	France	Germany	Italy	Japan	Sweden	U.K.	U.S.
Market capitalization (% of GDP)						
1990	24.15	21.78	12.74	91.53	38.57	79.71	53.51
1991	28.07	20.31	12.69	85.16	37.08	89.65	68.48
1992	27.05	17.71	11.97	61.41	38.13	101.02	71.31
1993	37.18	24.64	15.87	68.38	61.39	122.67	76.93
1994	32.30	22.80	18.37	74.76	61.03	108.42	71.27
1995	31.58	23.45	18.55	75.44	67.07	122.84	93.48
1996	38.67	28.75	20.67	69.82	94.03	128.43	108.17
1997	49.37	40.28	30.78	55.09	115.05	148.99	129.27
1998	64.85	47.96	45.42	56.57	118.84	168.05	144.39
Price–earnings ratio						
1990	10.2	11.6	16.5	11.0	39.8	10.6	14.8
1991	13.8	14.1	16.9	22.0	37.8	14.2	25.8
1992	15.4	22.0	25.8	60.0	36.7	17.5	22.7
1993	19.0	24.5	58.6	31.0	64.9	24.8	23.4
1994	14.0	25.2	136.9	14.0	79.5	17.4	18.2
1995	16.0	22.3	30.2	11.0	86.5	15.6	19.2
1996	N/A	20.7	18.9	17.0	79.3	15.9	20.6
1997	N/A	27.8	24.7	22.0	37.6	19.2	23.9
1998	N/A	30.6	25.0	21.0	103.1	23.3	27.2
Dividend yield (%)						
1990	4.0	3.78	3.3	3.6	0.6	5.7	3.7
1991	3.8	3.8	3.8	3.2	0.7	5.0	2.4
1992	3.8	4	4.1	2.7	0.9	4.3	3.0
1993	2.7	2.9	2.5	1.4	0.8	3.9	2.5
1994	3.2	3.32	1.6	2.0	0.8	4.3	2.9
1995	3.3	2.8	1.7	2.8	0.9	3.9	2.4
1996	2.7	1.8	2.4	2.4	0.8	3.9	2.1
1997	2.2	1.7	1.7	2.1	1.0	3.2	1.7
1998	2.1	1.3	1.4	2.2	1.2	2.8	N/A

Notes: Market capitalization for the United States is the sum of year-end market capitalizations of AMEX, NYSE, NASDAQ, and Chicago. U.S. price–earnings ratio and dividend yield are for NYSE only.
Sources: International Federation of Stock Exchanges (2000); International Monetary Fund's International Financial Statistics CD-ROM.

shift from defined-benefit to defined-contribution plans, especially in countries where private pensions are an important source of retirement income. Workers are therefore faced with the choice between lower risks and subsequently less retirement income or the possibility of higher retirement income at a significantly higher risk. Consequently, workers increasingly tend to invest their retirement savings in risky equity funds. About 75% of all 401(k) plan balances in the United States were estimated to be invested directly or indirectly in equities (VanDerhei, Holden, and Quick 2000). More specifically, plan holders in their 60s still have 39.2% invested in equities, whereas people in their 20s have 62.2% directly invested in equities. Similarly, in the United Kingdom, 80% of pension fund assets were invested in equity in 1994.

The promised rates of return for private accounts, particularly private equity accounts, are unlikely to materialize in the medium to long term because of slower expected GDP and productivity growth and because of the current market valuations. In addition, the costs associated with private pensions are substantially higher than the costs associated with public pensions for the same services. Furthermore, private pensions shift risks from the public to the individual. The risks for the individual seem to have especially increased in countries where the reliance on private pensions is most pronounced, the United States and the United Kingdom.

Conclusions

Public pensions have been a successful tool in combating poverty among the elderly. The commitment to provide the elderly with adequate retirement income seems to be intact in the industrialized countries. However, the question is whether governments should continue to provide public pensions as social insurance or whether private markets should take over. The evidence presented in this paper suggests that public pensions can be provided as a public good in the foreseeable future if policy changes are made and that private pensions would put the social insurance aspect of public pensions in jeopardy.

The financial needs of public pensions appear to have grown. Higher tax rates and benefit cuts have been the result. The evidence suggests that both economic factors and the particular design of each country's public pension system have led to greater financing needs. Especially slow employment and wage growth and possibly rising income inequality have adversely affected the finances of all public pension systems.

Projections of future problems rest to a large degree on rather pessimistic assumptions about economic trends and the unchanged structure of public pensions. Under more moderate assumptions, the burden
for workers of caring for the elderly grows more slowly or declines.
Finally, regardless of the underlying assumptions, the living standards of
future generations are likely to be substantially higher than those of current workers.

The changing demographics that exist in each country and that are
likely to continue can be compensated for by more rapid employment
growth and more rapid productivity and wage growth than is currently
expected. Thus, policy makers have the opportunity to influence forces
that can compensate for the continued increase in longevity and the
decline in population growth.

The goal of policies that ensure the future of public pensions should
be to raise employment and productivity. In particular, labor force participation could be boosted through family-friendly policies that allow
parents to combine child-rearing responsibilities and full-time jobs.
Even though raising the normal retirement age could increase labor
force participation, such a benefit is very regressive, puts the largest burden on low lifetime earners, and thus should not be further pursued.
Macroeconomic policies could be used, particularly in Europe, as a stim-
ulus to lower unemployment and raise employment growth. In particular, a less stringent monetary policy appears to be a means to achieve
lower unemployment. Finally, more equal earnings distributions can be
achieved through government policies, such as setting a minimum wage,
or through the strengthening of collective bargaining.

Aside from economic policies, changes in the structure of public
pensions may be necessary to ensure their long-term viability. First,
public pensions should be universal systems that require everybody to
participate. Second, public pensions should not serve as a substitute for
unemployment insurance. Third, the financing base of public pensions
should be stable. Thus, shifts in labor income as a percentage of national
income should not affect public pension finances. In particular, instead
of financing public pensions solely out of payroll taxes, other forms of
income, such as capital income, could also be taxed. Similarly, public
pensions could be financed out of general revenue.

Privatization of pensions, albeit increasingly popular, appears too
risky and too costly to be viable. Also, private pensions constitute only a
small addition to public pensions in many cases, with the exceptions of

the United Kingdom and the United States. While coverage of workers under private pension schemes seems to increase in countries where such plans are rather small, it is declining in the two countries where pension coverage is relatively large. Furthermore, a rapid privatization of a significant share of public pensions, which would be necessary to make privatization a viable option in theory, would most likely overwhelm private financial institutions and markets, possibly leading to financial instability and greater risks for workers.

It is time to put the debate over the future of public pensions into a serious framework. Thus, the pessimistic "gloom and doom" forecasts of those who want to see an end to government-administered and publicly supported social insurance have to be put in perspective. Where the underlying public pension structures are adversely affected, possibly even to a degree that magnifies existing trends, the solutions lie in both redesigning public pensions and in improving equality, productivity, and employment growth. No law of nature says that industrialized economies will be mired in slow growth and rising inequality in the long term. Policy makers have the option to improve the economic outcomes that can aid their public pension systems directly.

Appendix: Calculating Combined Tax Rates for OECD Countries

This section describes the calculation for the combined tax rates in table 2.

France

Government contributions are reported as share of benefit payments in 1969 and as share of income between 1989 and 1997. The reported figures for 1999 ("various subsidies") are assumed to be close to zero and are hence ignored. It is assumed that income and outgo are identical. Thus, the combined employer and employee contributions out of average earnings are scaled by the share made up by government contributions.

Germany

Government contributions are reported as share of benefit payments (1961–1969) and as share of total system (1971–1999). It is assumed that benefits and contributions are identical and that there are no other costs. Hence, the combined employer and employee contribution rates are scaled by the government contribution to arrive at the combined tax rate.

Italy

For 1997, employer contributions amounted to 8.89% for earnings up to 63,054,000 lire per year and to 9.9% for earnings above that but below 250,000,000. For 1997 and 1999, employee contributions are two tiered. Since the first tier is very close to the annual average wage rate of the business sector, only the first-tier tax rate is used for either employer or employee.

Government contributions are reported as share of total covered earnings (1961–1964), as share of costs (1967), or as lump-sum subsidies (1969–1999). For the years 1961 and 1964, the government's percentage contribution is added to employer and employee contribution rates, and for 1967, the combined employer and employee contribution rates are scaled by the government's contribution to arrive at the combined tax rates. In all other years, the government's contribution is set equal to zero.

Japan

Employee contributions are reported as a fixed yen amount. I divided them by the average annual wage rate of the business sector to arrive at the average tax rate. Complete data are available only from 1980 forward. Between 1980 and 1993, three tax rates (women, men, miners) are averaged (simple average), and between 1995 and 1999, two tax rates (women, men) are averaged for the welfare pensions. Finally, the tax rates for welfare pensions and for national pensions are added.

Both welfare and national pensions receive government contributions as a share of benefits. It is assumed that benefits are equal to contributions and that there are no other substantial costs. Hence, the combined employer and employee contributions are scaled—separately for each program—by the government contributions.

Sweden

Employer contributions are reported as share of payroll since 1975 for universal pensions and since 1983 for supplementary pensions. Before 1975, there are no employer contributions to universal pensions, and before 1983, employer contributions to supplementary pensions are reported as share of earnings between a lower and an upper bound. Tax rates that fall between an upper and a lower bound are scaled by the difference between the upper and lower bounds relative to the upper bound, which lies well beyond the average wage rate.

Government contributions to universal pensions are reported as share of benefits and other costs. It is assumed that benefit payments are equal to contributions. Combined employer and employee contributions to universal pensions are scaled by government contributions.

United Kingdom

Where ranges of tax rates are reported, the simple average is taken. If tax is payable only above a weekly earnings threshold (as was the case in 1999), the tax rates are scaled by average wage rates above the earnings threshold relative to average earnings.

Government contributions are reported as share of benefits and other costs between 1975 and as "various subsidies" after that. Hence, combined employer and employee contributions are scaled by government contributions between 1975 and 1991. Government contributions are assumed to be marginal thereafter and hence are set equal to zero.

United States

The average wage is below the point above which income is not subject to the payroll tax. Thus, the combined tax rate is simply the sum of employer and employee contribution rates.

The Ability to Pay and Changes in Living Standards

A country's ability to pay for its retirees depends on the number of workers relative to all retirees and on average wages and benefits. I first constructed a measure that adjusts each year's ratio of beneficiaries to workers by increases in before-tax real wages and by changes in benefit indexation, where necessary. I call this adjusted ratio the Care for the Aged and Retired by Employees Ratio (CARER).

CARER is defined as follows:

$$\text{CARER}_T = \frac{POP65+}{EMPLOYEES_T} \yen \frac{(newret) \yen \overline{(wage)_{T\text{-}n,T}}}{wage_T} \yen BenIndex \qquad (4)$$

where *POP65+* is the sum of all people above the age of 64, *EMPLOYEES* is total employment, and *(wage)T–n,T* is the average wage growth for the past *n* years (equal to the maximum of years needed for full benefits), which is scaled by the proportion of 65-year-olds relative to all elderly, *newret*. The number of employees is scaled by the real before-tax wages relative to their level in 2000, the base year. All economic variables are real; thus, in countries where benefits are indexed to inflation, the benefits indexation, *BenIndex*, is equal to 1. In countries where benefits are indexed to net wages (Germany, Japan), *BenIndex* is equal to the after-tax wage.

A few assumptions are necessary for this calculation. The number of public pension beneficiaries is equal to the number of those over 64 years old. Since all public pension systems offer not only retirement but also disability and survivorship benefits and in some cases welfare or poverty pensions (see the section "Country Experiences with Public and Private Pensions" for a detailed description of each country's benefits), the vast majority of those over 64 years old will receive benefits in one form or another.

To calculate changes in the net wage relative to its level in 2000, I proceeded as follows. The change in the after-tax wage is equal to the change in the before-tax wage minus changes in tax rates. I assumed that taxes other than public pension taxes remain constant over time. As a country's population ages, this assumption is likely to overstate the tax burden on workers because an aging population will most likely incur fewer costs for childcare, education, and other expenses related to the younger population. Furthermore, changes in public pension taxes were calculated by multiplying the cumulative percentage changes in the CARER by each country's combined tax rate in 1999 (see table 2 for details).

Different sources were used for the calculations. Demographic variables were provided by the U.S. Bureau of the Census International Database. All economic variables, with the exception of the CPI, are taken from the OECD's Economic Outlook Database, and the CPI is taken from the International Monetary Fund's International Financial Statistics CD-ROM.

Notes

[1] No data are available for Japan or Sweden. Also, the U.K. data include the supplementary pensions.

[2] Poverty rates vary from national measures because the Luxembourg Income Study (LIS) uses 50% of the median adjusted disposable personal income as the poverty threshold.

[3] See Turner et al. (1998) for a formalization of the connection between demographic changes and growth. Their predictions, however, are sensitive to assumptions about unemployment rates and labor force participation.

[4] If income is not capped, inequality has an ambiguous effect. Because of the redistributive functions of public pension benefits, a growing share of high-income earners may in fact help public pension finances. The exact effect depends on each system's benefit formulas.

[5] According to the OECD (1997), income inequality grew in France between 1986 and 1997; the Luxembourg Income Study (LIS 1999) indicates that income inequality grew in France in the early 1980s, remained stable in the late 1980s, and fell in the 1990s; and Atkinson (1998) found that income inequality continuously declined in France from 1977 to 1990. According to the LIS (1999), inequality rose in Germany from 1981 to 1995; the OECD (1997) indicates continuously rising income inequality in Germany between 1986 and 1991; Atkinson (1998) found rising income inequality in Germany from 1977 to 1995; and the Deutsches Institut für Wirtschaftsforschung (2000) reported increasing income inequality throughout the 1990s. The OECD (1997) found continuously growing income inequality in Italy between 1986 and 1991; Atkinson (1998) found that income inequality grew in Italy from 1991 to 1993; and the LIS (1999) showed that income inequality rose in Italy from 1991 to 1995. Also, income inequality appears to have grown in Japan in recent decades; Atkinson (1998) found growing income inequality between 1977 and 1991. The LIS (1999) showed that income inequality grew in Sweden from 1981 to 1992 and declined slightly by 1995. The OECD (1997) also found continuously growing income inequality in the United Kingdom between 1986 and 1991; the LIS (1999) showed rising income inequality in the United Kingdom between 1974 and 1995; and Atkinson (1998) found that income inequality grew in the United Kingdom from 1977 to 1995. Finally, income inequality has grown in the United States between 1986 and 1991 (OECD 1997) and between 1979 and 1997 (LIS 1999).

[6] See the appendix for a detailed description of the methodology and the assumptions used in the simulations.

[7] Because prefunded or partially funded systems impose a larger tax burden on capital than PAYG, my cost estimates likely overstate the future burden.

[8] It is common to assume that real wage growth is equal to productivity growth in the long run.

[9] A lower normal retirement age is different from early retirement. Under early retirement rules, benefits are reduced, generally in an actuarially fair way; but with a lower normal retirement age, full benefits are paid earlier.

[10] Sometimes the complementary mandatory pensions are considered employment-related pensions (OECD 1998c; Davis 1994). From a risk perspective, these schemes more resemble public pension systems than private pension systems.

[11] Compulsory membership in a company scheme as a condition of employment was abolished in 1998. Thus, personal pensions to which employers are not required to contribute have increased in number (Davis 1994).

[12] Productivity and profits may rise faster than expected, resulting in higher rates of return. At this point, however, forecasts for the future of public pensions would have to be revised, too. Significantly higher productivity growth rates would result in sharply declining burdens of caring for the elderly, as the simulations in the "Background" section showed.

[13] Administrative costs amount to 0.7% of benefit payments in Sweden (information provided by the National Social Insurance Board), 0.9% in the United States (SSA 2000a), 1.8% in Japan (Mitchell 1996), 1.9% in Italy (International Labor Organization [ILO] 2000), 2.1% in Germany (ILO 2000), 3.1% in the United Kingdom (Mitchell 1996), and 4.2% in France (ILO 2000).

[14] While not all privatization proposals would require the purchase of annuities, it is necessary to include them in a fair comparison between the costs of private and public pensions.

References

Abraham, Katharine, and Susan Houseman. 1995. "Earnings Inequality in Germany." In R. Freeman and L. Katz, eds., *Differences and Changes in Wage Structures*. Chicago: University of Chicago Press.

Ahrend, Peter. 1996. "Pension Financial Security in Germany." In Zvi Bodie, Olivia S. Mitchell, and John A. Turner, eds., *Securing Employer-Based Pensions: An International Perspective*. Philadelphia: University of Pennsylvania Press.

Atkinson, Anthony B. 1998. "The Distribution of Income in Industrialised Countries." Paper presented to the Symposium on Income Inequality: Issues and Policy Options, sponsored by the Federal Reserve Bank of Kansas City, Jackson Hole, WY, August.

Baker, Dean. 1997. *Saving Social Security with Stocks: The Promises Don't Add Up*. New York: Twentieth Century Fund.

———. 1998. *The Full Returns from Social Security*. A Century Foundation/Economic Policy Institute Report. New York: Century Foundation.

Baker, Dean, and Mark Weisbrot. 1999. *The Phony Crisis*. Chicago: University of Chicago Press.

Blanchet, Didier, and Louis-Paul Pelé. 1997. *Social Security and Retirement in France*. NBER Working Paper No. 6214. Cambridge, MA: National Bureau of Economic Research.

Blundell, Richard, and Paul Johnson. 1997. *Pensions and Retirement in the UK*. NBER Working Paper No. 6154. Cambridge, MA: National Bureau of Economic Research.

Board of Governors of the Federal Reserve. 1999. *Flow of Funds Statistics*. Washington, DC: Board of Governors of the Federal Reserve.

Börsch-Supan, Axel, Anette Reil-Held, Ralf Rodepeter, Reinhold Schnabel, and Joachim Winter. 2000. *Household Savings in Germany*. Levy Institute Working Paper No. 306. Annandale-on-Hudson, NY: Jerome Levy Economics Institute.

Börsch-Supan, Axel, and Reinhold Schnabel. 1997. *Social Security and Retirement in Germany*. NBER Working Paper No. 6153. Cambridge, MA: National Bureau of Economic Research.

Brugiavini, Agar. 1997. *Social Security and Retirement in Italy*. NBER Working Paper No. 6155. Cambridge, MA: National Bureau of Economic Research.

Bundesversicherungsanstalt fuer Angestellte. 2000. "Statistik." <http://www.bfa-berlin.de/>.

Bureau of Labor Statistics. 1999. *Employee Benefits in Medium and Large Private Establishments, 1997*. Bulletin 2517 (September). Washington, DC: Department of Labor, Bureau of Labor Statistics.

Commissariat Général du Plan. 1995. *Perspectives à long terme des retraites*. Paris: La Documentation Française.

Confederation of British Industry. 1994. *Pensions: A View from the Top*. London: Confederation of British Industry.

Congressional Budget Office. 1999. *Social Security Privatization: Experiences Abroad*. CBO Paper, January. Washington, DC: Congressional Budget Office.

Davis, E. Philip. 1994. *Pension Funds: Retirement-Income Security and Capital Markets: An International Perspective*. Oxford and New York: Oxford University Press, Clarendon Press.

Deutsche Bundesbank. 1984. "Company Pension Schemes in the Federal Republic of Germany." *Deutsche Bundesbank Monthly Report*, Vol. 39, no. 1, pp. 30–37.

Deutsches Institut für Wirtschaftsforschung. 2000. *Einkommensverteilung in Deutschland—Stärkere Umverteilungseffekte in Ostdeutschland*. DIW Wochenbericht 19/2000. Berlin: Deutsches Institut für Wirtschaftsforschung.

Diamond, Peter. 1999. *What Stock Market Returns to Expect for the Future?* Issue Brief No. 2, September. Boston: Center for Retirement Research at Boston College.

Diamond, Peter, and Johnathan Gruber. 1997. *Social Security and Retirement in the U.S.* NBER Working Paper No. 6097. Cambridge, MA: National Bureau of Economic Research.

Disney, Richard, Marco Mira d'Ercole, and Peter Scherer. 1998. *Resources during Retirement*. OECD Ageing Working Paper AWP 4.3. Paris: Organisation for Economic Co-operation and Development.

Edin, Per-Anders, and Bertil Holmlund. 1995. "The Swedish Wage Structure: The Rise and Fall of Solidarity Wage Policy?" In R. Freeman and L. Katz, eds., *Differences and Changes in Wage Structures*. Chicago: University of Chicago Press.

European Commission. 1999a. *Employment in Europe*. Brussels: European Commission.

Freeman, R., and L. Katz, eds. 1995. *Differences and Changes in Wage Structures*. Chicago: University of Chicago Press.

Gottschalk, Peter, and Timothy M. Smeeding. 1997. "Cross-National Comparisons of Earnings and Income Inequality." *Journal of Economic Literature*, Vol. 35, no. 2 (June), pp. 633–87.

Hauser, Richard. 1998. *Adequacy and Poverty among the Retired*. OECD Ageing Working Paper AWP 3.2. Paris: Organisation for Economic Co-operation and Development.

Herbertsson, Tryggvi Thor, Michael J. Orszag, and Peter R. Orszag. 2000. "Retirement in the Nordic Countries: Prospects and Proposals for Reform." Report to the Nordic Council of Ministers, May 10. London: Birkbeck College, University of London.

International Federation of Stock Exchanges. 2000. "Statistics." http://www.fibv.com/statistics.asp>.

International Labor Organization. 2000. "Cost of Social Security 1990–96." <http://www.ilo.org/public/english/protection/socsec/publ/css/cssindex.htm#point28a>.

International Monetary Fund. 2000. *World Economic Outlook* (September). Washington, DC: International Monetary Fund.

Katz, Lawrence, Gary Loveman, and David Blanchflower. 1995. "A Comparison of Changes in the Structure of Wages in Four OECD Countries." In R. Freeman and L. Katz, eds., *Differences and Changes in Wage Structure*, Chicago: University of Chicago Press.

Luxembourg Income Study. 1999. "LIS Inequality Indices." <http://www.lis.ceps.lu/ineq.htm>.

Ministry of Health and Social Affairs. 1998. "Pension Reform in Sweden: A Short Summary." Paper presented at the World Bank, Washington, DC, May 7, and at the Brookings Institution, Washington, DC, May 8. Washington, DC: Embassy of Sweden.

Mitchell, Olivia. 1996. *Administrative Costs in Public and Private Retirement Systems*. NBER Working Paper No. 5734. Cambridge, MA: National Bureau of Economic Research.

Mitchell, Olivia, James Poterba, and Mark Warshawsky. 1997. *New Evidence on the Money's Worth of Individual Annuities*. NBER Working Paper No. 6002. Cambridge, MA: National Bureau of Economic Research.

Murthi, Mamta, J. Michael Orszag, and Peter R. Orszag. 1999. *The Charge Ratio on Individual Accounts: Lessons from the UK Experience*. Birkbeck College Working Paper 99-2, March 2. London: University of London.

Office of Fair Trading. 1997. *Report of the Director General's Inquiry into Pensions*. London: Office of Fair Trading.

Olsen, Kelly A., Jack VanDerhei, Dallas L. Salisbury, and Martin R. Holmer. 1998. *How Do Individual Social Security Accounts Stack Up? An Evaluation Using the EBRI-SSASIM2 Policy Simulation Model*. EBRI Issue Brief No. 195, March. Washington, DC: Employee Benefits Research Institute.

Organisation for Economic Co-operation and Development. 1997. *OECD Employment Outlook* (July). Paris: Organisation for Economic Co-operation and Development.

———. 1998a. *Financial Market Trends*, no. 70 (June). Paris: Organisation for Economic Co-operation and Development.

———. 1998b. *Financial Market Trends*, no. 71 (November). Paris: Organisation for Economic Co-operation and Development.

———. 1998c. *OECD Economic Outlook*, no. 64 (December). Paris: Organisation for Economic Co-operation and Development.

———. 2000. *OECD Economic Surveys: Italy, May 2000*. Italy: Organisation for Economic Co-operation and Development.

Orszag, Peter. 1999. *Administrative Costs in Individual Accounts in the United Kingdom*. CBPP Report, March. Washington, DC: Center on Budget and Policy Priorities.

Oshio, Takshi, and Naohiro Yashiro. 1997. *Social Security and Retirement in Japan*. NBER Working Paper No. 6156. Cambridge, MA: National Bureau of Economic Research.

Palme, Mårten, and Ingemar Svensson. 1997. *Social Security, Occupational Pensions and Retirement in Sweden*. NBER Working Paper No. 6137. Cambridge, MA: National Bureau of Economic Research.

Prognos AG. 1998. *Asuwirkungen veränderter ökonomischer und rechtlicher Rahmenbedingungen auf die gesetzliche Rentenversicherung in Deutschland*. DRV-Schriften, Band 9. Frankfurt am Main: Prognos AG.

Sinn, Hans-Werner. 1999. *The Crisis in Germany's Pension Insurance System and How It Can Be Solved*. NBER Working Paper No. 7304. Cambridge, MA: National Bureau of Economic Research.

Sinn, Hans-Werner, and Marcel Thum. 1999. "Gesetzliche Rentenversicherung: Prognosen im Vergleich." *Finanzarchiv*, Vol. 56, pp. 104–35.

Smeeding, Timothy M. 1997. *Financial Poverty in Developed Countries: The Evidence from the LIS*. Luxembourg Income Study Working Paper no. 155. Syracuse, NY: Syracuse University.

Social Security Administration. Various years. *Social Security Programs throughout the World*. Washington, DC: Social Security Administration.

———. 1999. *Annual Statistical Supplement to the Social Security Bulletin 1999*. Washington, DC: Social Security Administration.

———. 2000a. *The 2000 Annual Report of the Board of Trustees of the Federal Old-Age and Survivors Insurance and Disability Insurance Trust Funds*. Washington, DC: Social Security Administration.

———. 2000b. *Income of the Population 55 and Older*. Washington, DC: Social Security Administration.

Turner, Dave, Claude Giorno, Alain De Serres, Ann Vourc'h, and Pete Richardson. 1998. *The Macroeconomic Implications of Ageing in a Global Context*. OECD Ageing Working Paper AWP 1.2. Paris: Organisation for Economic Co-operation and Development.

U.S. Department of Labor. 1999. *Private Pension Plan Bulletin*, No. 8 (Spring). Washington, DC: U.S. Department of Labor, Pension and Welfare Benefits Administration.

VanDerhei, Jack, Sarah Holden, and Carol Quick. 2000. *401(k) Plan Asset Allocation, Account Balances and Loan Activity in 1998*. EBRI Issue Brief, February. Washington, DC: Employee Benefit Research Institute.

CHAPTER 3

Diverting the Old-Age Crisis: International Projections of Living Standards

DEAN BAKER

Center for Economic and Policy Research

In recent years, a major topic of national debate has been the aging of the population. The media have presented numerous accounts of the costs associated with supporting the much larger population of retirees that the nation is projected to have in 20 or 30 years. Members of Congress have put forward numerous proposals to cut Social Security and Medicare to reduce the public-sector costs of supporting a larger elderly population. The cost of these programs is likely to be a major issue in future elections.

To a lesser extent this debate is also being carried on in other industrialized nations. All of the industrialized nations face the same "problem." Improvements in living standards and medical technology are allowing people to live longer. Therefore, all of these nations are looking at a future where the portion of the population over age 65 will be considerably greater than it is at present, although the exact timing of this demographic change differs among nations. Several years ago the World Bank devoted a volume to addressing this topic, *Averting the Old Age Crisis* (1994).

An increase in the relative size of the population of nonworking elderly people will impose costs on the rest of society. But it is not evident that these costs are of sufficient magnitude to warrant the attention that the issue has received. Nations have often absorbed much larger costs without viewing them as a "crisis." For example, in the United States, the increase in military spending associated with the Cold War was far larger measured as a share of GDP than the projected increase in spending associated with supporting a larger population of retirees. It is also worth noting that this increase took place over just a few years rather than several decades. Furthermore, in looking forward at future living standards, it is not evident that the aging of the population will loom as such an important factor. Other factors will also have a major impact on the living standards of future generations.

This chapter examines the impact of three of those factors—productivity growth, health care expenditures, and wage inequality—on living standards among nations and compares them with the impact of the aging of the population. This sort of cross-national comparison can help focus attention on what will actually be the most important factors determining living standards for typical families in the next century. It is also worth noting that, unlike the aging of the population, the other three factors examined in this paper can all be affected (albeit not easily) by policy. Insofar as it can be shown that these factors will have comparable or larger impacts on future living standards, it may be appropriate to focus public attention on these areas rather than a demographic phenomenon about which little can be done.

This chapter builds on an earlier study (Baker 1998) that constructed projections of income for families in the United States in the 21st century. This study relied on projections of wage and GDP growth from the Social Security Trustees Report (Social Security Administration 1999a) to project before-tax income at various dates in the 21st century. It used projections of the increase in Social Security costs from this report and Medicare and Medicaid costs from the Health Care Financing Administration to construct projections of after-tax income. It also used the Health Care Financing Administration's projections of health care costs to derive projections of after-tax, after-health-care income, the money that families will have left over after paying both their taxes and their health care expenses. Finally, it imposed on these growth patterns recent trends in wage inequality to determine how families at various points along the income ladder are likely to fare.

This chapter produces a similar set of projections for various Organisation for Economic Co-operation and Development (OECD) nations. These projections are intended only to give a general order of magnitude of the relative impact of these trends in each nation. Producing a more accurate projection of the expected impact would require considerably greater detail about each nation's institutional structure than is used in this paper. Nonetheless, the calculations produced here can be instructive because they provide both a preliminary estimate of the relative magnitudes of each of these factors among nations and a framework in which a more detailed analysis can be conducted.

The chapter has five parts. The first section constructs projections of wage growth for several OECD nations by extrapolating from past rates of productivity growth. The second section presents projections of after-tax wages that incorporate the impact of the aging of the population on national tax rates. The third section projects after-tax, after-health-care income based on recent trends in the growth of health care costs in both the private and public sector. The fourth section presents projections for the median family's after-tax, after-health-care income based on recent trends in wage inequality in each nation. The fifth section compares the relative importance of each of these factors and the differences in their impacts among nations.

Here is a summary of the findings:

- Differences in national rates of productivity growth, if they persist, will have a far larger impact on future living standards than any of the other factors examined. The impact of the variation in rates of productivity growth will be on average nearly four times as large as the impact of the higher projected tax burden associated with an aging population. This means that bringing productivity growth rates of the slower-growing nations, such as the United States, closer in line with the overall average will have far more impact on the living standards of future generations of workers than any savings that can be had by restructuring public pension systems.

- The impact of trends in wage inequality is potentially far larger for the typical family than the impact of tax increases associated with an aging population. In most OECD nations, there appears to have been some increase in wage inequality in the last two decades, with a larger share of wage income going to higher-wage workers. This trend has been particularly pronounced in the case of the United States and the United Kingdom. On average, the projected impact of recent trends in inequality on the income of the median worker is approximately 50% greater than the projected impact of the tax burden due to an aging population. In the case of the United States, the projected impact of inequality is more than three times as large as that of the tax burden associated with the aging of the population, and in the United Kingdom it is more than four times as large.

- The impact of growing health care costs on workers' after-tax, after-health-care income may be comparable in size to the impact of the increased taxes associated with an aging population. The trend in health care costs varies considerably across the OECD; many nations have been quite successful in containing the share of GDP that goes to health care expenditures. In the cases where costs have not been successfully contained, the continuation of past growth rates will pose a large burden on future living standards. In the case of the United States, the burden associated with rising health care costs is projected to be more than twice as large as the burden associated with the aging of the population.

Comparative Rates of Productivity Growth

A simple examination of the data reveals large and persistent differences in the rate of productivity growth among nations. This is striking because it might be expected that with increasingly mobile capital and a convergence of absolute levels of productivity, there would also be a convergence of growth rates. To date, this does not appear to have happened. The rate of productivity growth in several European nations that have largely caught up with the United States—most importantly France, Germany, and Italy—continues to be far more rapid than in the United States.[1] If this faster growth rate persists, these nations will have far higher levels of productivity than the United States by the middle of the next century.

Table 1 presents the reported rates of productivity growth in recent years for several OECD nations. It presents data from the OECD and the Conference Board. (The projections in this and other tables are explained in more detail in the appendix.) These sources use somewhat different methodologies, so the fact that they arrive at mostly similar results should provide a considerable degree of confidence in the measurements. As can be seen from the table, several nations have managed to maintain annual rates of productivity growth at or above 2.0%, compared to an annual rate of approximately 1.0% in the United States.[2] Some nations' rapid rate of productivity growth can be attributed to their low absolute level of productivity. These nations are in a process of catching up to the leaders, which allows them to borrow from the technological advances already achieved elsewhere.

But most of the nations with more rapid productivity growth can no longer be viewed as catching up. Table 2 presents data on output per worker hour from the Bureau of Labor Statistics (1999) and the Conference Board (1997). While nations such as Ireland and Japan are

TABLE 1
Trends in Productivity Growth

	OECD GDP per worker, 1979–96	OECD GDP per hour, 1979–96	Conference Board GDP per hour, 1973–95	Cumulative productivity growth, 2030 (1995 = 100)
Australia	1.2	1.3	1.4	162.7
Austria	1.8		2.2	214.2
Belgium	1.8		2.6	245.6
Canada			1.4	162.7
Denmark	1.7		1.7	180.4
Finland	2.6	2.8	2.3	221.6
France	1.8	2.4	2.5	237.3
Germany	1.9	2.6	2.6	245.6
Ireland	3.5		3.7	356.7
Italy	2.0		2.4	229.3
Japan	2.1	2.8	2.7	254.1
Netherlands	1.0		2.1	207.0
New Zealand	1.3			157.2
Norway	2.3	2.8	2.9	272.0
Portugal	2.0		1.3	157.2
Spain	2.4	3.0	2.9	272.0
Sweden	1.8	1.4	1.4	162.7
United Kingdom	1.8	2.1	2.1	207.0
United States	0.9	0.8	1.0	157.2
Average				**215.9**

Notes: All values are annual percentage change. Cumulative productivity numbers use the Conference Board data, except for New Zealand. The U.S. productivity projection is taken from the Social Security Administration (1999a).
Source: Schmitt and Mishel's (1998) analysis of OECD and Conference Board (1997) data.

clearly still in the catch-up phase, many of the nations experiencing significantly more rapid productivity growth than the United States already have achieved essentially the same absolute level of productivity. This is clearly true for the three largest economies in Europe: France, Germany, and Italy.

If the divergence in growth rates persists, several OECD nations will have significantly higher absolute levels of productivity than the United States by the middle of the next century. Table 3 combines the data on productivity growth and levels to project absolute levels of productivity for 2030. As can be seen, most nations will have far surpassed the United States in absolute levels of productivity if they maintain their recent pace of productivity growth and productivity growth in the United States follows the path projected by the Social Security Administration (1999a).

The last column in table 1 projects productivity levels in 2030, setting each nation's productivity level in the year 1995 at 100. This index of productivity growth can also be applied to the growth of before-tax wages. In long-term projections, it is usually assumed that the shares of

TABLE 2
Productivity Levels

	BLS GDP per worker, 1996	BLS GDP per hour, 1996	Conference Board GDP per hour, 1995
Australia	N/A	N/A	76
Austria	74.3	N/A	83
Belgium	75.9	N/A	97
Canada	76.2	N/A	85
Denmark	77.9	N/A	74
Finland	N/A	N/A	74
France	71.6	100.4	102
Germany (West)	80.2	106.8	101
Ireland	N/A	N/A	84
Italy	70.3	N/A	90
Japan	81.0	70.9	68
Netherlands	72.6	N/A	98
New Zealand	N/A	N/A	N/A
Norway	84.7	107.6	88
Portugal	N/A	N/A	38
Spain	N/A	N/A	70
Sweden	67.1	82.9	79
United Kingdom	65.1	N/A	84
United States	100.0	100.0	100

Source: Conference Board (1997) and Bureau of Labor Statistics (1999).

TABLE 3
2030 GDP per Worker Hour

	OECD growth rate	Conference Board growth rate
Australia	119.4	100.4
Austria	184.0	139.8
Belgium	194.0	200.8
Canada	120.4	108.5
Denmark	153.2	148.0
Finland	255.2	194.5
France	218.5	184.0
Germany (West)	148.1	314.7
Ireland	320.5	529.3
Italy	186.3	236.6
Japan	145.6	184.9
Netherlands	170.8	159.4
New Zealand	N/A	N/A
Norway	164.3	223.6
Portugal	87.2	45.2
Spain	184.0	249.7
Sweden	158.0	115.9
United Kingdom	156.8	156.8
United States	157.2	157.2

Note: United States in 1995 = 100.
Source: Conference Board (1997), Bureau of Labor Statistics (1999), and author's calculations.

income going to labor and capital stay constant, which means that real wages will rise at the rate of productivity growth.[3] As can be seen, in most nations, real wages will have doubled by 2030. In the United States, they will have risen by slightly more than half if the Social Security Administration's (1999a) projections for wage growth are correct.[4]

Projections of After-Tax Wages

This section incorporates the impact of an aging population to derive projections of after-tax wages. This projection combines the earlier projections of productivity and wage growth shown in table 1 with projections of the increase in national tax burdens due to a larger elderly population.

The projected tax burden used to calculate after-tax wages assumes that the share of GDP devoted to supporting retirees will increase in proportion to the elderly population. This increase is then assumed to be passed on in the form of a higher tax burden. This additional tax burden is assumed to be borne disproportionately by labor. The reason for this assumption is that most nations fund their public pension systems at least in part from a payroll tax, which is generally assumed to be a deduction from wages. While some amount of revenue from other sources generally supplements this tax, the share of pension benefits paid out of taxes on labor is considerably higher than for most other forms of government spending. For purposes of this analysis, it is assumed that the capital share of the incremental tax burden is only half of its share of income (which is assumed to be 30% of GDP). The labor share of the tax burden is therefore correspondingly larger.

These projections involve several important simplifying assumptions. First, the assumption that expenditures on the elderly will increase in proportion to their share of the population is likely to exaggerate the actual increase. Many countries, such as the United States, have already increased the age of retirement for future beneficiaries or taken other measures to reduce future benefit levels. For this reason, the numbers in these projections are likely to lead to an overstatement of the actual tax burden that would be projected given current law.

The second key assumption in this calculation is that the proportion of GDP going to other categories of government spending stays constant. This is also likely to lead to a considerable overstatement of the increase in the tax burden. Government spending in many areas is almost certain to fall as a share of GDP. The flip side of an increasing population of retirees is a smaller share of children in the population. In the United States, the percentage of the population that is under 20 is projected to fall from 28.9% in 1990 to 24.3% in 2030. Other things being equal, this would be expected to lead to a proportionate reduction in education, childcare, and other government expenditures associated with raising children. In 1990, government expenditures on education in the United States were equal to 5.1% of GDP. The projected decline in the proportion of the population under age 20 in 2030 would imply a reduction of approximately 0.8 percentage points of GDP in government spending on education if spending per pupil grew at exactly the rate of GDP over this period. By failing to include the impact of the decline in spending on education and other categories of expenditures related to raising children, these projections substantially overstate the expected increase in the tax burden.

The assumption that the additional tax burden will be disproportionately borne by labor may also lead to an overstatement in some cases. Several nations, such as Sweden and Denmark, are now partially prefunding their retirement systems through the purchase of private equities. Other countries, including the United States, are considering prefunding through equity ownership. This in effect amounts to a tax on capital since a portion of future profits will be paid out to the government to support the public pension system. This will lower the return available to other holders of private equities. The United States has also partially prefunded its system by having a payroll tax that is higher than would be needed under a strictly pay-as-you-go system. This has allowed a surplus to be built up in the public fund, which will be repaid from general revenue rather than the payroll tax. The primary sources for general revenue are the individual and corporate income tax. These taxes are borne primarily by higher-wage earners and owners of capital. This means that as general revenue starts to be an important source of funding for Social Security, the tax burden for most workers will not rise as fast as spending on the program.

These projections also assume that the public sector's share of health care spending is not affected by the aging of the population, except in the United States. The reason for this assumption is that most health care spending in other OECD nations is already paid by the government. In these countries, aging would lead to increased spending only insofar as an older population will have higher per-person costs. While there is some evidence that this is the case, the impact of an aging population on total health care costs is ambiguous. It is not easy to disentangle the impact of an aging population from rising health care costs more generally (Getzen 1992). For purposes of the projections of after-tax income, it is assumed that the impact of higher health care costs due to aging is zero.[5]

In the United States, the vast majority of health care spending for most of the population is private. However, most health care spending for the elderly is provided publicly through Medicare and Medicaid. This means that as the population ages, the government will incur larger health care expenses simply because the health needs of a larger segment of the population are being paid for by the government. Therefore, the aging of the population will lead to a significant increase in government spending on health care.

To distinguish between the impact of rising per-person health care costs and the aging of the population, the projected impact of aging on public-sector health care expenditures is a simple extrapolation based on the percentage of the population over age 65. This projection assumes that public-sector spending on health care rises in proportion to the increase in the share of the population over age 65. The base is Medicare spending in 1990 plus 60% of Medicaid spending (approximately the share spent on people over age 65).

Table 4 shows the projected increase in government spending on public pensions due to the aging of the population as a percentage of GDP between 1990 and 2030. As noted earlier, given the appropriate simplifying assumptions, these numbers can be viewed as the additional tax burden that will be borne by workers. The unweighted average for the group is 4.9 percentage points, although this number is boosted nearly a quarter of a percentage point by the jump of 9.0 percentage points for Italy. The U.S. increase in spending attributable to Social Security alone is among the smallest. (Factoring in the impact of the scheduled increase in the retirement age would lessen the impact of aging through this period by just over 0.5 percentage point of GDP.) However, when the projected increase in public-sector health spending is included, the U.S. increase is just about in the middle.

Table 5 combines the projected increases in tax burdens shown in table 4 with the projected increase in real wages shown in table 1 to produce projections for increases in after-tax wages. As can be seen, the relatively slow projected rate of productivity growth for the United States

TABLE 4
Public Pension Spending as a Share of GDP

	1990 share (includes public employees)	Public employee share of pension spending	SS-type pension	Increase by 2030
Australia	3.9	19.3	3.15	2.66
Austria	14.8	29.9	10.37	7.34
Belgium	11.0	30.6	7.63	4.24
Canada	4.2	5.8	3.96	3.70
Denmark	9.9	11.8	8.73	5.14
Finland	10.3	19.3	8.31	5.65
France	11.8	20.5	9.38	5.56
Germany	10.8	17.7	8.89	6.57
Ireland	6.1	19.3	4.92	5.60
Italy	14.4	15.6	12.15	9.03
Japan	5.0	2.5	4.88	4.42
Netherlands	9.8	19.3	7.91	6.93
New Zealand	7.5	19.3	6.05	4.62
Norway	10.1	19.3	8.15	3.23
Portugal	7.7	19.3	6.21	4.04
Spain	7.5	19.3	6.05	4.06
Sweden	11.6	19.3	9.36	4.54
United Kingdom	9.5	19.3	7.67	3.24
United States	6.5	25.9	4.82	3.37
United States with Medicare			6.93	4.84

Source: World Bank (1994: table A-5) and author's calculations.

TABLE 5
Projections of Before- and After-Tax Wages for 2030

	Before-tax	After-tax
Australia	162.7	154.5
Austria	214.2	175.5
Belgium	245.6	220.0
Canada	162.7	150.0
Denmark	180.4	155.7
Finland	221.6	188.4
France	237.3	202.5
Germany	245.6	207.4
Ireland	356.7	318.7
Italy	229.3	178.4
Japan	254.1	233.0
Netherlands	207.0	172.8
New Zealand	157.2	140.9
Norway	272.0	252.7
Portugal	157.2	143.0
Spain	272.0	248.8
Sweden	162.7	138.9
United Kingdom	207.0	193.5
United States	157.2	147.8

Note: 1995 = 100.

has far more impact than the aging of the population in determining after-tax income. The United States is near the bottom in the projected growth of after-tax wages, with slightly more than half the projected growth for Italy and the United Kingdom and slightly less than half the projected growth of France and Germany.

The Impact of Health Care Costs

The OECD nations have had very different experiences with growth in health care costs over the last quarter century. In 1973, the United States already topped the OECD in the portion of GDP spent on health care, 7.5%. However, six other OECD nations spent at least 6.5% of their GDP on health care, so health care expenditures in the United States would not have seemed exceptional at the time. But in the years since 1973, health care costs have grown far more rapidly in the United States than in any other OECD nation. By 1997, health care spending as a share of GDP was more than 3.0 percentage points higher than in any other OECD nation. Several OECD nations, such as Belgium, Denmark, Italy, and Japan, manage to provide health care to their populations while spending less than 60% as much as the United States, measured as a share of GDP.[6]

The rapid increase in the cost of health care in the United States has had a significant impact on the income that workers have left over after paying their health care expenses. To some extent, these higher costs have been reflected in tax rates, most importantly the Medicare tax on wage income. The Medicare payroll tax has gone from 1.2% on the first $33,700 (in 1999 dollars) of wages in 1970 to a 2.9% rate on all wages. Higher health care costs have also pushed up the portion of labor compensation going to nonwage benefits as employers deduct more from wages to pay for workers' health care coverage. In 1972, 5.9% of labor compensation went to nonwage benefits. By 1997, the share of labor compensation going to nonwage benefits had risen to 11.8%. Rising health care costs were the main factor fueling this growth. If the share of nonwage benefits had not risen over this period, wages would have been more than 6.0% higher in 1997. Of course, people are also dealing with the increase in costs by going without health care insurance altogether. More than 40 million people now lack health insurance coverage at any point in time.

Other OECD countries have had problems containing health care costs, but in no case has the increase been of the same magnitude. In

Germany, health care costs rose by 3.0 percentage points of GDP between 1973 and 1997. This is a large increase but less than half the 6.5-percentage-point rise in the United States. In France and Italy, the increases were 3.7 and 1.7 percentage points, respectively. These increases in health care spending, and others throughout the OECD, clearly impose some burden on national budgets, but in no case is that burden comparable to the burden that the population of the United States has experienced.

It also is not clear that the United States has much to show for its expenditures in terms of the health of its population. In life expectancy at birth, the United States ranks behind most of the other OECD nations. Its standing is somewhat better in the category of life expectancy at age 65, although even in this category it is not at the top of OECD.[7] Part of the explanation for the relatively short life expectancies of people in the United States may lie in economic factors, such as high poverty rates and high levels of income inequality, or in social factors, such as crime, all of which could be expected to have negative effects on health. However, even if these factors explain a lower level of health in the United States, it would be reasonable to expect that the extremely rapid growth of health care spending in the United States would have led to some improvement in its health care statistics relative to other nations. This appears not to have been the case. While life expectancy at birth increased by 4.5 years between 1973 and 1995 in the United States, it increased by 5.3 years in Germany, 5.5 years in Finland, and 5.8 years in Austria over the same period, all countries with higher life expectancies than the United States. It is possible that the social environment in the United States deteriorated over this period (there was a large increase in inequality) so that its relative health statistics would have fallen even more without this increase in spending, but this would be a difficult claim to evaluate. In any case, it is at least not evident what benefit people in the United States are receiving from its extraordinary level of health care spending.[8]

Regardless of the actual benefits received from health care spending in the United States, it is still worth examining trends in living standards net of health care spending. In other words, health care spending can be viewed as a sort of tax, which, like any other tax, may or may not provide benefits for its payer. However, without passing judgment on the worthiness of the tax, it is still possible to assess trends in workers' disposable income, their income net of the tax. Similarly, it is possible to examine trends in the income workers will have left after paying their health care expenses.

To construct these projections, it is assumed that, in the period from 1995 to 2030, health care expenses will increase at the same rate, measured as a share of GDP, as they did in the period from 1973 to 1995. This assumption takes into account the extent to which health care costs exceed the overall rate of economic growth, regardless of whether the reason is higher-than-average inflation in the health care sector, the increased use of medical services by all segments of the population, or an increase in medical services due to the aging of the population. In most OECD nations, there was a considerable increase in the portion of the population over age 65 in the years from 1973 to 1995. In most cases, the rate of increase of the elderly population will not be very different in the years from 1995 to 2030.

Table 6 shows the projected increase in health care costs measured as a share of GDP for each nation and as a share of projected after-tax, after-health-care income in the year 2030. The third column gives an index for the projected level of after-tax, after-health-care income for each country in the year 2030.[9] The fourth column presents the index for projected after-tax income from table 5, and the fifth column shows

TABLE 6

Growth Projections for After-Tax, After-Health-Care Wages

	Growth in health care spending as share of GDP	Growth as share of after-tax, after-health-care wages	After-tax, after-health-care wages (1995 = 100)	After-tax wages (1995 = 100)	Before-tax wages (1995 = 100)
Australia	3.5	7.1	143.5	154.5	162.7
Austria	3.6	11.1	156.1	175.5	214.2
Belgium	4.4	12.0	193.6	220.0	245.6
Canada	3.5	8.3	137.5	150.0	162.7
Denmark	1.7	5.4	147.3	155.7	180.4
Finland	2.0	6.4	176.4	188.4	221.6
France	5.4	17.2	167.7	202.5	237.3
Germany	4.4	12.5	181.5	207.4	245.6
Ireland	0.7	1.6	313.7	318.7	356.7
Italy	2.5	7.9	164.4	178.4	229.3
Japan	4.1	8.4	213.5	233.0	254.1
Netherlands	2.6	7.6	159.6	172.8	207.0
New Zealand	3.0	7.7	130.0	140.9	157.2
Norway	2.8	6.6	236.0	252.7	272.0
Portugal	6.2	16.2	119.8	143.0	157.2
Spain	4.5	10.5	222.8	248.8	272.0
Sweden	1.9	7.2	128.9	138.9	162.7
United Kingdom	3.0	6.6	180.7	193.5	207.0
United States	9.4	20.5	127.3	147.8	157.2

Source: OECD (1998) and author's calculations.

the index for projected before-tax wage growth from table 1. As can be seen, the projected impact of rising health care costs on after-tax, after-health-care income is substantial. For several countries, it is considerably larger than the projected impact of the tax burden associated with the aging of the population, and in almost every case, the impact is at least of comparable magnitude.

These projections make the same assumption about the division of taxes associated with health care costs as the earlier set of pension projections did. In both cases, it is assumed that capital's share is half its proportion of national income.

The Impact of Wage Inequality

In projecting future living standards, it is important to consider trends in wage inequality since most workers will not benefit if wage gains are concentrated at the top end of the distribution. This analysis focuses on the impact of wage inequality on the wages of the median worker because this should provide a basis for assessing how a typical worker will be living. In principle, it is possible to do a more detailed analysis, in which trends could be projected by wage quintile or decile (see Baker 1998). The projections for the median worker developed in this section should at least be an improvement over an analysis that focuses exclusively on average wages without regard to distribution.

There has been a tendency toward increasing wage inequality in several OECD nations over the last two decades. This trend has been most pronounced in the United Kingdom and the United States. In the case of the United States, the increase in inequality has been sufficiently large that real wages have actually fallen for the median worker, in spite of a cumulative rise in productivity of more than 20% over this period. In other OECD countries, the trend in relative wages is less clear. Italy may have also experienced a significant increase in inequality, although its starting point was a position of relative equality. There was some rise in inequality in most countries, although generally the increase was not large and may be sensitive to the endpoints chosen or the yardstick used to measure inequality. Germany and Belgium actually experienced a decline in inequality over the last 20 years.[10]

This analysis assumes that the trends in wage inequality from the last 20 years will continue for the next 35 years. Using data from the United States, this analysis assumes that the impact of changes in the level of inequality on the wages of the median worker in other nations will be proportionate to those in the United States. (The methodology is explained in more detail in the appendix.)

The projections of the impact of the continuation of recent trends in wage inequality are shown in table 7. The first column shows the percentage rise in the ratio of weekly wages for workers at the ninth decile to the weekly wages of workers at the fifth decile over the period from 1979 to 1996.[11] The second column shows the implied percentage-point reduction in the growth rate of wages for the median worker. The third column shows the projection of before-tax wages in 2030 from table 1. These numbers effectively assume that workers all benefit equally from productivity growth. The fourth column shows the impact that the continuation of recent trends in inequality will have for the median worker. The fifth column shows projections of the after-tax wage for the median worker, applying the same methodology that was used to construct table 5.[12] The sixth column shows projections for after-tax, after-health-care wages, applying the methodology used to construct table 6.

As can be seen, for several nations the projected impact of the continuation of recent trends in inequality is quite large. In the case of the United States, the median worker would lose more than two thirds of the projected growth in the average wage if inequality continues to grow at its recent pace. After factoring in the impact of higher taxes due to aging and projected increases in health care costs, the median worker is actually projected to have a lower after-tax, after-health-care wage in 2030 than at present. In the United Kingdom, projecting the continuation of recent trends in inequality will cost the median worker more than half the increase in the average wage over this period. In Portugal, the impact of growing inequality is actually projected to be larger for the median worker than the growth in the average wage, leading to a projected 24.5% decline in the median wage by 2030, although the data that provide the basis for this projection is not very solid.

Comparing the Impacts

The previous sections calculated the impact of national differences in productivity growth, aging and the generosity of public pension systems, the growth in health care costs, and trends in wage inequality on future living standards for the typical worker. Having generated these projections, it is now possible to compare their relative importance for future living standards.

Table 8 presents a comparison of the impact of each factor on the standard of living projected for the typical worker in each nation. Table

TABLE 7
Growth Projections for After-Tax, After-Health-Care Wages with Inequality

	% Change in inequality, 1973–95	Implied reduction in annual wage growth rate (percentage points)	Before-tax wages, no inequality (1995 = 100)	Before-tax wages, with inequality (1995 = 100)	After-tax wages, with inequality (1995 = 100)	After-tax, after-health-care wages, with inequality (1995 = 100)
Australia	5.98	0.40	162.7	147.2	139.8	129.8
Austria	0.78	0.05	214.2	207.0	169.6	150.8
Belgium	-3.30	-0.22	245.6	262.9	235.4	207.2
Canada	3.44	0.23	162.7	174.3	160.6	147.3
Denmark	5.26	0.35	180.4	157.2	135.7	128.3
Finland	3.46	0.23	221.6	207.0	176.0	164.8
France	2.75	0.19	237.3	221.6	189.1	156.6
Germany	-1.96	-0.13	245.6	254.1	214.5	187.8
Ireland	N/A	N/A	356.7	N/A	N/A	N/A
Italy	10.67	0.72	229.3	180.4	140.4	129.3
Japan	5.45	0.37	254.1	221.6	203.2	186.2
Netherlands	4.39	0.30	207.0	186.7	155.8	143.9
New Zealand	5.65	0.38	157.2	136.8	122.6	113.1
Norway	2.99	0.20	272.0	254.1	236.1	220.5
Portugal	30.84	2.08	157.2	75.5	68.7	57.6
Spain	N/A	N/A	272.0	N/A	N/A	N/A
Sweden	1.57	0.11	162.7	157.2	134.2	124.6
United Kingdom	13.33	0.90	207.0	151.8	141.9	132.5
United States	11.42	0.77	157.2	119.1	111.9	96.4

9 provides the same information focusing specifically on the United States to make the meaning of table 8 clearer. The implicit counterfactual assumption in table 8 is a world where all nations had exactly the same rate of productivity growth, no increase (or decrease) in wage inequality, no increase in taxes due to the aging of the population, and no increase in health care costs as a share of GDP. The numbers in each column are the percentages by which a median worker's after-tax, after-health-care wage will be higher or lower in 2030 as a result of the country-specific trends in the factor shown in each column.

The impact of productivity growth, shown in the first column of table 8, was calculated as the percentage by which wages will be higher or lower for the median worker in each nation in 2030 as a result of the fact that productivity growth in that nation is projected to exceed or trail the OECD average over the period from 1995 and 2030. The average of 35.5% shown at the bottom is the average absolute value of the differences for the 19 nations. In other words, the differences in projected productivity growth in individual nations, compared with the OECD average, will on average leave wages 35.5% higher or lower in 2030 compared with a scenario in which productivity growth in each nation tracked the

TABLE 8
Comparative Impacts on Living Standards of Median Worker

	Differences in productivity growth	Effect of changing inequality	Effect of higher taxes	Effect of increased health care costs
Australia	−45.9	−13.5	−5.0	−7.1
Austria	−1.5	−0.8	−18.1	−11.1
Belgium	25.6	6.2	−10.4	−12.0
Canada	−45.9	−7.4	−7.8	−8.3
Denmark	−30.6	−10.5	−13.7	−5.4
Finland	4.9	−7.4	−15.0	−6.4
France	18.5	−7.4	−14.7	−17.2
Germany	25.6	6.2	−15.6	−12.5
Ireland	121.5	N/A	−11.7	−1.6
Italy	11.6	−22.0	−22.2	−7.9
Japan	33.0	−10.5	−8.3	−8.4
Netherlands	−7.7	−10.5	−16.5	−7.6
New Zealand	−50.6	−13.5	−10.4	−7.7
Norway	48.4	−7.4	−7.1	−6.6
Portugal	−50.6	−52.0	−9.0	−16.2
Spain	48.4	N/A	−8.5	−11.5
Sweden	−45.9	−4.1	−14.6	−7.2
United Kingdom	−7.7	−27.2	−6.5	−6.6
United States	−50.6	−22.0	−6.0	−13.8
Average	**35.5**	**13.4**	**11.6**	**9.2**

Note: All values are percentage change.

TABLE 9
Comparative Impacts on Living Standard of Median Worker in the United States in
1999 Dollars

Median wage, 1995	Median wage, 2030	Adjusted for productivity differential	Adjusted for trend in wage inequality	Adjusted for tax increases due to aging	Adjusted for increasing medical costs
$15,741	$33,985	$24,753	$19,307	$18,149	$15,645
Lost after-tax, after-health-care income due to:		Slower productivity growth	Increasing wage inequality	Tax increases due to aging	Increasing medical costs
		$9,232	$5,446	$1,158	$2,505

OECD average. As can be seen, differences in productivity growth are
projected to have more than twice as much impact as any of the other
three factors. Even if Ireland, with its extraordinary projected productivity growth, is pulled out of the sample, the average difference would
be 30.7%. This is still more than twice as large as the impact of any of
the other three factors.

This finding suggests that productivity growth will continue to be
the key to maintaining significant improvement in living standards in the
future. While this conclusion should not be surprising, it is perhaps
unfortunate because the factors explaining national differences in productivity growth are still not well understood. While differences in
national rates of saving and investment clearly account for part of the
differences in productivity growth, there is a considerable gap that cannot be readily explained. The projections in the table imply a serious
need for more research on the differences in national rates of productivity growth.

Table 9 illustrates the impact of differential productivity growth in
the United States. If the United States could maintain the average rate
of productivity growth for the whole OECD over the next 35 years, then
the median after-tax, after-health-care annual wage would be $33,985.
However, the rate of productivity growth assumed by the Social Security
Administration (1999a) implies an annual wage of $24,753, a loss of
$9,232.

The projected impact of trends in inequality is the second most
important factor affecting the living standard of the typical worker; the
average absolute size of the impact is 13.4%. This number is driven up
by the –52.0% projection for Portugal. However, even if Portugal is
removed from the sample, the average impact is still 11.0%, leaving
inequality firmly in second place for its relative impact.

As noted earlier, the projected impact of inequality on the living standards of the typical worker is particularly large in the United Kingdom and the United States, in both cases reducing the wage gains that would otherwise be obtained from productivity growth by more than half. As shown in table 9, the continuation of recent trends in productivity growth will cost the median worker in the United States $5,446 a year by 2030. The trend toward increasing inequality in these nations could perhaps be justified if it was associated with more rapid productivity growth. In fact, productivity growth in both nations is projected to be below the overall average, with the cumulative growth in the United States projected at less than half the average. In short, the factors that are leading to increasing inequality in the United States and the United Kingdom do not appear to be producing dividends in the form of more rapid productivity growth. This suggests that redressing the sources of inequality may have significant payoffs for the typical worker, without leading to costs for the economy as a whole.

The impact on future living standards of tax increases associated with the aging of the population has the third greatest significance, averaging 11.6%. In other words, on average, workers will have 11.6% less after-tax income because of tax increases attributable to the aging of the population. This is almost certainly a significant overstatement, as was noted in the construction of this projection, since the projections do not take account of many of the changes in public pension systems that have already been implemented. Most of these changes would reduce the impact of the aging of the population.

The projected impact of increases in health care costs is slightly less than the impact of aging, with an average projected reduction in after-tax, after-health-care income of 9.2%. However, for many nations, the projected impact of rising health care costs is far larger. The United States stands out in this respect; the projected impact of rising health care costs is a reduction in after-tax, after-health-care income of 13.8%. Table 9 shows that this rise in health care spending as a share of GDP will reduce the after-tax, after-health-care wage for the median worker by $2,505 in the year 2030. This is more than twice as large as the 6.0% ($1,158) reduction projected in 2030 as a result of the taxes needed to support a larger population of retirees.

Most nations appear to have been relatively successful in getting their health care costs under control. The projected rates of growth of health care spending are exaggerated somewhat by using the longer period from 1973 to 1996 as the basis for the projections. If a shorter period, such as the last decade, were used, the projected increase in health care costs would be considerably more modest, with several nations, such as Denmark, Ireland, and Sweden, actually showing declines in the share of GDP devoted to health care expenditures over this period.

The contrasting experiences with containing health care costs suggest that this should be an important area of focus for public policy in nations that have been less successful. As noted earlier, the higher level and growth rate of expenditures in the United States are not associated with any obvious improvement in health care statistics relative to other nations. Clearly, some nations are able to achieve comparable health outcomes at considerably lower costs than others. If lessons from the relatively successful nations can be transferred across national boundaries, there are potentially large payoffs for future living standards.

Conclusion

The problems of dealing with an aging population have been given considerable attention in many OECD countries since the last decade. The projections in this paper suggest that this concern may be somewhat misplaced. While paying for a proportionately larger population of retirees will place some burden on future generations of workers, in no nation will the cost be so large that it will be close to offsetting projected gains in productivity. Workers in the future should still enjoy considerably higher living standards than workers do presently, even if they face a higher tax burden to support the elderly.

Furthermore, the projections in this paper suggest that the aging of the population will not be the largest factor affecting the living standards of workers in the future. National differences in rates of productivity are projected to have an impact on future living standards that is at least three times as large on average as the impact associated with tax increases needed to support a larger population of retirees. Trends in inequality, particularly in the United States and the United Kingdom, are also projected to have a far larger impact on the living standards of the typical worker. In addition, the projected growth in health care costs will have a comparable, or in the United States far larger, impact on the income left over after paying taxes and health care expenses.

The relative impacts of these factors suggest that the attention focused on dealing with the problems of paying for a growing population of retirees may be better directed elsewhere. From a policy standpoint, it should be possible in principle to adopt policies that affect productivity growth, wage inequality, and health care costs. No obvious policy can reverse the aging of the population, although policy can affect the distribution of costs borne publicly and privately.

Even in this respect, there appears to be considerable confusion in the debate. Many proposals for "privatizing" pension systems do not really change the extent to which retirees may pose a burden on the rest of the population—they just change the form this burden takes. For example, if workers' pension contributions are placed in funds that own private assets, such as corporate equities, this is really just a different way to impose a claim on the earnings of capital in a future period. (This can be done either collectively through a central fund or individually through private accounts.) A country that chose to go this route, with no other change in tax or spending policy, would find itself with the same capital stock and GDP in the future, as if it had kept an entirely public system.[13] (In other words, the money used to buy private assets for the pension system is either borrowed by the government or not used to pay down government debt.) In this case, it would not be necessary to fund the pension system out of taxes directly because the money would be paid out of corporate profits. However, this would lower the returns to other holders of capital by exactly the amount paid out to retirees through such a mandated pension system.[14]

This approach may have some political advantages over a pay-as-you-go system, primarily because it may allow a redistribution of the burden from future workers to future owners of capital. It may also have the effect of providing a more solid political footing for future pension benefits, making them more immune to cutbacks. But such a system does not change the extent to which retirees will impose an economic burden on future generations.

In determining the best approach for dealing with an aging population, it is important that policy be guided by the evidence, not fear tactics. There is no "crisis" in the sense that the prospective burdens are particularly large compared with other costs imposed on society in recent decades or other costs that may be imposed in the future. Nor is aging a new phenomenon. The industrialized nations have been substantially increasing the share of GDP going to support retirees for decades. In some cases, a pronounced acceleration of this trend is not even projected for the future. In short, we've been here and dealt with this problem. There is no reason to believe that we will be unable to deal with it in the future.

Appendix

Table 1 uses OECD data on productivity growth that appears in Schmitt and Mishel (1998) and data from the Conference Board (1997). The cumulative productivity growth calculation is based on the productivity growth rate estimated by the Conference Board.

Table 2 presents data on productivity levels that can be found in BLS (1999) and Conference Board (1997). Table 3 projects productivity levels using both the OECD and Conference Board growth rates shown in table 1 and the levels estimated by the Conference Board shown in table 2.

The calculations in table 4 for the increase in the share of GDP needed to pay for public pensions first assume that the increase in expenditures on the elderly will be proportionate to the increase in the share of the population over 60 between 1990 and 2030 (World Bank 1994:349). The analysis used the World Bank data for the share of GDP being paid as pensions (1994:358). (This calculation excludes any growth in the cost of pensions for public-sector workers. It is assumed that this expense will be taken directly from these workers' wages.)

The after-tax wage calculations that appear in table 5 assume that taxes (at all levels of government) are presently proportionate to the income shares of labor and capital, for which a 70-30 split assumed in all cases. It is assumed that labor will bear most of the additional taxes associated with supporting the elderly, with capital paying only a half share, or 15%, of any additional taxes. (In other words, if the additional tax burden due to aging will be 5.0% of GDP, it is assumed that workers will pay an additional amount equal to 4.25% of GDP in taxes.) The current tax burden on workers is assumed to be proportionate to the share of GDP going to government expenditures (OECD 1998). (This will lead to a significant overstatement of tax rates, and therefore future tax burdens, in nations where government enterprises constitute a large portion of GDP.) The increase in the tax rate is then calculated as a percentage of the after-tax GDP currently going to the working population. This percentage is deducted from the projected growth in the before-tax hourly wage to obtain the projected after-tax wage.

The calculation of the impact of the increased cost of health care on after-tax, after-health-care wages shown in table 6 uses essentially the same procedure as that used to construct the impact of increasing public pension expenditures on after-tax wages. The growth rate in health expenditures as a share of GDP over the period from 1973 to 1996 is projected to continue in the years from 1995 to 2030. This additional cost is assumed to be borne by workers and capital in the same proportion as the additional cost of public pension expenditures.

The calculation of the impact of the continuation of recent trends in wage inequality that appears in table 7 uses the U.S. experience as a base. For the United States, it uses the same methodology as Baker (1998), who assumed that the absolute size of the gap between the rate of average hourly wage growth and the rate of hourly wage growth for the median worker will stay the same over the period from 1995 to 2030 as it was for the years 1973 to 1995. This rise in inequality created a gap of 0.77 percentage points between the annual growth rate of the average hourly wage and the median hourly wage. In the United States, this rise in inequality was associated with an increase in the ratio of the hourly wage for workers at the ninth decile to workers at the fifth decile from 1.91 in 1973 to 2.21 in 1995 (Mishel, Bernstein, and Schmitt 1996:143).

To calculate a comparable figure for other OECD nations, the change in the ratio of the wage for workers at the ninth decile to workers at the fifth decile was calculated for each country over the years from 1979 to 1995 or for the years available (OECD 1996:61–62). The rate of change in this ratio was divided by the rate of change in the ratio in the United States over this period. This number was then multiplied by the difference between the rate of growth of median hourly wage and the average hourly wage in the United States to determine the projected difference in each nation. This calculation is clearly quite limited because arguably the trend in inequality should be a multiplicative function of inequality so that the absolute divergence between the median and average wage would be larger in a nation with more rapid wage growth and slower in a nation with less rapid wage growth. It is also important to note that the effect of the rate of divergence between the ninth-decile worker and the fifth-decile worker on the wages of the median worker will also depend on the absolute levels. If there is already a high degree of inequality, further divergence will have more of an impact on the wages of the median worker (since a larger share of wage income will be siphoned away by high-wage workers) than if wages were initially distributed relatively equally. This analysis ignores this difference among nations. It is worth noting that according to the OECD data, the level of inequality is greater in the United States than in any of the other OECD nations included in this analysis (except Portugal) so that by effectively treating all other nations as having the same initial level of inequality as the United States, this analysis overstates the impact of projected future increases in inequality in other nations.

The calculations of the relative impact of different factors on living standards in table 8 rely on the data from previous tables. The impact of productivity differences, which appears in the first column, is the difference between each nation's projected cumulative productivity growth and the average for the whole set of nations. The second column shows the projected percentage change in the median worker's wage if recent trends in inequality continue. The third column shows the projected percentage reduction in after-tax wages due to the projected increase in the cost of the public pension system. The fourth column shows the projected reduction in after-tax, after-health-care wages as a result of the projected growth in health care costs. At the bottom are the average absolute values of the impact on individual nations.

The starting point for table 9 is the median after-tax, after-health-care wage in the United States in 1995. This is obtained by first calculating a median before-tax annual wage, using the median hourly wage in Mishel et al. (1996) and multiplying by 2,000. The ratio of the after-tax, after-health-care wage to the before-tax wage is assumed to be the same as the ratio of after-tax, after-health-care income to before-tax income for the median family in Baker (1998). This is a considerable simplification, but for purposes of this analysis, the inexactness of the procedure should not pose a problem. The second column, the median wage for 2030, is a projection that assumes that wages rise in step with the average rate of productivity growth for all OECD nations over the period from 1995 to 2030, as calculated in table 1. The third column shows the projected wage based on the assumption that the wage grows at the rate projected by Social Security Administration (1999a). The fourth column shows the projected median wage for 2030 after incorporating the impact of the continuation of recent trends in wage inequality, as calculated in table 7. The fifth column shows the projected after-tax wage after incorporating the impact of higher taxes due to an aging population, as calculated in table 5. The sixth column shows the after-tax, after-health-care wage after incorporating the extent to which health costs rise for reasons other than aging, as calculated in table 6. The second row of numbers assigns a dollar value to the annual income lost to each of these factors.

Notes

[1] As a result of its recent acceleration, productivity growth in the United States has been more rapid than in most other OECD nations over the last five years. However, in most cases the acceleration has not been enough to offset the relatively slow growth of the prior 15 years. It is also worth noting that the Social Security and

Medicare trustees have not raised their projections for future productivity growth as a result of this acceleration.

[2] The comprehensive revisions to GDP numbers published in October 1999 show considerably more rapid productivity growth than the previously published numbers. However, this revision has had little impact on official projections. The Social Security Administration (1999b), which had a general knowledge of the nature of the revisions prior to issuing its report, projected future productivity growth for the United States of 1.35% annually.

[3] The assumption that the labor share of income remains constant is made explicitly by the Social Security Administration (1999a:148–49).

[4] This actually overstates wage growth somewhat since a portion of productivity gains will be taken in the form of shorter working hours and nonwage benefits. However, for purposes of these comparisons, wage growth can be viewed as being equal to productivity growth.

[5] The effect of an aging population on health care costs can be ambiguous for two reasons. First, as society gets wealthier and healthier, it may cost less to care for a person at the same age because that person is likely to be healthier. Second, rising cost pressures due to an aging population may lead to more effective means to control costs. This appears to have been the pattern in most OECD nations.

[6] Information on health care expenditures can be found in OECD (1998).

[7] According to OECD data, life expectancy at age 65 in the United States in 1995 was 17.4 years. This is somewhat higher than the 16.9 year life expectancy in France but below the 17.6 and 18.3 year life expectancies in Belgium and Canada, respectively.

[8] It appears that higher physician salaries, larger expenditures on pharmaceuticals, and greater use of expensive procedures and equipment are the main factors that explain the higher health care costs in the United States (Anderson and Poullier 1999). The higher administrative costs associated with a decentralized system are also an important factor.

[9] The projection for after-tax, after-health-care income for the United States is taken from Baker (1998:17; the exact procedure is explained in the study's appendix). This projection was used in order to avoid the double counting of the impact of aging on health care expenditures that the method used in this paper would imply. The methodology used in this paper produces a substantially lower measure of after-tax, after-health-care income for the United States, 115.3.

[10] These comments are based on the data on earning dispersion that appear in OECD (1996:61–62).

[11] The wages for decile levels refer to workers at the cutoffs. In other words, the wage for a worker in the ninth decile is the wage for a worker in the 90th percentile of the wage distribution.

[12] Neither this projection nor the one for impact of health care costs takes into account the possible interaction between changes in wage distribution and tax rates or health care costs. These interactions could be important. For example, if a country

has a very progressive tax structure, then lower wages due to increasing inequality may be partly offset by a reduction in taxes. Similarly, the government may also pick up a larger portion of health care expenditures for the median wage earner in response to a relative decline in his or her wage.

[13] This ignores the possible incentive effects on workers' willingness to work that may result from seeing a more direct link between their pension contributions and their eventual benefits. This effect may not be inconsequential (see Diamond and Geanakoplos 1999; Feldstein and Samwick 1998).

[14] The government would also have a larger public debt to finance in this situation. It is logically possible to eliminate this additional debt through inflation. Under such circumstances, the transfer of the tax burden to capital through a mandated saving system can be seen most clearly.

References

Anderson, George, and Jean Poullier. 1999. "Health Spending, Access, and Outcomes: Trends in Industrialized Countries." *Health Affairs*, Vol. 18, no. 3, pp. 178–92.

Baker, Dean. 1998. *Defusing the Baby Boomer Time Bomb: Projections of Income in the 21st Century*. Washington, DC: Economic Policy Institute.

Bureau of Labor Statistics. 1999. *Comparative Real Gross Domestic Product per Capita and per Employed Person: Fourteen Countries 1960–1996*. Washington, DC: Bureau of Labor Statistics.

Conference Board. 1997. "Perspectives on a Global Economy: Understanding Differences in Economic Performance." Conference Board Report No. 1187-97-RR. New York: Conference Board.

Diamond, Peter, and Jean Geanakoplos. 1999. "Social Security Investment in Equities I: Linear Case." Unpublished paper, Massachusetts Institute of Technology, Department of Economics.

Feldstein, Martin, and Andrew Samwick. 1998. "Potential Effect of Two Percent Personal Retirement Accounts." *Tax Notes*, May 4, pp. 615–20.

Getzen, T. 1992. "Population Aging and the Growth of Health Expenditures." *Journal of Gerontology*, Vol. 47, no. 3, pp. S98–S104.

Mishel, Larry, Jared Bernstein, and John Schmitt. 1996. *The State of Working America 1998–99*. Armonk, NJ: M.E. Sharpe.

Organisation for Economic Co-operation and Development. 1996. *Employment Outlook* (July). Paris: Organisation for Economic Co-operation and Development.

———. 1998. *OECD Health Data 1998*. Washington, DC: Organisation for Economic Co-operation and Development.

Schmitt, John, and Larry Mishel. 1998. *An Evaluation of the G7 Economies in the 1990s*. Washington, DC: Economic Policy Institute.

Social Security Administration. 1999a. *Annual Report of the Board of Trustees, Federal Old-Age and Survivors Insurance and Disability Insurance Trust Funds, 1999*. Washington, DC: U.S. Department of Health and Human Services, Social Security Administration.

————. 1999b. *The 1999 Technical Panel on Assumptions and Methods: Report to the Social Security Advisory Board*. Washington, DC: Social Security Administration.

World Bank. 1994. *Averting the Old Age Crisis*. Oxford: Oxford University Press.

Chapter 4

Social Security: A True Family Value

Valerie Rawlston and William Spriggs
National Urban League

Introduction

Recent questions raised about the solvency of Old-Age, Survivors, and Disability Insurance (OASDI)—more commonly known as Social Security—became a major topic of political debate. In light of the aging baby-boom generation and the impact their retirement is expected to have on the Social Security Trust Fund, some have suggested that we should convert Social Security to a system of privately held accounts. Unfortunately, among other shortcomings, most of these privatization schemes are devoid of any real consideration of how those dependent upon disability and survivors' benefits—primarily women, minorities, and children—would be affected.

The Old-Age, Survivors, and Disability Insurance Program, Social Security's formal name, is about more than old age. For purposes of clarity, OASD Insurance, as its full name implies, is an insurance program. The tax collected to support the program comes from the Federal *Insurance* Contribution Act. It can best be described as a life insurance product, with disability benefits indexed to inflation and family size, and an annuity fully indexed to inflation and marital status. What makes OASD Insurance unique is that it insures families. The benefits of the program are not just for the worker but also for the worker's dependents and spouse.

The premium that American workers pay each year in the form of the FICA tax insures workers and their families against three things. One is a drop in earnings because of disability. The second is a loss in earnings because of the death of a family's breadwinner. The third is a drop in earnings because of old age.

The concept of private accounts in effect changes what is an insurance program, in which all American workers are in the risk pool, into an individual retirement plan that would leave the families and children of the individual worker out. Therefore, comparing rates of return between the current system and a privatized system is completely misleading. Calculations of private "rates of return" on the program miss that point and remove both the "social" and the "security" aspects from the program.

As with any other form of insurance, OASD Insurance works because it pools individuals who face each of these risks to varying degrees. Therefore, by putting all American workers into the risk pool, OASD Insurance works to the benefit of all Americans.

Motivation for This Research

Unfortunately, all Americans are not spread equally across each of the risk pools. Evidence of the risk pool disparity is clear from observing the distribution of recipients among each type of insurance. Data from the Social Security Administration's (SSA) 1999 *Annual Statistical Supplement* reveals that out of over 44 million OASDI beneficiaries, 86% were paid benefits from the Old Age and Survivor Trust Fund, and 14% were paid from the Disability Trust Fund. However, when beneficiaries were evaluated by race, disproportionate shares of African Americans (26%) and those classified as some race other than white or black (34%) were receiving benefits from the Disability Fund.

When we look at the distribution of new white and African American recipients for the year 1998, as illustrated in figures 1 and 2, we find similar racial differences in the types of benefits received. For example, retirement beneficiaries were clearly the majority of new white OASDI recipients. However, new retirement and disability recipients constitute virtually equal shares of new African American beneficiaries. While there is less difference between the shares of whites and African Americans receiving survivor benefits, further decomposition reveals that over half of African American survivors' insurance recipients are children under 18.

This analysis of *new* Social Security recipients is different from an analysis of *all current* recipients (both new and existing), which were previously discussed. When we refer specifically to the most vulnerable members of families, the children, it is more pertinent to look at *new* recipients because children stop receiving survivor benefits when they reach age 18, so there is less of a cumulative stock of child recipients over time than old-age recipients.

FIGURE 1
New African American OASDI Recipients, 1998

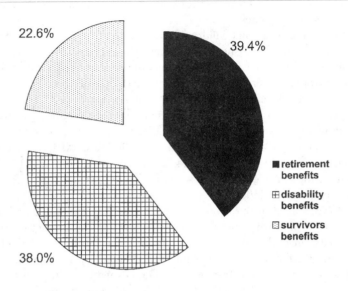

FIGURE 2
New White OASDI Recipients, 1998

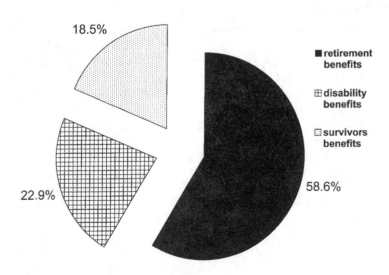

Differences in the distribution of beneficiaries reveal that while Social Security itself is sex, race, and age neutral, many of life's misfortunes—poverty, disability, and early death—tend to visit people of color with greater frequency.

Despite the fact that children represent significant portions of Social Security recipients in the African American and Latino communities, analyses of how Social Security affects dependent children have been absent from the literature and much of the discussion. Based on data for 1998 in the March 1999 Current Population Survey (CPS), 26% of African American Social Security recipients were children, 20% of Latino recipients were children, and 10% of white recipients were children. These data also show that in 1998, 36.7% of African American children under 18 years of age, 34.7% of Latino children, and 15.1% of white children lived in homes where family income was below the poverty threshold index.

Given the disproportionate levels of OASDI recipients and child poverty in minority communities, we examine the impact of Social Security on child poverty among families in the lower 40% of the income distribution in 1998. While Social Security by no means eradicates poverty among extremely poor families with children, this report provides evidence that without Social Security benefits not only would there be more children living in poverty but the depth of their poverty would be much greater.

Methodology

We used household data from the 1999 March CPS, which provided information on income sources and other relevant demographics for families in 1998. To get a clear picture of how OASDI benefits affect poverty, families with children were divided into five groups (quintiles) based on their annual family income. The first quintile represents the poorest 20% of families, whose annual family income was between $0 and $21,188. Families with negative income (denoting a loss) were excluded. The second quintile represents the next 20% of families, with annual family income between $21,189 and $36,550. We refer to the first group as low-income families and the second group as lower-middle income. Only the lowest two quintiles were used in this analysis because none of the families with income greater than $36,550 lived below the poverty threshold.

We used the official federal poverty level for this study. The poverty threshold index provides a range of income cutoffs, or poverty thresholds, adjusted to account for family size, number of children, farm versus nonfarm residence, and age and sex of the family household head. That is, for each family, given information on the combination of the preceding characteristics, the government uses a defined level of income to determine need and eligibility for assistance. If the family's actual income is below this level (threshold), the family is considered to be living in poverty. The current official measure takes into account money income before taxes. It does not include capital gains, noncash benefits (such as public housing, Medicaid, and food stamps), or the Earned Income Tax Credit, which might add income to some families. As an example, in 1998 the poverty threshold for an urban family of two adults and two children was $16,450.

A two-step process was used to determine the effect of Social Security benefits on poverty rates among families with children. The first step involved calculating the share of families with children whose total annual income was below the poverty threshold index. This was labeled the actual poverty rate. Next, an adjusted poverty rate was estimated by calculating the share of families with children whose total annual income *minus Social Security benefits* was below the poverty threshold index. The percentage reduction in poverty due to Social Security benefits was calculated using the following formula:

$$(1) \text{ \% reduction in poverty due to OASDI} = \frac{\text{Adjusted poverty rate} - \text{Actual poverty rate}}{\text{Adjusted poverty rate}}$$

We recognize that in the true absence of Social Security benefits, some individuals might compensate with some other form of income. Therefore, equation 1 measures OASDI's current effect on poverty barring any other adjustments or changes to income, and our results should be interpreted as upper bounds. However, in terms of family well-being, this is a good measure. That is, because work undertaken to replace Social Security benefits would come at the expense of current time allocation between work and family duties, the substitution of work for income may lead to less family well-being if family duties are reduced.

We examined poverty and the impact of Social Security separately for the two income groups. Within the two income groups, we analyzed the effect of Social Security on poverty for three different racial and ethnic groups (whites, African Americans, and Latinos), *all* families with children, and the subgroup *OASDI recipient* families with children. Results for both the composite group of all families as well as the subgroup of recipient families are included so that the effect of Social Security can be put in proper context.

First, are there measurable effects among those families who receive OASDI? Second, are those effects significant enough to decrease the poverty rate among the larger body of all (both OASDI recipients and nonrecipients) low- and lower-middle-income families? Finally, how do we apply our results to some remaining issues such as the effect Social Security has on those families who were not lifted out of poverty and how differential mortality rates for African American workers would impact on the effectiveness of President Bush's proposal to allow workers to divert two percentage points of their Social Security payroll tax into private accounts?

First-Quintile Families

All First-Quintile Families with Children

Represented within the 6.1 million families who earned $21,188 or less were 14 million children under age 18. Three out of four children whose families were in the lowest-income group lived in poverty. For Latino children, the share was four out of five. Latino families experienced the greatest incidence of poverty, despite the fact that African Americans, not Latinos, were the lowest earners. This is because on average Latino families were larger than African American and white families. White families with children were more likely to receive benefits of some type than either African Americans or Latinos. Still, less than one tenth of low-income families of any race with children received Social Security. Summary statistics are presented in table 1.

The analysis of the overall effect of Social Security benefits on poverty rates for families with children in the first quintile shows that white families with children experienced the greatest reduction in poverty (5%) as a result of receiving Social Security benefits. This follows from whites having the highest average annual earnings. Their

TABLE 1

Summary Statistics for Low-Income[a] Families with Children

	1998 poverty rate	Receiving OASDI	Average annual family income
All families	66.4%	7.7%	$11,446
White families	59.9%	8.4%	$11,792
African American families	69.1%	7.9%	$11,008
Latino families	73.6%	6.0%	$11,445

[a]Annual family income of $0 to $21,188.

higher earnings in turn result in higher Social Security benefits, which were more effective in raising them above the poverty threshold. Furthermore, since white families were more likely to receive benefits than any other group, we'd expect the program to have a greater impact on them. Similarly, as the group with the highest rates of poverty and lowest dollar amount of benefits, Social Security benefits were less effective in lifting Latino families out of poverty. These changes are presented in table 2.

TABLE 2

Impact of OASDI on Poverty among Low-Income[a] Families with Children

	1998 adjusted poverty rate (excluding OASDI)	1998 actual poverty rate	Reduction in poverty due to OASDI benefits
All families	68.6%	66.4%	3.3%
White families	62.8%	59.9%	4.6%
African American families	71.2%	69.1%	3.0%
Latino families	74.9%	73.6%	1.6%

[a]Annual family income of $0 to $21,188.

First-Quintile OASDI Families with Children

Next, we isolated only those families with children in the lowest-income group who actually received Social Security benefits in 1998. Their actual poverty rates were slightly lower than the overall average of low-income families, and their average annual incomes were greater. For example, 64% of OASDI-recipient families in the low-income group were in poverty compared with 66% of *all* low-income families. On average, the annual family incomes of OASDI-recipient families exceeded the average for all low-income families by $1,500. White families remained the highest-income earners within this subgroup, but Latinos instead of African Americans were the lowest earners. Social Security represented over 50% of the annual income of low-income OASDI-recipient families. This equates to an average of $7,187 per year, or almost $600 per month. In most American cities, the average family benefit is enough to pay the rent of an apartment for a year.

Because Social Security constituted half of the family's income, we found that it had significant effects on poverty rates for all racial groups. Had these families not received their benefits, an additional 390,000 children would have been in poverty in 1998. Those families on whose poverty status Social Security had an impact tended to have annual incomes and benefit levels that were higher than the average for all families in this group. These results are reported in tables 3a and 3b.

TABLE 3a

Impact of OASDI on Poverty among Low-Income[a] Recipient Families with Children

	1998 adjusted poverty rate (excluding OASDI)	1998 actual poverty rate	Reduction in poverty due to OASDI benefits
All families	92.9%	63.9%	31.2%
White families	94.0%	59.1%	37.1%
African American families	95.1%	68.4%	28.0%
Latino families	91.3%	71.0%	22.3%

[a]Annual family income of $0 to $21,188.

TABLE 3b

Income Statistics of Low-Income[a] OASDI-Recipient Families with Children

	Average annual family income	OASDI share of annual family income	Average annual family income for families moved out of poverty	OASDI share of annual family income for families moved out of poverty
All families	$12,996	55.3%	$17,243	61.6%
White families	$13,241	54.9%	$17,660	63.8%
African American families	$13,117	54.2%	$16,423	56.7%
Latino families	$11,999	61.3%	$16,180	63.1%

[a]Annual family income of $0 to $21,188.

Second-Quintile Families

All Second-Quintile Families with Children

Let's now move the discussion to those families with annual income between $21,189 and $36,550. As we would expect, the incidence of poverty was lower among this group, but there were still nearly 130,000 lower-middle-income families with almost 460,000 children under 18 years of age living in poverty in 1998. Again, Latino families with children experienced the highest incidence of poverty, 5%.

Income demographics changed very little for the second-quintile families, in that white families with children were the highest earners and African American families with children were the lowest earners. However, unlike the first-quintile group, the racial group with the largest share of Social Security recipients in the second quintile was African Americans. Nearly 11% of lower-middle-income African American families with children received Social Security. Latinos remained the least likely to receive benefits. Summary statistics for this group are presented in table 4.

TABLE 4

Summary Statistics for Lower-Middle-Income[a] Families with Children

	1998 poverty rate	Receiving OASDI	Average annual family income
All families	1.8%	6.6%	$28,857
White families	0.5%	6.3%	$29,063
African American families	2.9%	10.7%	$28,429
Latino families	5.0%	4.6%	$28,594

[a]Annual family income of $21,189 to $36,550.

In the analysis of the overall effect of Social Security benefits on poverty rates for families with children in the second quintile, we found again that white families with children experienced the greatest reduction in poverty as a result of receiving Social Security benefits, African American families had the second highest reduction, and Latino families the lowest. Compared with the actual rates presented in table 4, these adjusted rates (excluding Social Security) are clearly as much as two to six times higher than the actual rates. These changes are presented in table 5. Though the poverty rates for this group (actual and adjusted) are more modest than those for the poorest 20% of families, we found that Social Security was more effective in lifting families in this group out of poverty. That is because this group is more likely to have other income that lifts them closer to the poverty threshold.

TABLE 5

Impact of OASDI on Poverty among Lower-Middle-Income[a] Families with Children

	1998 adjusted poverty rate (excluding OASDI)	1998 actual poverty rate	Reduction in poverty due to OASDI benefits
All families	4.1%	1.8%	56.0%
White families	2.8%	0.5%	83.1%
African American families	7.3%	2.9%	59.9%
Latino families	5.9%	5.0%	14.3%

[a]Annual family income of $21,189 to $36,550.

Second-Quintile OASDI Families with Children

We repeated the process of isolating only those families with children who actually received Social Security benefits in 1998 for the second income group. The actual poverty rates for second-quintile white and Latino OASDI families with children were only slightly higher than their overall poverty rates. However, for second-quintile African American OASDI families, the actual poverty rate was almost 10 percentage points higher than the overall poverty rate for lower-middle-income African Americans. This implies that the lowest-income African American families with children in the second quintile were those who received Social Security. Because the average annual family income for African American OASDI families was $27,245—over $1,100 less per year than the overall African American average—we discovered that this is indeed the case. For all lower-middle-income families, Social Security represented over 30% of their annual income, roughly $10,275 per year or $856 each month.

Looking specifically at those families with children in the second quintile who received benefits, we again found that Social Security had significant effects on poverty rates for all racial groups. Had these families not received their benefits, 88% more lower-middle-income families with children would have had annual incomes below the poverty threshold. This translates to an additional 570,000 children who were rescued from poverty last year by virtue of the fact that their families received Social Security benefits. For all racial groups except African Americans, those families who were moved out of poverty by Social Security tended to have annual incomes that were lower than the overall average for their particular race. All had higher than average benefit levels. These results are reported in tables 6a and 6b.

TABLE 6a

Impact of OASDI on Poverty among Lower-Middle-Income[a] Recipient Families with Children

	1998 adjusted poverty rate (excluding OASDI)	1998 actual poverty rate	Reduction in poverty due to OASDI benefits
All families	39.7%	4.8%	87.9%
White families	37.4%	0.8%	97.9%
African American families	53.4%	12.8%	76.1%
Latino families	26.2%	7.7%	70.6%

[a]Annual family income of $21,189 to $36,550.

TABLE 6b

Income Statistics of Lower-Middle-Income[a] OASDI-Recipient Families with Children

	Average annual family income	OASDI share of annual family income	Average annual family income for families moved out of poverty	OASDI share of annual family income for families moved out of poverty
All families	$28,385	36.2%	$26,901	58.9%
White families	$28,656	37.6%	$26,248	63.7%
African American families	$27,245	37.7%	$27,442	50.3%
Latino families	$29,311	30.7%	$29,194	68.4%

[a]Annual family income of $21,189 to $36,550.

Extensions of the Results

The Impact of OASDI on Families below Poverty

Despite the fact that nearly one million children were lifted out of poverty by Social Security, there still remained millions more who were not. However, in some cases where Social Security did not keep a family out of poverty, it was instrumental in keeping large numbers of people out of *extreme* poverty. For our purposes, extreme poverty is defined as having an income of less than half the applicable poverty threshold index. For example, figure 3 depicts the overall effect of Social Security benefits on extreme poverty among families with children. While these overall differences are relatively meager (two to three percentage points), figure 4 illustrates the more striking differences among OASDI-recipient families.

The subgroup of OASDI recipients experienced reductions in extreme poverty ranging from 74% among Latino families to 80% among white and African American families. Therefore, Social Security not only was successful at moving families on the margin completely out of poverty but it also moved a number of families out of extreme poverty (i.e., above half the poverty threshold).

The Effect of Differential Mortality Rates among African Americans

Replacing the current Social Security system with a privatized system would be an especially harsh prospect for black America. Two thirds of African American and Latino children in our sample—compared with 31% of white children—live in families who earned less than

FIGURE 3
Reduction in Extreme Poverty for All Families with Children

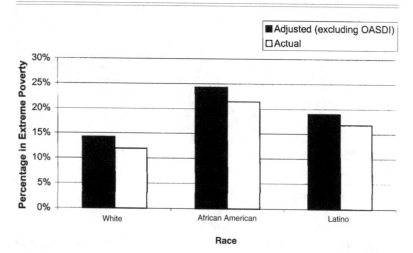

FIGURE 4
Reduction in Extreme Poverty for OASDI-Recipient Families with Children

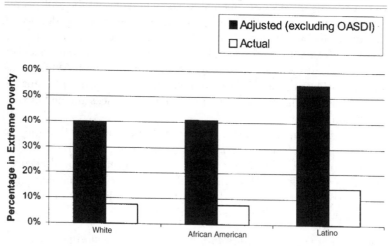

$21,188 in 1998. About 9% of African American children—compared with 6% of white and Latino children—lived in families receiving Social Security benefits. Since a greater share of African American children are living closer to the poverty line than their white counterparts, African American children are almost four times more likely to be lifted out of poverty by Social Security than are white children.

Again, it is important not to forget that for the most part these are young families. Differences in mortality, and hence life expectancy, between whites and African Americans are greatest for African Americans in their 20s and 30s. Those recipients are young widows and younger disabled workers whose lifetime earning capacity has been severely limited by misfortune—the same misfortune that would limit their ability to accumulate large balances in private retirement accounts. These are the people who are helped by disability and survivors' benefits—the very portions of the program that private account proposals have failed to specifically and adequately address.

The Social Security Administration Office of Research, Evaluation, and Statistics (ORES) released a report in November 2000 comparing the earnings of African American and all other workers who died or were disabled in 1996 and 1997 (SSA ORES 2000). In this report, the SSA acknowledges the same conclusion that we arrived at from our research: that some solvency proposals (privatization in particular) could affect African Americans differently than other races. Using data from the SSA's 1% Continuous Work History Sample, they discovered that African American workers in every age group were more likely to die or become disabled and had lower average lifetime Social Security taxable earnings even when they worked a similar number of years as whites worked. This pattern is particularly obvious for African American workers under age 50 in 1996 who had died by the end of 1997. The ORES found that this group had much lower average annual earnings than those who continued living. For example, the average annual earnings of African American workers who died before their 50th birthday were more than $2,000 less than the earnings of those from the same age group and race who lived, compared with a difference of about $1,200 between the average earnings of living and deceased workers in all other races for the same age group. Regretfully, these also happen to be the ages at which people are most likely to have children under 18 years old.

President Bush has proposed allowing workers to divert part of their Social Security payroll taxes (two percentage points) into private accounts. He has also promised to maintain current-law Social Security benefits for disabled workers and survivors. Based on research by Henry Aaron, Alan Blinder, Alicia Munnell, and Peter Orzag (2000), Bush's proposal would not be feasible without higher payroll taxes, investing part of the trust fund in higher-yielding assets, transferring general revenue to Social Security, and/or cutting Social Security benefits. Aaron and co-workers suggest that under the most plausible phased-in benefit-cut scenario, the average total retirement benefit would fall by 20% relative to current law for single earners who are age 30 in 2002. Therefore, we examined whether the surviving families of workers who died at ages 25, 35, and 45 would be able to maintain or improve their current level of benefits if 2% of taxable earnings were diverted into a private account, without any other adjustments to the system.

First, we used the SSA Benefits Calculator to calculate the maximum family benefit under the current system based on average annual lifetime earnings and the median age of each age grouping (25, 35, and 45) from the ORES report. That value is used to represent the current maximum monthly benefit.

Next, we calculated private savings, using 2% of mean indexed lifetime Social Security taxable earnings. We assumed a 5.5% per year net real rate of return.[1] This assumes a fee of 40 basis points to convert the personal savings account into an annuity; the balance in the private savings account at the time of the worker's death is turned into an annuity for the family. The average age of a child of a householder of a given age and race in our sample was used to determine the duration of the children's annuity. There are a number of ways in which the annuity could be structured, but we examined three scenarios.

1. The entire balance of the account is exhausted during the time period from the worker's death until the children turn 18, with no provisions for the surviving spouse's retirement.
2. The children's annuity is such that when they reach age 18, a balance of 50% of the nominal value of the account at the time of the worker's death is maintained for an annuity for the surviving spouse to receive on retirement.
3. The children's annuity is such that when they reach age 18, a balance of 100% of the nominal value of the account at the time of the worker's death is maintained for an annuity for the surviving spouse to receive on retirement.

Table 7 shows the value of the annuity under each of the three scenarios as well as the percentage of the current-law benefit this annuity represents. Presenting the data in this way makes it easier to get an understanding of how much benefits could be cut without making a family worse off.

TABLE 7

Comparison of Current System and "2% Plan" under Three Annuity Scenarios, by Race

Median age of deceased worker	Current maximum monthly family benefit	Real value of annuity (% of current maximum monthly family benefit)		
		Scenario 1	Scenario 2	Scenario 3
African Americans				
25	$454.90	$6.04 (1.3%)	$4.62 (1.0%)	$3.22 (0.7%)
35	$859.00	$62.98 (7.3%)	$42.49 (4.9%)	$22.28 (2.6%)
45	$1,053.00	$248.16 (23.6%)	$158.17 (15.0%)	$69.30 (6.6%)
All others				
25	$801.00	$14.57 (1.8%)	$11.33 (1.4%)	$8.14 (1.0%)
35	$1,035.10	$86.89 (8.4%)	$61.51 (5.9%)	$36.54 (3.5%)
45	$1,435.00	$377.15 (26.3%)	$240.38 (16.8%)	$105.32 (7.3%)

Under current law, the family of an African American worker who dies at age 25 and earned the average for those who die would receive $454.90 a month while the children were under age 18. If 2% of their lifetime earnings were set aside in a private account, the value of the annuity would be $6.04 a month while the children were under age 18, leaving nothing in the balance for a surviving spouse's benefit at retirement. That would replace 1.3% of the current guaranteed benefit. So if the current benefit level was reduced by more than 1.3% to offset the transition cost to a privatized system, the family would be worse off while the children were under 18, and the surviving spouse would be left with a reduced benefit with no offset at retirement. She would have to qualify under either her own earning record or that of a subsequent spouse.

This picture would be only slightly different for older workers. The annuity of African American workers who die at 35 could replace 7.3% of their current guaranteed benefit, and the annuity of those who die at 45 could replace 23.6%. However, even for those who die at age 45, to ensure that there would still be a sizable annuity left for the surviving spouse after the children reach age 18, the annuity would replace only 6.6% of the guaranteed benefit for African Americans and 7.3% for all other workers. In other words, guaranteed benefits under a privatized system cannot fall below 93% of the current-law level without seriously jeopardizing the families of those who die before reaching retirement age.

Thus, Social Security would have to be reformed by changing its current structure, with a new set of separate equations to address survivors' benefits, dependent benefits for disabled workers, disabled workers' benefits, and benefits for retirees. That would set in motion a set of very difficult moral choices that the system currently avoids by grouping all workers under one benefit equation.

What happens if a worker is worth more to his or her family dead than alive? if a worker's family is better off if the worker is disabled than if the worker retires? If there is a separate formula to ensure the benefits of survivors at the current-law level, then what happens to the worker's private savings account?

Maintaining the insurance and family-based benefit structure of the OASDI program is vital for the fairness of the program to African Americans. These calculations suggest that it would be hard to do that without making the private accounts an addition to the existing program instead of a substitution for a part of the program. In short, African Americans would be better off only if a program outside the existing OASDI framework were added to OASDI—not by altering the existing structure.

Conclusion

Although the majority of families with children do not receive Social Security, for many of those who do, the benefits are significant enough to prevent the family from slipping into poverty. The greatest impact are seen among families who are closer to the poverty threshold. This group consists mainly of those on the high end of the low-income group and the low end of the lower-middle-income group, the majority of whom are white families. Although the greatest percentage of recipients are white families with children in the first quintile, African Americans have the highest concentration of recipients among second-quintile families with children. Almost one million children are lifted out of poverty because of Social Security benefits. For families receiving Social Security benefits, this means a drop of 31% in child poverty for the poorest families and 56% for lower-middle-income families. This is significant to the African American community because more than one fourth of African Americans who get Social Security are children.

The CPS data used in this study did not permit us to differentiate among types of benefits (i.e., retirement, disability, or survivors' insurance). However, data from the *Social Security Bulletin Annual Statistical Supplement, 1999* (SSA 1999) confirm that the majority of children under 18 years of age who receive benefits are receiving either disability or survivors' benefits.

As discussions about how to strengthen Social Security continue, it would be wise to broaden the scope beyond retirees. We cannot emphasize enough that Social Security is more than a retirement program; it is a family insurance program. As our research demonstrates, Social Security is important not only to adults but to children as well. The broad-based support for the program comes from the many ways it touches the lives of American families. For some families, it is in the receipt of disability benefits. For some it is in the receipt of dependent survivor benefits. For some, it is in the receipt of old-age retirement benefits. Any program that separates the treatment of retirement from the family insurance part of the program cannot have such a universal family focus. Therefore, any changes made to the system must carefully consider dependent children and their families. Policy makers must be careful not to cut the line that holds nearly one million children above the poverty threshold. Rather, they must consider how more children can be helped.

Note

[1] Rate-of-return assumptions and administrative-cost assumptions are the same as those used by Aaron et al. (2000), which were taken from assumptions used in several papers by Martin Feldstein, a leading Bush adviser. Feldstein assumes a gross rate of return of 5.9% and administrative costs of 40 basis points, resulting in a net rate of return of 5.5%.

References

Aaron, Henry J., Alan S. Blinder, Alicia H. Munnell, and Peter R. Orzag. 2000. "Governor Bush's Individual Account Proposal: Implications for Retirement Benefits." *Social Security Network Issue Brief Series*, no. 11 (June).

Social Security Administration. 1999. *Social Security Bulletin Annual Statistical Supplement, 1999* (November). Washington, DC: Social Security Administration.

Social Security Administration Office of Research, Evaluation, and Statistics. 2000. *Earnings of Black and Nonblack Workers Who Died or Became Disabled in 1996 and 1997, Research and Statistics Note.* Note no. 2000-01 (November). Washington, DC: Social Security Administration.

CHAPTER 5

Issues in Social Security Reform

PETER DIAMOND
Massachusetts Institute of Technology

Changes in social security are on the agendas of many countries. Discussions vary among countries as the finances of social security, the state of the economy, and the details of politics all vary among countries. While these discussions include medical care and provision of income to both the elderly and the disabled, this essay focuses on some of the many issues in the provision of income to the elderly, without in any way discounting the importance of the provision of income to the disabled and the provision of medical care.

Primarily, this essay discusses some basic differences between defined-benefit (DB) and defined-contribution (DC) pension systems. That is, I contrast systems built around a benefit formula (like traditional systems) with systems built around mandatory contributions (like the reform in Chile). Along the way, I also touch on issues of funding and the contrast between centralized investment and individual accounts. But first I consider some issues in moving from an old system (or no system) to a new, different system that is intended to last for a long time. The paper concludes with a brief discussion of some reform issues in the United States other than the central issues of funding and introducing individual accounts—indexing, universal coverage, and protection of widows.

Transition to a New System

Regarding the transition to a new system, the message is relatively simple. Short-run and long-run circumstances are often very different. Therefore, it is important to consider the design of short- and long-run systems separately and the process of changing from one to the other, rather than simply selecting a single system and tinkering with it to try to make it fit both circumstances. This is part of my view that designing a retirement income system well, rather than poorly, is likely to be more important than whether the system is DB or DC. Both DB and DC systems can be designed well or poorly. This will be illustrated with some examples. Indeed, adaptation of a system designed for the long run to the short run has been done poorly in some countries. The converse is also true: letting short-run concerns dominate the design of a long-run system can also be costly.

The United States in the 1930s and Canada in the 1960s set up defined-benefit systems. Their benefit formulas were designed to eventually use average earnings over nearly a full career. This approach to a DB system is widely seen to be the right approach since the use of a short averaging period for determining benefits both highly distorts the labor market and is easy to manipulate, resulting in an excess of undesirable income redistributions and also public disdain. When these systems were new, workers had far fewer years under the system than the averaging period to be used eventually. In both the United States and Canada, the answer was simply to use a short (but growing) averaging period until the system became mature. There were two consequences of this approach. One was a large redistribution to retirees when the system was immature, leaving a large unfunded liability for future generations. The second was that this redistribution went particularly to high earners, not low earners. While the first consequence might be an appropriate response to the low incomes of retirees when a system is immature, as was true in the United States, the second consequence seems to me to be bad policy. In both the United States and Canada, this effect was compounded by also starting with a low tax rate, which was steadily increased over time.

Let me spell out how this works. When the system is young, retirees have paid taxes for a short period of time, may have paid a low tax rate, and yet get benefits from a formula that is designed to make sense when the system is mature. Thus, collectively, these early retirees are getting a large rate of return on the taxes they have paid. In aggregate they receive a large transfer from future generations. But which members of the generation get the most? In an earnings-related system, the higher the earnings, the larger the transfer received. A progressive system reduces the extent of such redistribution, but the presence of larger transfers to the better-off continues.

How could this result have been avoided while retaining a reasonable level of administrative complexity? There are many answers. Let me give one. The DB system could have used a long earnings history right from the start, with legislatively chosen earnings levels used for years when the system did not exist. For example, everyone could have been given average earnings for earlier years. Or everyone could have been given zero earnings, and this could have been combined with a uniform flat benefit. Initially, the level of such a flat benefit should reflect the level of resources that society is willing to make available for retirees. The initial legislation would include a declining level of the flat benefit relative to earnings in the economy as the earnings-related DB system grew. There are other answers to this adaptation problem, such as heavy reliance on means-tested benefits in the short run. But good answers are likely to recognize explicitly that there is a need for two systems plus an adaptation rather than a single system designed for very different circumstances.

A similar problem arises from the system that was common in communist countries. Commonly, communist systems based benefits on years of work and average earnings in a very short averaging period. In consequence, detailed earnings records were not kept. As an aside, let me say that I cannot see any virtues in a mature national system that uses years of service as an important variable in determining benefits; this seems an odd way to base benefits on the history of earnings (and credited non-earning years).[1] The issues in the former communist countries are somewhat different after the start of a new system because workers have a long history of coverage under the old system. This creates both a moral obligation and political pressure to recognize that history when determining benefits. But the question is similar: What to do about the absence of earning records? Excessive reliance on earnings after the setup of a new system has similar problems to the errors made in the United States and Canada. The implied income patterns do not do a good job of reflecting history but rather reward those who do well in the new system, not necessarily those who are more in need of benefits. So again, an explicit adaptation mechanism is needed to adjust to the lack of records in the short run but still provide a good system for the long run.

Another source of poor design is the use of a system for the long run that has been particularly adapted to short-run circumstances. An economy may choose to encourage early retirements at a time of considerable unemployment rather than relying on an unemployment insurance mechanism aimed at older workers. But such an economy should not assume that it will always have a large unemployment problem and so design a system that discourages work by older workers indefinitely. It may be very difficult to remove the incentives for early retirement once they have functioned for some time. Similarly, the fact that earnings records are limited in the short run is not a good reason to set up a system that uses a short averaging period for determining benefits in the long run because a short averaging period is a poor design.

In designing redistribution into the system, there are likely to be important differences over time. There is always a tension between wanting to provide more resources to those with greater needs and wanting to provide resources in response to previous expectations and legislation, possibly with a strong past-earnings-related benefit pattern. Recognizing needs is of obvious importance. Recognizing past earnings represents both the ethical claims in justified expectations and the importance of labor market incentives and tax compliance incentives staying roughly within the rules previously legislated. Although the past is past, expectations about the future are affected by how past expectations are honored or not honored. This is relevant for how much benefits should vary with earnings in the short run after a new system is in place.

Similarly, the rules possibly relating benefits to assets and asset income have implications for the incentive to save, just as rules about earnings have implications for labor supply. That is, if saving for retirement lowers benefits, then there is a disincentive to save. To the extent that redistribution depends on total incomes and not just mandatory pension benefits, there is a disincentive for savings. This suggests the advantages of a system with multiple parts (or multiple systems), one part that provides one (low) level of guaranteed income based on total income and a different mechanism that addresses redistribution across pension levels based on past earnings. Such a split approach is common; examples include the United States and Chile, countries with very different pension systems in almost every other way. The degree of reliance on the different parts should plausibly vary over time. If administratively feasible, more use of income testing early and more use of pension-level testing later is probably a sensible part of adapting to changing circumstances. That is, as a country goes from a system in which benefits are not closely tied to past earnings to one in which benefits are closely tied to past earnings, the basis for redistribution should move from heavier reliance on total income to heavier reliance on benefits based on earnings.

In some countries, the short run is a time of poorly functioning markets and very limited regulatory ability of the government. At a time of limited regulatory ability, social security should try to economize on regulatory effort, concentrating regulatory effort on problems that are more pressing, such as tax collection.

As an aside, I want to mark the important philosophical debate about whether redistribution within social security should be merely an attempt to reduce the level of poverty or whether redistribution up and down the income distribution is a central issue for retirement-income determination. Some people view the first, limited objective as the only philosophically legitimate policy issue. Others, including me, support the utilitarian approach, which recognizes income distribution more widely as the proper concern of government. This view is related to the underlying justifications of the role of government in mandating retirement income systems. Some of those who view poverty as the only issue also view the attempt to free-ride on the altruism associated with reducing poverty as the only legitimate basis for a social security mandate. Others, including me, view the widespread tendency of many people to undersave for retirement and the extremely limited use of annuities (reflecting both very low demand and very limited and expensive supply of different annuity products) as a better philosophical basis, leading to a broader program. Moreover, as with the income tax, progressivity in the social security system provides insurance against income fluctuations as well as being redistributional. Let us note that democratic societies have generally gone for the broader program.

Over time, current legislation does not necessarily commit future resources—the political process can change the system. So the real issue is how current legislation sets the political default and thus influences future political outcomes. Indeed, predicting how the political process will adapt the retirement income system to changing economic and demographic circumstances and to changing political forces is central for considering alternative systems.

Defined Benefit versus Defined Contribution

Now, let me turn to a central issue in social security design: the choice between DB and DC systems for some or all of the retirement income system.[2] Since the Chilean social security reform, a number of countries have legislated systems similar to that in Chile. Moreover, some economists in the World Bank are particularly enamored with the

Chilean approach (World Bank 1994). In this section, I contrast DB and DC systems in general and then discuss the experience in Chile for concreteness.

It is important in this discussion to compare systems on similar footings. One can compare idealized DB and DC systems. One can compare politically plausible, well-designed DB and DC systems (and the option of no economy-wide earnings-related system). But one should not compare a well-designed system of one kind with a poorly designed system of the other. That sort of comparison may be the stuff of polemics but does not belong in good policy analysis. It is worth noting that some imitators of Chile have done less well than Chile in their designs.

Before comparing DB and DC systems, let me first define terms. There are many ways in which systems differ from one another. I want to single out the element that seems most important in how the overall system is likely to work. The central element in a DB system is that the level of benefits is given by a formula (preferably indexed in some way) that depends on the history of earnings that have been subject to tax. The benefits might be annuitized or might have a lump-sum option (or a phased withdrawal mechanism). The central element in a DC system is a level of mandatory contributions that determine benefits. Thus, one critical element in the extent of difference between systems is whether the tax rate will be stable. If so, this aspect of difference may be small. If not, differences in intergenerational redistribution will be present. Of course, a DC system may also have some form of minimum benefit guarantee or some redistribution without altering the central design characteristic.

Both systems can have any degree of actual funding, although the political outcome for funding is likely to vary with type. Both systems can provide redistribution and protection of family members. In practice, the different systems lend themselves to, indeed frame, the political process to result in different levels of redistribution both intra- and intergenerationally. The presence of redistribution affects labor market incentives, and both systems can combine redistribution and incentives roughly equally well. Both systems can make benefits available beginning at a certain age without any retirement test or only in conjunction with some degree of retirement. Insofar as access to benefits is delayed, there must be rules or market determination of the extent to which benefits are increased as a consequence of their delayed start. Again, the two systems can function very similarly. Both systems can be set up to work along with private provision of retirement income through both individual and corporate efforts.

Thus, the central differences between the systems are how they affect the political process that determines the details of the system, how they adapt to variable and changing circumstances, and how much they cost to administer.

Given the unpredictability of the future, a DB system needs to be adjusted from time to time in order to preserve the level of funding designed for the system (whether it is positive or zero). Similarly, given the unpredictability of the future, a DC system needs to be adjusted from time to time in order to deliver the level of benefits expected from the system. That is, with a DC system, both the risk in the return on assets and the risk of changing life expectancy fall directly on individual workers without a mechanism for wider risk sharing. Insofar as the funding for a DC system is notional, actual funds may also need adjusting. For both DB and DC systems, we should think of initial legislation as analogous to an incomplete contract—there are elements that will be worked out later. In principle, there can be a variety of degrees of automatic adjustment in either type of system. In practice, use of automatic adaptation (or indexing mechanisms) has been quite limited. A DB system's financing issues and a DC system's level-of-benefit issues may generate very different pressures for legislative change. That there is more pressure on a DB system to respond to changed circumstances is a plus if the response is well managed and a minus if it is not.

In practice, either system can be designed well or badly. Some countries have used multiple DB systems as a mechanism for redistribution in ways that are viewed as perverse by those not receiving the redistribution, hence the importance of a single DB system. Many DB systems have a powerful disincentive to work past the initial age of eligibility for benefits, creating sizable labor market distortions. But other DB systems are close to actuarially fair on average and do not create excessive distortions. While many DB systems have very low administrative costs (less than 1% of annual benefits), others manage to be expensive. All DC systems relying on individual choice in the market are expensive, but some of them have design features that result in much larger administrative costs. For example, the U.K. system of opt-out accounts is estimated to use up 40% to 45% of potentially accumulated resources in administrative costs (Murthi, Orszag, and Orszag 1999).[3] I consider the role of analysts in encouraging good design to be at least as important as the basic choice of system type.

Given the centrality of the experience of Chile in the widespread interest in DC systems, I next consider the accomplishments and short-comings of the reform in Chile and note how these might or might not apply to other countries.

Chile

Chile had a poorly designed set of DB systems before reform.[4] Switching to a DC system included phasing out the previous systems (except for the military), with their poor design elements. In Chile, it was certainly not politically necessary to switch to DC to reform a poor system. For other countries with DB systems in need of reform, switch-ing to a DC system may or may not help with the politics of reform.

Chile had a government budget surplus at the time of implementa-tion of the change. The surplus has been used to finance many of the transition costs for the increased funding in the DC system. In Chile, it may well have been the case that the financing needs of the transition helped preserve a larger contribution of the government budget to national savings. Some other countries may also have a surplus that is more easily protected by switching to a DC system. On the other hand, in some countries it may be possible to preserve higher national savings by increased funding of a DB system, as President Clinton proposed. However, in many countries the political problem is how to deal with deficits, not how best to use surpluses. At a time of overall deficits, it is unclear how increasing demands on the government budget for funding social security helps with budgetary politics. Of course, a DC system can be set up without increasing national savings, but then increased savings are not an advantage of such a change.

Since initiation of its pension reform, Chile has gone through many legislated changes in the implementation of the system. By and large, these have been improvements, and the pension system has not been used for other purposes. Success in insulating the pension system from political use for other purposes will vary country by country. There is no guarantee that the future politics of DC systems will be better than those of well-constructed DB systems. For example, a DC system may end up requiring high levels of investment in government debt at below-market rates, high taxation of portions of accounts (e.g., through taxing "excess accumulations" defined in some way), or heavy taxation of what may be the most readily available tax base in the country.

The funds accumulated in the Chilean accounts have earned a high rate of return overall, although there have been poor years as well as good ones. This is a reflection of high rates of return in Chile generally, including the return on government debt, and not a sign of particularly good investment choices. Investments in below-market return opportunities have not been politically required. Protecting the rate of return from political interference may be made to work for a funded DB system. In particular, a country with active index funds may be more likely to set up a transparent indexed investment mechanism. It will be interesting to follow how Switzerland and Canada do with their investment of DB funds in a diversified portfolio.

The presence of pension investments in Chile (and insurance company investments as backing for annuities) has strengthened the hand of capital-market reformers, leading to capital markets that function better than before. No doubt some other countries could benefit from pension investments in the same way, whether under a DB or DC system. However, some countries already have capital markets that function well. Since significant regulatory oversight is needed for capital markets to work well, some other countries do not have the regulatory abilities to have well-functioning capital markets in the near term, with or without pension investments.

While some people expected that switching from a DB to a DC system would result in dramatic improvements in the efficiency of the labor market, this has not happened in Chile. There is some evidence that there has been some shrinking of the informal sector in Chile compared with what might otherwise have occurred. However, this may have resulted more from the large decrease in the payroll tax rate than from the change in the form of the system. Indeed, Argentina, which initiated a similar reform but without a tax rate decrease, has not had even the modest labor market improvements that appear to have occurred in Chile.

In a DB system, there is intergenerational risk sharing of the return on any portfolio that exists. DC systems are designed to concentrate portfolio risk on the holders of the assets, which can lead to sizable fluctuations over short periods in anticipated retirement incomes. Indeed, the Chilean equity market has shown significant swings. This can be both an economic and a political problem. Unlike most other aspects, this concentration of rate-of-return risk is an inherent difference between DC and DB systems.

In addition, the high cost and only partial use of annuities reflects another shortcoming in risk sharing in Chile. Design of annuitization appears to be an afterthought in some reforms rather than a central element in any retirement-income system. In general, reliance on the market to supply annuities, even mandatory annuities, will involve a considerable cost from marketing and the attempt to sell to attractive (short-lived) customers.[5] This problem is further compounded by the failure of many to understand the role of annuitization and the benefits of alternative annuity design, particularly indexing for inflation. Thus, current voluntary markets include both significant costs and many choices that seem very poor from the perspective of economic theory (e.g., wide preference for nominal over indexed annuities and wide use of guaranteed payments, decreasing the extent of annuitization).

The redistribution in Chile is in the form of a minimum benefit guarantee paid from general revenues; there is no explicit redistribution within the individual accounts. As with the income tax, progressivity in a social security system provides insurance against income fluctuations and is redistributional.

Being a DC system, Chile's will adapt to longer life expectancy by cutting benefits. This raises the issue of whether benefits will be large enough when people are living considerably longer. A DB system could index to life expectancy to produce the same outcome. However, this seems to me to be poor design: longer lives should result in a combination of both greater taxes and lower benefits, not just lower benefits. If indexing is used, which is probably politically expedient, more complex indexing is called for.

Like any DC system, the system in Chile leaves considerable funds in estates, whether individuals value that as much as potentially larger retirement benefits or not. A DB system puts all the available resources into retirement benefits and explicit survivors' benefits. Those interested in larger estates can purchase life insurance. In contrast, it is harder to use rolling annuitization to convert accumulations that would go to an estate in the event of death before retirement into larger benefits given survival until retirement. Given variation in life expectancy, how to deal with the consequences of early death is an important part of the redistributional pattern of a system.

Lastly, the administrative costs in Chile have been considerably larger than anticipated. Fifteen to 20% of what would otherwise be available for benefits goes to administrative costs. Some have argued that it is the nature of the regulations in Chile that has resulted in high costs. I believe that this is not correct—that, in fact, the Chilean regulations have held costs down relative to less-regulated systems (such as the voluntary opt-out individual account in the United Kingdom), which have considerably higher costs.

I think that high administrative costs are part and parcel of any private-market-investment system that is organized around individual choice from a wide market. Indeed, the voluntary equity mutual fund market for individuals in the United States has higher costs (in percentage terms) than the Chilean system (Rea and Reid 1998). It is true that a centralized DC system can function with significantly lower costs than a decentralized system, possibly only one fifth as much or less. However, in some countries, the concern about political interference with investment is similar for centralized DC systems and DB systems.

Organizing Individual Account Investments

Because organizing individual account investments is a central issue, let me spell it out in more detail. One can have a DC system in which workers have no choice whatsoever in the investment of the funds—a provident fund system. Indeed, there may not be any funds; benefits may be based on rates of return that may or may not reflect market rates. But such an approach goes against the underlying motivation of such systems: to move investment choices from government to workers and thus to channel the funds through private institutions. I therefore want to discuss different ways of designing the choice of portfolios. Here I draw heavily on the report of an expert panel of the National Academy of Social Insurance (1999), which I chaired.

The report distinguished between government-organized DC accounts and individually organized DC accounts. Government-organized accounts are those where the government makes available a small number of alternative investment vehicles. The government negotiates contracts with private firms to manage these investment vehicles. The pricing that occurs is the pricing that the market provides to large investors, referred to as institutional pricing in the United States. These prices are considerably lower than the prices offered to individuals. Interestingly, Bolivia used competitive bidding for each half of its market when setting up its new DC system. The costs are very low, but as with other bidding settings, Bolivia now needs a mechanism to ensure that adequate services are provided in return for the charges.

In contrast, the Chilean approach leaves individuals free to deal with any approved investment vehicle provided in the market, and the approval mechanism is meant to be quite easy and open so as to hold down market power. Thus, the mandatory markets, although highly regulated, are meant to mimic voluntary capital markets. But voluntary capital markets that deal with individuals are expensive everywhere in the world. In the United States, which has the best-developed capital markets in the world, the typical individual who invests in equity mutual funds pays nearly 1.5% of the value of assets in annual charges. Over the course of a 40-year career, such charges will cut the value of the accumulation by roughly 30%. That is, these annual charges on benefits compound over time because deposits are subject to annual charges each year until retirement.

This is what the voluntary market does when it functions well. Can a mandatory, more highly regulated market do better? The U.K. experience suggests that it can indeed do worse, as it draws on investors who are inexperienced. Chilean experience suggests that higher regulation that effectively limits both portfolio choice and the pricing structure can do better, but still at considerable expense. An interesting question is whether there are really benefits to the Swedish approach, which is to give workers access to the entire market, but with centralized record keeping and aggregated investments, not separate individual investments, and with government negotiation of allowable charges.[6]

There is no question that centralized record keeping can be cheaper if the government does it well itself or does a good job of taking bids for privatizing this function. But the key questions are the incentive for firms to hold down prices as a method of attracting more business and the role of advertising to try to take advantage of the markups that happen given limited worker response to differences in prices. First, let us be clear that the evidence in both the U.S. voluntary market and the Chilean mandatory one is that individual workers are not very sensitive to price differences. This is not surprising. First, at any moment in time, there is not much at stake to warrant continuous serious attention by a typical worker. Second, the choices may be complex, either because the pricing structure is not transparent (as has been the case in the United Kingdom) or because alleged differences in performance draw attention away from cost issues (as is the case in the United States). The highly stochastic nature of investment returns makes it hard to judge the quality of portfolio management.

It is hard to know, but I do not see anything in the Swedish system that will make demand more price sensitive and thus competition more concentrated on low prices rather than on heavy advertising. That the investment firms may not know who their customers are will change advertising but may not lower its overall cost. Thus, I see no reason to think that this form of organization itself will result in a particularly cheap system.

Another approach is to limit the market to firms that have very low charges. Both the apparent intent of access to the full current Swedish market and the likely political pressures from investment firms suggest that mandating very low charges is not likely to be a viable political solution. Effectively, this would be a form of price regulation, and price regulations generally do not work well. So I look for the Swedish example to be as expensive as is the Chilean—much more expensive than government-organized systems need to be.

Hallmarks of a market with limited pressure on pricing are the presence of prices above marginal costs and very similar products charging different prices at the same time. Idealized markets satisfy the law of one price: you can't sell the same item as someone else at a higher price. But real markets fail this test of idealized markets. Whether in a regime of price posting or bargaining, real markets have different prices—and wide differences. Since retail markets generally are far from ideal markets, it is useful to review why the case for limited choice and a large role for the government does *not* extend to consumer goods generally. First, we are considering a mandated market. A mandate is needed because workers do not do an adequate job of saving for retirement, which creates an obligation for the government to see that the mandate does not lead to inferior outcomes. Second, saving for retirement during a working career is something people do just once. There is no opportunity to learn to do it better the next time. Third, the principles of investment in the presence of risk are not simple to master. Fourth, as long as the mandate is small enough that many people are saving outside the system, portfolios held outside the system can be adjusted to offset some of the limitations on choices for portfolios held inside the system. And fifth, the presence of the government is not likely to stifle innovation in financial markets because the mandated savings remain only a part of overall savings and investment.

I have not used one basis of comparison that one sometimes hears about because it is not valid. Some people argue that if the rate of return on assets is greater than the rate of growth of the economy, then a DC system is better than a DB system. This argument is wrong on two counts. One count is that access to market rates of return can be done through funding either DB or DC systems. Indeed, because of administrative costs, the rate of return available on assets held by a DB system is considerably larger than the rate available on assets in a DC system with wide individual choice. The second count on which the argument is wrong is that there is a transition cost in order to generate funding. Once the cost of financing the funding is included, a funded system overall does not have a higher rate of return than an unfunded system. What is true is that eventually there can be a higher rate of return for some workers, but that comes at a cost of a lower rate of return for other workers while the funding is being built up. One therefore must consider both the cost of funding and the return from funding. It is wrong to consider just the return without considering the cost; it is wrong to consider the long run without considering the short run.

My essential point is that one can design a good DC system. One can also design a good DB system. Good design is the important element, and DC systems do not guarantee good design, nor do they live up to the overselling that has occurred. High costs and poor risk sharing seem to me inevitable parts of reliance on DC systems because countries seem to select high-cost approaches and because intergenerational risk sharing is not possible with a standard DC system. On the other hand, the quality of a DB system, particularly the quality of intertemporal risk sharing, also depends on the quality of political decision making, about which one naturally has worries. Analysts and international organizations should push for good designs. The system most likely to come out better from the political process is likely to vary across countries. One size does not fit all.

Some Reform Issues in the United States: Indexing, Universal Coverage, and Protection of Widows

Much of the recent debate in the United States is on the problem of restoring actuarial balance and whether to introduce a DC element into the system. These questions have received considerable attention.[7] But some reforms are also needed as part of making the system function better. I identify three for which there are easy solutions: indexing, universal coverage, and the protection of widows. I also raise two issues involving more complex analysis: treatment of the family and use of all earnings in determining benefits.

At the time of 1972 legislation that indexed Social Security, it was understood that the system was not correctly indexed for inflation. Congress proceeded with the legislation anyway in the expectation that the flaws in the indexing would not matter greatly. That expectation proved to be false as inflation soared. The 1977 legislation that overhauled Social Security changed the inflation indexing in the system. However, it remains the case that indexing is not correct. While this has far less potential importance, there is no reason to continue with an incorrectly indexed system. There are two places where indexing is done incorrectly, and I describe what it would take to fix each of them. Each of these fixes can be done in a revenue-neutral way if that is desired.

In determining the average indexed monthly earnings (AIME), which is the first step in determining benefits, earnings in all earlier years are indexed up to the year in which the worker turns 60 by means of an average earnings index (with benefits related to the index in the year in which a worker turns 60). Benefits are increased to reflect increases in the cost of living after age 62. Thus, there is a two-year gap in the indexing: a wage index is used until age 60, and a price index is used after age 62. This is an unfortunate feature in the system because two years of high inflation would adversely affect a cohort. Thus, there is the potential for an unfortunate shock to real benefits. There is no reason not to have a smooth transition between indexing methods. The simplest adjustment would be to start the price indexing of benefits in the year a worker turns 60, rather than the year he or she turns 62. Benefit levels could be adjusted to be revenue neutral on an expected-value basis.

As stated earlier, for determining the AIME, earnings in all earlier years are indexed up to the year in which the worker turns 60. Earnings in later years enter the formula without any indexing correction. This approach represents an enhanced incentive for continued work compared with uniform indexing. There is no apparent virtue in having this incentive fluctuate with the level of nominal earnings growth. It would be better to index all earnings to the same base year and enhance the incentive for additional work in an explicit way. This can be done in a variety of ways. While some other ways might be better, the current pattern could be imitated without the dependency on nominal wage growth by multiplying later earnings by an age-related factor before beginning the process of determining AIME. Delays in the availability of the average earnings index would require some adjustment, such as a conservatively estimated adjustment followed by a correction. This method would maintain the current approach to work incentives, the approach of increasing future benefits as a consequence of continued work. It might be useful to enhance incentives by allocating part of the return on continued work to contemporaneous partial benefits, while preserving the rest for larger future benefits (Diamond 1982).

At present, roughly four million state and local workers are not covered by Social Security (Munnell 1999). Universal coverage is an obvious feature of good design of a national social security system. Omission of state and local workers means that they are at risk from lapses in coverage as they move between state or local jobs (with those retirement systems) and jobs in the private sector covered by Social Security. Also, some state and local systems do not contain the protections against inflation and for surviving spouses that are part of Social Security. Omission of state and local workers also means that they do not pay their fair share of the unfunded liability of Social Security as a consequence of the generosity to early cohorts. Also, since state and local workers are above-average earners, they do not pay their fair share of redistribution to contemporary lower earners. There is no good reason not to phase in universal coverage for state and local workers.

It is widely recognized that the poverty rate for elderly widows is much higher than the poverty rate for elderly married couples. While many steps could be taken to change the treatment of the family, to design such a wide reform of the system to both work well and be politically acceptable is difficult. As an example of the difficulty of finding an acceptable reform, note the long list of reports that grappled with this problem: Consultant Panel on Social Security to the Congressional Research Service (1976); U.S. Department of Health, Education, and Welfare (1979); U.S. Department of Health and Human Services (1985); Congressional Budget Office (1986); U.S. House of Representatives Select Committee on Aging (1992). One proposal to address just the position of widows without considering wider issues is to base the benefits for a survivor on the benefits of both husband and wife (Burkhauser and Smeeding 1994). This can be done with or without adjusting benefits when both are alive. A simple rule would give the survivor 70% to 75% of what the couple received (apart from actuarial adjustments). Since this would cost revenue, a revenue-neutral proposal requires some decrease in some benefits. There are a variety of ways to do that. Another approach is to base benefits of both the couple and the survivor on the AIMEs of both husband and wife (Consultant Panel on Social Security to the Congressional Research Service 1976).[8]

At present, benefits are based on the best 35 years of indexed (and partially unindexed) earnings. There are proposals to increase this to 38 years. Additional years of earnings give no additional benefits, although early earnings years potentially contributed to the determination of benefits either as a result of disability or low earnings later on. Similarly, many spouses receive no additional benefits as a consequence of additional earnings. In contrast, some systems, such as those of Italy and Sweden, count all years of earnings by cumulating all earnings, using an average earnings index, as the first step in determining benefits. Both of these approaches consider only simple combinations of earnings in different years. Consideration of providing insurance against low-earnings years and of labor market incentives suggests that one might do better by giving some, but not full, credit to additional years of earnings. This approach is worth researching to see whether a better pattern of benefits and incentives would result.

When the United States comes to grips with the long-run fiscal problems of Social Security, it would be wise to make further changes to improve the overall system.

Acknowledgments

An earlier version of this paper was presented as the Opening Lecture of the 55th Congress, International Institute of Public Finance: Public Finance and Transitions in Social Security, Moscow, August 23–26, 1999. The author is grateful to Henry Aaron and Sheldon Friedman for comments and to the National Science Foundation for research support under grant SBR-9618698.

Notes

[1] It is common for employer-provided DB systems to multiply average earnings over a short time period by the number of years of service as part of determining benefits. This same approach has been used in some national systems (Sweden, until its recent reform, as well as former communist countries). Yet for an economy with labor mobility, such an approach for a national system has very poor labor market incentives. It is necessary to pay attention to the level of earnings in many years in order to have good incentives.

[2] For more on this comparison, see Bodie, Marcus, and Merton (1988) and Diamond (1995, 1997).

[3] In the United Kingdom, an individual can leave the government-provided DB system for either an employer-provided system or an individual account held with a financial intermediary. In addition, individuals can leave an employer-provided system for an individual account.

[4] For a detailed view of Chilean pension developments, see Diamond and Valdes-Prieto (1994).

[5] On the cost of annuities in the United States, see Mitchell, Poterba, Warshawsky, and Brown (1999).

[6] That is, in Sweden the government keeps all records for the 2.5% of payroll devoted to individual accounts. Financial firms negotiate a price structure with the government to become eligible to accept deposits, and those deposits are made in bulk by the government, not separately by individual workers.

[7] See, in particular, Arnold, Graetz, and Munnell (1998) and National Academy of Social Insurance (1999).

[8] For discussion of how reform proposals might affect widows, see Holden (forthcoming).

References

Arnold, R. Douglas, Michael J. Graetz, and Alicia H. Munnell. 1998. *Framing the Social Security Debate, Values, Politics, and Economics*. Washington, DC: National Academy of Social Insurance, distributed by Brookings Institution Press.

Bodie, Zvi, Alan J. Marcus, and Robert C. Merton. 1988. "Defined Benefit versus Defined Contribution Plans: What Are the Real Trade-Offs?" Chapter 5 in Z. Bodie, J. Shoven, and D. Wise (eds.), *Pensions in the U.S. Economy*. Chicago: University of Chicago Press.

Burkhauser, Richard V., and Timothy M. Smeeding. 1994. *Social Security Reform: A Budget Neutral Approach to Reducing Older Women's Disproportionate Risk of Poverty*. Policy Brief 2/1994. Syracuse, NY: Center for Policy Research, Syracuse University.

Congressional Budget Office. 1986. *Earnings Sharing Options for the Social Security System*. Washington, DC: Congressional Budget Office.

Consultant Panel on Social Security to the Congressional Research Service. 1976. *Report Prepared for the Use of the Committee on Finance of the U.S. Senate and the Committee on Ways and Means of the U.S. House of Representatives*. Washington, DC: U.S. Government Printing Office.

Diamond, Peter. 1982. "Social Security: A Case for Changing the Earnings Test but Not the Normal Retirement Age." Unpublished paper, Massachusetts Institute of Technology.

————. 1995. "Government Provision and Regulation of Economic Support in Old Age." In Bruno and Pleskovic (eds.), *Annual Bank Conference on Development Economics*, 1995. Washington, DC: World Bank, pp. 83–103.

————. 1997. *Macroeconomic Aspects of Social Security Reform*. Brookings Papers on Economic Activity, 2. Washington, DC: Brookings Institution.

Diamond, Peter, and Salvador Valdes-Prieto. 1994. "Social Security Reform." In B. Bosworth, R. Dornbusch, and R. Laban (eds.), *The Chilean Economy*. Washington, DC: Brookings Institution.

Holden, Karen. Forthcoming. "Women as Widows under a Reformed Social Security System." In Olivia S. Mitchell, Robert Myers, and Howard Young (eds.),

Prospects for Social Security Reform. Philadelphia: University of Pennsylvania Press, Pension Research Council.

Mitchell, Olivia, James Poterba, Mark Warshawsky, and Jeffrey Brown. 1999. "New Evidence on the Money's Worth of Individual Annuities." *American Economic Review*, Vol. 89 (December), pp. 1299–318.

Munnell, Alicia. 1999. "The Impact of Mandatory Social Security Coverage of State and Local Workers: A Multi-state Review." Unpublished report for AARP.

Murthi, Mamta, J. Michael Orszag, and Peter R. Orszag. 1999. *The Charge Ratio on Individual Accounts: Lessons from the UK Experience.* Birkbeck College Working Paper 99-2. London: University of London.

National Academy of Social Insurance. 1999. "Evaluating Issues in Privatizing Social Security: Report of the Panel on Privatization of Social Insurance." <http://www.nasi.org/publications2763/publications_show.htm?doc_id=56732&name=Social%20Security> Also available as Peter A. Diamond (ed.), *Issues in Privatizing Social Security: Report of an Expert Panel of the National Academy of Social Insurance.* Cambridge, MA: MIT Press.

Rea, John D., and Brian K. Reid. 1998. "Trends in the Ownership Cost of Equity Mutual Funds." *Investment Company Institute Perspective*, Vol. 4, no. 3.

U.S. Department of Health and Human Services. 1985. *Report on Earnings Sharing Implementation Study.* Washington, DC: U.S. Department of Health and Human Services.

U.S. Department of Health, Education, and Welfare. 1979. *Social Security and the Changing Roles of Men and Women.* Washington, DC: U.S. Department of Health, Education, and Welfare.

U.S. House of Representatives Select Committee on Aging. 1992. *Congressional Symposium on Women and Retirement.* Hearing, Comm. Pub. No. 102-897. Washington, DC: U.S. Government Printing Office.

World Bank. 1994. *Averting the Old Age Crisis.* Oxford: Oxford University Press.

CHAPTER 6

The State of Private Pensions

DALLAS L. SALISBURY
Employee Benefit Research Institute

Introduction

A review of the state of private pensions must begin with a clear understanding of what a pension plan is. The legal meaning has clearly changed over the past 25 years. The Employee Retirement Income Security Act of 1974 (ERISA) gives this definition:

> any plan, fund, or program which was heretofore or is hereafter established or maintained by an employer or by an employee organization, or by both, to the extent that by its express terms or as a result of surrounding circumstances, such plan, fund, or program—

> (A) provides retirement income to employees, or results in a deferral of income by employees for periods extending to the termination of covered employment or beyond, regardless of the method of calculating the contributions made to the plan, the method of calculating the benefits under the plan or the method of distributing benefits from the plan.[1]

This represented an expansion in concept from the first full version of the legislative proposal, HR 2, which limited plans to those "for the purpose of providing for its participants or their beneficiaries, by the purchase of insurance or annuity contracts or otherwise, retirement benefits, [including] any deferred profit-sharing plan which provides benefits at or near retirement." HR 2 was closer to the traditional dictionary definition of a pension: "a retirement or disability allowance."

Today, the term *pension plan* is used to describe any employer- or government-sponsored capital accumulation program that has a stated purpose of providing funds for retirement. Defined-benefit plans, defined-contribution plans, annuity payments, and lump-sum distribution plans are all within the new-age definition.

ERISA created requirements and standards for vesting, funding, participation, and fiduciary behavior; established a termination insurance program for private employer and union employee benefit plans; and exempted public-employee plans from its jurisdiction. ERISA was the end result of a 1963 report from a cabinet committee on pensions appointed by President Kennedy, work by career civil servants throughout the Johnson administration, and a single-minded drive by Republican Senator Jacob Javits to convince the Nixon administration that this new law was needed. The Nixon administration worked with Congress to frame the legislation, which was ultimately signed by President Ford as one of his first acts in office. ERISA has met its primary objective: protecting existing covered workers. Expansion of pension coverage was not an objective of ERISA. The state of private employer pensions today is the result of ERISA rules, interacting with economics, demographics, and competition.

ERISA's expansion of the definition of *pension plan* to include capital accumulation plans with lump-sum distributions at "termination of covered employment," as opposed to "at or near retirement," actually serves to highlight the state of private pensions in the United States. Both the public and private sector have moved in the direction of sponsoring fewer plans that pay benefits only "at or near retirement" and have created more and more plans that pay at "termination of covered employment." The result has been dramatic change in defined-benefit pension plans, those that promise a fixed accrual and benefit, and growth in the number of defined-contribution plans, those that promise payment of funds contributed, adjusted for investment earnings, but guarantee no fixed benefit.

This paper does not provide a normative assessment of whether these trends are good or bad for employers, unions, individuals, or public policy. It merely describes the reality.

Where Did We Start?

The first reported pension plan in the United States was established in 1636 as the Plymouth Colony settlers' military retirement program for soldiers' widows. In 1759 a pension plan was established to benefit the widows and children of Presbyterian ministers. Gallatin Glassworks established a profit-sharing plan in 1797. The U.S. government provided pensions to soldiers' widows following the Civil War. In 1875 the American Express Company established a formal corporate pension plan (Allen, Melone, Rosenbloom, and VanDerhei 1992; Employee Benefit Research Institute [EBRI] 1995; Rosenbloom 1996).

The statutory tax treatment of pensions was formally legislated through the Revenue Act of 1921, which exempted interest income on stock-bonus and profit-sharing plans from current taxation and deferred tax to employees until distribution. Statutes enacted since 1921 have permitted employers to deduct a reasonable amount in excess of the amount necessary to fund current pension liabilities (1928), made pension trusts irrevocable (1938), and established nondiscriminatory eligibility rules for pension coverage, contributions, and benefits (1942). These provisions were incorporated into the Internal Revenue Code of 1954 and amended substantially by the Employee Retirement Income Security Act of 1974 and several added statutes, including the Tax Reform Act of 1986.[2]

The most rapid growth in plans occurred during the 1940s and 1950s in response to collective bargaining activity. When there were wage and price controls during this period, expenditures for employee benefits could still increase, providing a strong impetus for plan establishment. Table 1 provides a summary of public and private plan growth. As this table shows, early growth was dramatic. While it combines "private industrial pension and deferred profit-sharing plans," Holland (1966), from whose work the table is taken, did not view both to be "pensions." Today, the definition of pension has changed to include both defined-benefit and defined-contribution plans. The U.S. Bureau of the

TABLE 1
The U.S. Pension System, 1940–1999

	1940	1950	1960	1979	1993	1999
Participants (millions)	5.5	12.4	25.7	43.5	51.7	61.4
Private	4.1	9.8	21.2	32.5	36.9	46.6
Public	1.4	2.6	4.5	11	14.8	14.8
Fund assets (billions)	2.5	12.3	53.0	684	4,187	5,750
Private	2.4	12.0	52.0	517	2,932	4,905
Defined benefit	N/A	N/A	N/A	N/A	1,232	2,215
Defined contribution	N/A	N/A	N/A	N/A	1,043	1,845
Other	N/A	N/A	N/A	N/A	657	845
Public	0.1	0.3	1.0	167	1,255	2,385
Total workforce (millions)	56.0	63.8	72.1	95.0	121.5	131.5
Percentage participating	9.8	19.4	35.6	45.8	42.6	46.7
Private net flows (billions)	0.3	2.0	5.4	N/A	451	419
Private net contributions (billions)	0.2	1.7	3.7	N/A	12	-12

Sources: Data from Holland (1966, 1970); Employee Benefit Research Institute (1995); Ture and Fields (1976); Salisbury and Jones (1994); and Salisbury (1995).

Census combines all 1996 data on plan types under the single heading of "pension," as does the Federal Reserve. The table shows the impact of a maturing pension system, with the divergence of net flows and net contributions. Net flows are a measure of new contributions plus all investment earnings less benefit payments. Net contributions are a measure of benefit payments less new contributions. The fact that net contributions are negative while net flows are positive underlines the primary virtue of advance funding, compound interest, and investment earnings (see Holland 1966, 1970; Ture and Fields 1976; Salisbury and Jones 1994; Salisbury 1995).

Types of "Pension" Plans

Defined-Benefit Plans

In a defined-benefit plan, the employer agrees to provide the employee a nominal benefit amount at retirement based on a specified formula and, increasingly, to provide lump-sum payment of the accrued present value at termination of employment. The formula is usually one of three general types: a flat-benefit formula, a career-average formula, or a final-pay formula.

Flat-benefit formulas. These formulas pay a flat dollar amount for each year of service recognized under the plan.

Career-average formulas. There are two types of career-average formulas. Under the first type, participants earn a percentage of the pay recognized for plan purposes in each year they are plan participants. The second type of career-average formula averages the participant's yearly earnings over the period of plan participation. At retirement, the benefit equals a percentage of the career-average pay multiplied by the participant's number of years of service.

Final-pay formulas. These plans base benefits on average earnings during a specified number of years at the end of a participant's career; this is presumably the time when earnings are highest. The benefit equals a percentage of the participant's final average earnings multiplied by the number of years of service. This formula provides preretirement inflation protection to the participant but can represent a higher cost to the employer.

Flat-benefit formulas are common in collectively bargained plans or plans covering hourly paid employees. Career-average and final-pay formulas are most common in plans covering nonunion employees. Under pay-related formulas, an employer has some discretion in defining pay for plan purposes, provided that the definition does not discriminate in favor of highly compensated employees, subject to the statutory and regulatory definition of compensation used in testing for nondiscrimination. Under ERISA's minimum standards, there is also some leeway in determining what employment period is recognized in the benefit formula. The benefit may be based on only the plan participation period or on the entire employment period.

Bank of America instituted the first cash-balance defined-benefit plan in 1985. Now, approximately 14% of defined-benefit plans are of this type. They generally use a career-average formula and communicate the benefit as present value of an individual account (see Quick 1999). These plans have become quite controversial (see Salisbury 2000). The primary motivation for the movement to such plans has been the desire for a defined-benefit plan that workers appreciate, which the individual account balance has accomplished. At the same time, however, transition to the plans can involve losses for older workers. The *Wall Street Journal* highlighted these issues in a series of articles in 1999, Congress held hearings in 1999 and 2000, and the Clinton administration explored issues of possible age discrimination and desirable levels of disclosure.

Defined-Contribution Plans

In a defined-contribution plan, the employer makes provision for contributions to an account established for each participating employee. The final retirement benefit reflects the total of employer contributions, any employee contributions, and investment gains or losses. As a result, the level of future retirement benefits cannot be calculated exactly in advance. Sometimes the accumulated amount is reduced by forfeitures of employer contributions by employees who leave before becoming vested. Employer contributions to defined-contribution plans are generally based on a specific formula, such as a percentage of participant salary or of company profits, but whether or not a contribution is made in a given year is generally discretionary. The plans may be designed to include pretax or after-tax employee contributions, which may be voluntary or mandatory.

There are several types of defined-contribution plans. In a money-purchase plan, employer contributions are mandatory and are usually stated as a percentage of employee salary. In a profit-sharing plan, total contributions to be distributed are often derived from a portion of company profits. Stock-bonus plans usually make contributions and benefit payments in the form of company stock. A target-benefit plan is a cross between a defined-benefit plan and a money-purchase plan: a targeted benefit is used to determine the level of contributions, but contributions are allocated to accounts as in a money-purchase plan. A thrift, or savings, plan is essentially an employee savings account, often with the employer's matching contributions. In a 401(k) arrangement, an employee can elect to contribute, on a pretax basis, a portion of current compensation to an individual account, thus deferring current income tax on the contribution and on the investment income earned. In an employee stock ownership plan (ESOP), employer contributions to employee accounts must be primarily in company stock.

For the individual worker, the move to defined contributions stimulates a number of needs:

- A need for basic financial literacy education

- A need to understand that savings represent a trade-off between lifestyle today and money to live tomorrow

- A need to understand investing, fees, returns net of fees, and so on

- A need to evaluate the importance of the benefits that come with a job and the degree to which they may determine happiness for a lifetime

What Is the Pension Landscape Today?

Congress acted in 1984 to change the pension system for federal civilian employees. Prior to 1987, the only retirement plan was a final-pay defined-benefit plan. For those hired after the 1984 act, a new, reduced, defined-benefit plan was accompanied by a generous 401(k)-type plan. Those already working have the option of remaining in the old plan or shifting to the new plans. Congress also acted in 1978 to add two new sections to the Internal Revenue Code, sections 125 and 401(k). Regulations in 1981 led to a massive transition of traditional profit-sharing plans into 401(k) plans, which meant that employees could contribute pretax dollars. State and local governments and nonprofit organizations had this type of opportunity in 457 and 403(b) plans. Legislation since 1986 has moved all these so-called salary-reduction plans closer together in design and rules; nearly all employers are now able to establish 401(k) plans. Recent years have seen debates in a number of states over proposals either to introduce expanded, supplemental salary-reduction plans or to replace defined-benefit plans with defined-contribution plans. Demographic change and economic competition make it likely that these debates and trends will continue.

Table 2 presents data from the U.S. Department of Labor on the number of private employer pension plans. The trend lines are clear: defined-benefit plans are on the decline, and salary-reduction plans are becoming the primary "pension" plans in the nation. The numbers on multiemployer plans reinforce the trend line of increasing use of supplemental and primary defined-contribution programs ("Abstract" 1999; Olsen and VanDerhei 1997).

TABLE 2
Number of Qualified Private Pension Plans, 1975–1999

	1975	1985	1995	1999 (est.)
Single-employer defined-benefit	101,214	167,911	67,682	40,000
Single-employer defined-contribution	207,437	461,158	622,584	700,000
Multiemployer defined-benefit	2,132	2,261	1,810	1,800
Multiemployer defined-contribution	311	805	1,328	1,500

Sources: U.S. Department of Labor and author's estimates.

As the number of plans has changed, so have the numbers of participants. Table 3 underlines the shift in primary retirement plan type from 1975 to 1995, based on annual plan filings and analysis of the U.S. Department of Labor (1999). The Department of Labor defines a defined-contribution plan as supplemental when the worker also has a defined-benefit plan. The participation data underline that not only has the number of defined-benefit plans fallen but the number of participants who have them as their primary plan has fallen as well. More recent data from the Federal Reserve Survey of Consumer Finance document this trend through 1998 (Copeland and VanDerhei 2000). Considering all families reporting at least one worker with some type of

TABLE 3
Qualified Private Pension Participation of Total Private Workforce by Plan Type, 1975–1995

	1975	1985	1995
Number of W/S workers	68,104	88,293	102,162
Participate in primary DB plan	39%	33%	23%
Participate in primary DC plan	6%	13%	23%
Participate in supplemental DC plan	9%	18%	16%

Source: U.S. Department of Labor (1999).

pension coverage, the number of those families with at least one worker participating in a defined-contribution plan only was 57% in 1998, compared with 38% in 1992. Families with at least one worker participating in a defined-benefit plan declined only from 40% to 21%, while families with both stayed steady at 22%.

Unions, participant advocates, and many others have not been happy with these trends. Traditional defined-benefit plans, as noted, provide annuity income, which assures some level of economic security for the remaining lifetime of the participant and, frequently, the beneficiary. This in fact represents the old definition of a pension. Unions have traditionally viewed pensions as a method of seeking to achieve security against the risk of economic loss resulting from factors over which the worker has no control (employer commitment to provide a predetermined income stream under certain circumstances; Duzak 1982), such as

- Unanticipated expenses or income loss
- Layoff or termination
- Retirement with inadequate savings to maintain real income for the remainder of one's lifetime

One union counselor noted in 1982:

> Defined contribution plans which determine the amount of income to the employee as a function of the employer's profit, or the price of the company's stock, or the investment yield of a fixed pool of assets, are not compatible with the concept of a wage versus income security trade-off. . . . It is virtually impossible to construct plans which provide desirable levels of income replacement and which also represent an equivalent value to all employees in the covered population. . . . The collective bargaining process requires a pooling of economic strength in order to achieve an objective which is determined by the group as a whole; but at the same time, the process dictates a sacrifice of individuality. . . . Secure protection against the consequences of management's actions. (Duzak 1982)

While many unions have negotiated defined-contribution plans since 1982, it is my sense that those concerned about pensions providing economic security in retirement continue to hold these views.

Employer preferences for pensions focus more on economic performance than retirement income security. Pensions are viewed favorably if they serve to

- improve corporate efficiency (Rosenbloom and Hallman 1991),

- enhance morale,

- keep channels for promotion open,

- facilitate workforce reduction,

- enhance employee identification with profit,

- offer a most cost-effective and least administratively intense form of capital accumulation, or

- attract and hold capable employees (Andrews 1989: chap. 4; Ippolito 1986, 1997).

A Society for Human Resource Management survey found in 1998 that higher salaries elsewhere and dissatisfaction with potential career development at an organization are the most significant threats to employee retention, with only 11% citing benefits as a job-change motivator. A senior corporate executive noted in 1998 that "not having benefits at some threshold level will repulse employees, but the mere presence of a more generous benefits package will not attract and retain employees" (Tharp 1998). This view explains the movement in recent years toward flexibility and the effort to respond to environmental factors with program design. This includes responding to

- favorable tax laws that provide an incentive to provide a pension program,

- demands in labor negotiations,

- social and indirect government pressures,

- inherent advantages of group purchase or provision, and

- shareholder desires and competition.

The noted trends have occurred in spite of the relatively consistent philosophy by union leaders and those focused on retirement income delivery, and the factors driving employers and individuals seem to be accelerating. Taken together, these facts can be viewed as showing that it is unlikely that the movement toward individual accounts and individual control will end. I do not believe the baby boomers will demand a return to the days of "gold watches," and I expect the pressure for individual control to continue.

Borrowing While Still Employed

The availability of loans to participants is an exception to ERISA's general principle that transactions between a plan and parties in interest, such as participants, are prohibited because of potential abuse of funds earmarked for retirement.

A 1999 report found that loans in today's plans are very common ("401(k) Plan" 1999). Over half of 401(k) plans now offer a loan option, 70% of participants are in plans offering loans, and 18% of participants borrowed in 1996. The average unpaid balance as a percentage of account balances was 16%. Loan ratios tend to decrease with age, dropping from 30.0% for participants in their 20s to 9.8% for those in their 60s.

The primary public policy and plan-design argument for loans is that low-income workers are more likely to contribute to a plan if they can access the funds when needed. The primary argument against loans is that they mean that the plan is less a retirement plan than a savings plan. The belief that access to funds is desirable was evidenced by the proposal by the Clinton administration in 2000 for the creation of a new Retirement Savings Account that included the ability to withdraw funds for home purchase, the college expenses of children, or medical emergency, without the requirement of repayment.

Rollovers upon Lump-Sum Distribution

In general, lump-sum distributions from a qualified pension plan may be rolled over tax-free into an IRA or another retirement plan. The transfer must be made within 60 days of the participant's receipt of the distribution from the first plan. The most recent comprehensive data on lump-sum distributions and rollovers is from the 1993 Current Population Survey. Nearly half of those with recent distributions reported having rolled over all of the funds into a tax-qualified program, compared with 17% of those with such distributions prior to 1960. The mean amount of recent distributions was $11,237, and the median amount $3,496 (Salisbury 1995).

A recent analysis by John Sablehaus of the Congressional Budget Office looked at the proportion of Individual Retirement Account (IRA) balances that had come from rollovers as opposed to contributions. By the end of 1997, IRAs held over $1.948 trillion in assets. Of this, $182.9 billion was from direct contributions, $747 billion from rollovers, and the balance from investment earnings ("Projecting" 1999). These numbers suggest that, as a vehicle for new savings, IRAs have not proven particularly popular, but as a vehicle for portability and preservation, the IRA is proving quite useful. As the baby boom moves into retirement and takes lump-sum distribution from both defined-benefit and defined-contribution plans, the assets in IRAs will grow rapidly. There is a lack of good microdata on how IRA assets are invested; this remains important for the capital markets and the economy. There are detailed data on 401(k) plans, which can provide insight because the investments in both are controlled by the individual.

How Are Plan Assets Being Allocated among Investments?

Traditionally, assets in most pension plans were invested on a pooled basis, with plan sponsors or trustees making allocation decisions among managers, equities, bonds, and so on. That has now changed, and the investment of 401(k) assets can tell us a great deal about future investments. With the combination of the growth of mutual funds, 401(k) plans, and computer advances, individual participants now make most of the allocation decisions. The *EBRI-ERF Pension Investment Report* (1999) provides summary data on allocation from 1950 to 1997 (for public plans) and to 1998 (for private plans). The January 1999 *EBRI-ERF Issue Brief* ("401(k) Plan" 1999) provides data on asset allocation within 401(k) plans. Table 4 summarizes aggregate allocation at

TABLE 4

Pension Fund Investment Trends, 1985–1998

	Private trusteed DB	Private trusteed DC	Public plans	401(k)
1985				
Equity	41	38	58	N/A
Bond	29	17		N/A
Other	30	45	11	N/A
1990				
Equity	34	35	32	N/A
Bond	40	17	43	N/A
Other	26	48	25	N/A
1996				
Equity	46	43	56	10
Bond	32	12	28	
Other	22	45	16	22
1998				
Equity	53	48	68	72
Bond	27	10	25	9.5
Other	20	42	7	18.5

Note: All figures are percentages.

the end of several years and individual allocation at the end of 1998 for private trusteed defined-benefit and defined-contribution plans and for public plans.

These average allocations hide variation across plans and participants. They suggest at least two things: first, that asset allocation shifts a lot over time, and second, that individuals invest more aggressively than the average plan board. For example, some public plans have had legal prohibitions against investment in equities, while others have been able to be very aggressive. Large trusteed private plans tend to be more heavily invested in equities than small plans, and there is substantial variation among individual 401(k) participants when one looks at the numbers by age, income, and tenure. Looking at detailed statistics is beyond the scope of this paper, but it is essential that one look at these details in making policy.

Corporate Governance and Plan Assets

As assets in pension plans have grown, many organizations and individuals have tried to figure out how to use the money to advantage. EBRI sponsored a policy forum in 1979 that explored whether pension assets should be managed for social and political purposes (Salisbury 1980). The conclusion then, and now, is that when "all other things are equal in terms of risk and return," then social considerations can be part of a final decision. The voting of proxies has also arisen as an issue; the Department of Labor holds that fiduciaries must vote proxies if they can be used to enhance the value of shares held on behalf of participants and that proxies cannot be voted in a way that harms participants. Throughout the 1980s and 1990s, many pension funds—particularly those related to higher education, unions, and public employees—have sought to proactively vote proxies and invest assets in ways that do not increase risk or reduce return but that provide a second level of good to participants, for example, funding construction that creates jobs.

Another way in which pension assets have acted to attract investors was featured in the movie *Wall Street*, which highlighted the potential to use surplus pension assets to actually help finance the purchase of a company from shareholders. This actually happened in the sale of A&P in 1983 and ultimately led Congress to enact an excise tax that effectively ended plan terminations as a means of making use of surpluses for other corporate purposes.

Plan Termination

Although pension plans must be established with the intent that they will be permanent, employers are permitted to terminate their plans. As table 1 showed, terminations have been heavy. If a defined-benefit plan terminates with assets greater than the amount necessary to pay required benefits, the employer may recover the excess assets and use them for business or other purpos es. ERISA established plan termination insurance to protect participants' defined benefits in the event that a defined-benefit plan terminates with insufficient assets to pay benefits. The program does not apply to defined-contribution plans. There are separate programs for single-employer and multiemployer plans (see Pension Benefit Guaranty Corporation [PBGC] 1998). As noted earlier, a 50% excise tax, in addition to regular income taxes, is now imposed on the amount recovered.

With a strong economy, strong markets, and many large employers remaining in the PBGC premium pool by moving to cash-balance plans rather than to defined-contribution programs, the PBGC has had several good financial years. As of September 30, 1998, PBGC's single-employer program had $17.6 billion in assets, against $12.6 billion in current liabilities. However, PBGC notes exposure to likely future terminations of an additional $20 billion. Should future government action make it legal to shift to defined-contribution plans but not to cash-balance plans and should this action combine with a period of weak markets, the PBGC could well see a flood of new terminations.

Meeting Changing Needs with Plan Design Changes

The preceding sections have highlighted with numbers the changes taking place in pension coverage, asset allocation, and relative levels of net contributions to plans. The numbers further show that the proportion of the workforce covered by plans is slowly growing and that IRAs are proving effective as portability devices, in accord with demographic changes in the American workforce and general population, which have influenced and are likely to continue to influence the provision and design of pension plans.

One change in progress is the shift in the U.S. population's age distribution. Members of the large baby-boom cohort (individuals born between 1946 and 1964) currently compose a disproportionately large part of the overall workforce, especially in new and fast-growing industries. As this cohort ages and the smaller baby-bust cohort (individuals born between 1964 and 1975) has entered the labor force, the age distribution of the workforce has shifted toward older workers, whose needs and preferences may differ from those of younger workers. As the baby-boom cohort begins to retire, an increasing proportion of Americans will be elderly, will live longer, and will depend on sources other than employment for income and vital services. These forces will affect both income security and health care insurance programs.

Developments in the retirement-plan market represent a response to workforce changes. Many employers have always been characterized by high turnover, and few workers have spent 25 years or more with one employer. Defined-contribution plans provide a career average benefit and deliver more to workers with relatively short service with a given employer than do defined-benefit plans. For the employer they provide a known cost, which can be budgeted. The defined-benefit cash-balance plan does the same, while giving the participant less investment risk. Both plans provide lump-sum distributions, which are popular with workers. They are portable, and once a lump-sum distribution is taken upon job termination, they eliminate any risk related to the former employer going out of business or running off with the money because the participant already has the money.

The employer, the worker, and the union gain flexibility. The potential for workforce mobility is enhanced, and more workers build assets. A public policy issue would arise if the intent of the programs was the provision of lifetime income support during retirement. This has not been the public policy, as I understand it.

What Income Do Plans Provide?

Worth Magazine ran a cover in 1996 with the words, "Why Retire?" With the cover went an upbeat article on all the reasons one should view retirement as unnecessary in a future of longer life, better health, better medical care, and multiple careers. Many other publications have run stories with themes such as "Will you be able to afford to retire?" "Will you retire in poverty?" "Why aren't you saving enough?" and "The end of retirement!" These stories tend to be negative about the future and tend to paint the past as one in which all achieved the great American Retirement Dream with little effort.

The American workforce, from an income perspective, is a pyramid: there is only one Bill Gates at the point, but there are over 25 million below the poverty level, creating a very wide pyramid base. The pattern of asset distribution is the same. Three and a half million households, or

3.5% of households, have a net worth of $1 million or more, compared with the pyramid base of over 60% of households that have a net worth of effectively zero or are in debt. While saving would be desirable for those in this 60% of the pyramid, they have never done it. This lack of savings shows up among retirees today.

Contrary to the picture often painted by the popular media, most of today's retirees did not prepare for retirement. The 1999 EBRI Retirement Confidence Survey found that just under one third of present retirees had done any financial or life planning prior to retirement. Among workers, 32% report having done nothing to date, and less than half of these consider what they have done to be adequate.

Census data tell us that today's retirees are well off financially compared with those before them, but the media picture of a generation of retirees on golf courses and cruise ships represents a telescope focused on the tip of the iceberg. Fully 80% of retiree households today have total income of less than $23,000 per year. For the top 25%, nearly 25% of income still comes from Social Security, 25% from working, 25% from savings, and the final 25% from employment-based pensions. These income data underline a critical fact: for today's retirees, continued work after age 65, personal savings, and an employer plan are what make it possible to be in the top 20% by income. The contention by some that work after 65 is what will be different for the baby-boom and "X" generations ignores the facts: work after 65 is already essential for millions in order to have a "decent" income. Table 5 underlines the importance of Social Security and work for today's retirees. While there are no good matched data available on pre- and postretirement income by individual, this table does show income by age, including relative levels for those over 65. It shows that median income drops substantially and that income from continued work is substantial. It also confirms the importance of Social Security, pensions, and income from assets. Table 6 paints an even clearer picture of economic well-being and the relative role of different income sources. Table 6a tells us how many get income from each source. Table 6b tells us how much of the income comes from each source. Those with income only from Social Security are concentrated in the lowest income quintiles. Those who also have savings, pensions, and continued earnings move to the top.

What is true for retirees today will be true for retirees tomorrow: Social Security alone does not provide an adequate income by any standard other than a high replacement rate for some. Is 120% of $5,000 an adequate income, or a guarantee of poverty? The issue is

TABLE 5

Median Income of the Population Aged 55 and Over by Age and Income Source, Selected Years 1974–1994 (constant 1992 dollars)

Year	Aged 55+	Aged 65+	Age 55–61	Age 62–64	Age 65–69	Age 70–79	Age 80+
Total income							
1974[a]	$11,425	$8,674	$20,490	$14,653	$ 9,676	$8,600	$7,492
1979	10,793	8,795	17,812	13,214	10,127	8,743	7,517
1984	11,349	9,659	16,536	13,039	11,081	9,657	7,977
1989	12,509	10,765	18,356	14,478	12,423	10,749	9,083
1992	11,842	10,200	18,043	13,620	11,302	10,361	8,947
1994	12,521	10,982	19,000	14,400	12,242	11,228	9,613
OASDI[b]							
1974	5,854	6,033	5,601	4,778	5,806	6,306	5,746
1979	5,674	5,798	5,598	4,522	5,643	5,989	5,691
1984	6,045	6,234	5,757	4,710	6,118	6,270	6,121
1989	6,332	6,504	5,884	5,011	5,886	6,789	6,618
1992	6,348	6,420	6,000	5,143	6,015	6,514	6,681
1994	7,225	7,453	6,870	5,665	6,960	7,561	7,693
Pensions and annuities[a,c]							
1974[a]	5,464	5,123	8,538	6,010	5,362	5,123	3,961
1979	5,658	4,824	9,025	6,957	5,338	4,638	4,402
1984	5,476	4,694	8,733	7,025	5,476	4,350	3,896
1989	5,920	5,211	9,504	7,673	6,291	4,874	4,073
1992	6,000	5,076	10,000	8,000	6,204	5,024	3,600
1994	6,600	5,800	12,000	9,600	6,600	5,775	4,079
Income from assets							
1974	1,423	1,821	1,110	1,352	1,708	1,958	1,779
1979	966	1,353	696	966	1,248	1,366	1,353
1984	1,499	2,067	987	1,362	1,831	2,213	2,283
1989	1,436	1,923	987	1,245	1,707	2,086	1,980
1992	989	1,200	572	750	1,083	1,210	1,300
1994	795	1,000	500	696	951	1,048	1,000
Earnings							
1974	17,075	6,113	22,767	19,921	6,830	5,123	4,354
1979	17,393	6,646	21,654	18,939	7,730	5,539	3,247
1984	15,647	5,858	19,559	16,905	6,817	4,564	3,260
1989	16,972	7,694	22,063	16,972	9,052	5,657	4,526
1992	15,840	7,000	20,200	15,000	8,300	6,000	5,000
1994	17,000	8,000	22,000	16,000	9,600	6,120	5,000
Other[a,d]							
1974[a]	2,739	2,669	3,039	2,869	2,732	2,598	2,732
1979	2,213	2,125	2,319	2,763	1,980	2,114	2,300
1984	2,086	1,956	2,477	2,086	2,034	1,964	1,784
1989	2,263	1,989	2,715	2,608	2,172	1,926	1,901
1992	2,400	2,264	2,628	3,334	2,400	2,172	2,100
1994	2,688	2,400	3,311	3,010	2,436	2,386	2,394

Notes: Medians are not additive as not all individuals have each income source. Thus, median for those with earnings can exceed median total income for all individuals.

[a]In 1974, the percentage of income of the older population represented by pension income may be overstated, and the percentage of income represented by "other" income sources may be understated. Total private pension income of individuals aged 55 and over in 1974 was $10,451 million; however, because some sources of income in the "other" category are included in private pension income, the actual pension total is overstated by between 2% and 12%, or between $9,221 million and $10,243 million. Similarly, public pension income in 1974 was $13,603 but is potentially overstated by between 7% and 18%,

TABLE 5 (*Continued*)
Median Income of the Population Aged 55 and Over by Age and Income Source,
Selected Years 1974–1994 (constant 1992 dollars)

or between $11,226 million and $12,638 million. Income from "other" income sources is
understated by the amount pension income is overstated.
[b]Old-age, survivors', and disability insurance; includes railroad retirement.
[c]Includes pension, annuity, survivors', and disability benefits.
[d]Includes public assistance, Supplemental Security Income, unemployment compensation, workers' compensation, veterans' benefits, nonpension survivors' benefits, nonpension disability benefits, educational assistance, child support, alimony, regular financial assistance from friends or relatives not living in the individual's household, and other sources of income.
Source: Employee Benefit Research Institute tabulations of the March 1970, March 1975, March 1980, March 1985, March 1990, March 1993, and March 1995 Current Population Surveys.

TABLE 6a
Percentage of Individuals Aged 65 and Over with Income from Specified Sources by
Income Quintile, Selected Years 1974–1995

	Total	Lowest	2	3	4	Highest
OASDI[a]						
1974	88.6%	82.0%	90.4%	94.8%	94.3%	79.6%
1979	91.0	82.5	96.6	95.5	95.6	83.9
1984	92.6	87.7	96.1	96.9	95.6	86.7
1989	92.5	89.7	95.7	96.5	95.5	85.1
1994	93.2	87.3	96.2	97.4	95.7	89.0
1995	93.8	91.0	97.6	97.5	95.6	87.3
Pensions and annuities[b,c]						
1974[b]	24.0	2.2	5.0	14.5	40.0	50.8
1979	26.6	2.4	21.0	6.6	45.2	54.6
1984	30.1	3.2	10.5	29.0	52.3	53.5
1989	34.7	4.9	13.0	35.8	58.3	59.9
1994	35.9	5.0	12.4	32.9	58.9	65.8
1995	35.8	4.7	12.3	31.8	59.0	63.9
Income from assets						
1974	47.4	16.6	23.4	42.1	62.8	81.6
1979	68.9	43.9	70.2	51.8	82.8	92.3
1984	69.4	42.1	49.1	73.2	85.2	95.0
1989	70.3	44.6	53.1	72.6	85.4	94.3
1994	69.3	48.9	51.5	68.3	82.9	91.9
1995	69.3	46.4	51.9	69.5	82.7	90.6
Earnings						
1974	21.9	8.8	8.6	13.6	25.8	48.1
1979	17.5	4.5	10.8	5.9	23.1	41.4
1984	15.2	4.6	5.7	12.0	19.8	33.0
1989	16.4	4.5	6.1	12.8	20.0	37.8
1994	15.7	4.5	4.6	10.2	20.9	36.3
1995	16.1	4.6	5.2	9.6	19.4	38.6
Other[b,d]						
1974[b]	17.3	14.5	27.2	21.8	13.8	8.3
1979	15.3	18.7	16.3	24.7	9.7	8.0
1984	13.6	20.0	21.6	11.7	7.5	7.7
1989	13.4	18.2	18.6	9.9	9.7	11.1
1994	11.7	13.2	16.2	8.1	10.2	11.2
1995	6.7	3.1	5.0	5.8	7.8	11.1

TABLE 6b

Percentage Distribution of the Older Population's Income by Source and Quintile, Selected Years 1974–1995

	Total	Lowest	2	3	4	Highest
OASDI[a]						
1974	42.0%	88.6%	77.7%	74.6%	55.4%	19.9%
1979	42.7	79.1	71.9	78.7	51.9	20.5
1984	40.5	80.2	79.7	68.1	48.0	19.6
1989	38.6	81.5	78.8	65.2	45.8	17.9
1994	44.4	84.8	82.4	74.5	52.4	23.2
1995	43.7	88.8	84.6	74.7	51.3	21.1
Pensions and annuities[b,c]						
1974[b]	14.0	1.5	2.3	4.6	14.4	18.8
1979	14.8	1.1	5.6	2.1	15.7	20.6
1984	15.0	1.2	2.8	8.2	18.5	18.9
1989	17.5	2.0	3.8	10.6	21.1	21.6
1994	20.0	1.8	3.5	9.0	21.6	26.7
1995	18.6	2.3	3.6	8.3	21.9	24.3
Income from assets						
1974	18.2	3.8	4.4	7.4	14.1	25.7
1979	21.5	7.1	13.1	9.1	19.5	28.4
1984	28.2	7.4	8.5	16.5	23.5	38.6
1989	25.2	6.7	9.1	16.1	22.4	33.2
1994	17.6	6.3	7.2	10.6	14.8	23.3
1995	17.7	6.1	8.2	11.6	16.0	23.3
Earnings						
1974	21.3	-3.2	2.8	4.8	11.4	33.8
1979	17.3	0.3	3.9	1.6	9.9	28.8
1984	13.3	0.2	1.5	3.7	8.2	21.3
1989	15.8	0.2	1.7	5.0	8.6	25.3
1994	14.9	-0.6	1.2	3.7	8.5	24.0
1995	17.8	1.7	1.6	3.7	8.4	28.8
Other[b,d]						
1974[b]	4.5	9.3	12.8	8.6	4.7	1.7
1979	3.6	12.3	5.5	8.5	3.0	1.7
1984	2.9	11.0	7.5	3.6	1.8	1.7
1989	2.9	9.7	6.6	3.1	2.1	2.0
1994	3.2	7.6	5.8	2.2	0.3	2.8
1995	2.2	1.0	1.5	1.7	2.3	2.4

[a]Old-age, survivors', and disability insurance; includes railroad retirement.
[b]In 1974, the percentage of income of the older population represented by pension income may be overstated, and the percentage of income represented by "other" income sources may be understated. Total private pension income of individuals aged 55 and over in 1974 was $10,451 million; however, because some sources of income in the "other" category are included in private pension income, the actual pension total is overstated by between 2% and 12%, or between $9,221 million and $10,243 million. Similarly, public pension income in 1974 was $13,603 but is potentially overstated by between 7% and 18%, or between $11,226 million and $12,638 million. Income from "other" income sources is understated by the amount pension income is overstated.
[c]Includes pension, annuity, survivors', and disability benefits.
[d]Includes public assistance, Supplemental Security Income, unemployment compensation, workers' compensation, veterans' benefits, nonpension survivors' benefits, nonpension disability benefits, educational assistance, child support, alimony, regular financial assistance from friends or relatives not living in the individual's household, and other sources of income.
Source: Employee Benefit Research Institute tabulations of the March 1970, March 1975, March 1980, March 1985, March 1990, March 1995, and March 1996 Current Population Surveys.

important for workers, who must be concerned with the income of parents and grandparents; for employers, who need to sell product; for unions, which need employers to sell product in order to need workers; and for the retired, who need income to live.

Retirement Planning Is Needed throughout the Pyramid

The data just reviewed make it clear that many of today's retirees saved little themselves and did not accumulate pension value beyond Social Security. The data highlight the importance of the Social Security program to the vast majority of today's retirees. There is little reason to believe that this will change dramatically in the future.

A 1996 survey from the National Endowment for Financial Education found that the average financial planner's client has median net worth of $400,000, median annual gross income of $75,000, and median annual discretionary income of $10,000 (income that the respondent said could be saved or spent but was not needed for fixed expenses). In other words, such clients are near the top of the pyramid. Yet many report that clients have difficulty saving enough to meet retirement income goals. It is interesting to look at why this is believed to be the case. The top two barriers reported by planners were (1) procrastination and (2) confusion over how to begin planning for retirement. Behind these were (3) lack of information or awareness, (4) poor cash management, (5) paying off debt, and (6) college education funding. A 1999 report from Fidelity Investments found that among 401(k) participants, fewer than 10% were very confident that they would be economically prepared for retirement. These are the haves!

For the population at large, the 1999 Retirement Confidence Survey (RCS) found similar barriers, but one third of the respondents to that survey said that they simply did not have any money they could save, another third said that they did not have enough to save regularly, and one third reported saving regularly.

The planners' survey found that clients generally expected the same standard of living during retirement, not better or worse. The RCS found that 18% expected better, 20% less, and 62% about the same. Social Security was expected to be the primary source of income.

The public does not feel prepared financially for retirement, while most planners think that the average client is. The fact that clients already have high net worth probably makes this inevitable. Why doesn't the baby boomer save more today? A series of surveys have come up with common findings on barriers: the high cost of education, the amount of personal debt, the potential for job loss and downsizing, and meeting daily living expenses. Fully 25% of workers state simply that they will live for today, each day, and worry about retirement income should they ever retire. The Retirement Confidence Survey found that the reasons retirees gave for not saving more for retirement were very much the same.

For retirees, common concerns include meeting health care costs, the prospect of long-term care costs, and outliving what assets and income sources they have. These retiree concerns provide a partial list of items that should be more heavily stressed to workers today. It is very clear that in the new millennium these concerns have to be emphasized, as the prospects for longer life make savings and retirement planning all the more essential. For the lowest-income workers, these concerns underline the importance of Social Security, Medicare, and Medicaid; the virtue of seeking work that brings a pension plan of some type with it; and saving even a little each month and year to ensure some cushion beyond what the "system" has provided in the past.

Will Retirement Planning in the New Millennium Be Easier?

Several factors combine to promise better retirement planning across the pyramid in the new millennium:

- Savings education is now beginning in kindergarten and is taught through grade 12.

- Debt management gets regular attention.

- Medical miracles and life extension are around us every day as reminders.

- Technology makes it easier and easier to collect the information needed for planning and to do it.

- The infrastructure of organizations, individuals, and machines to assist in financial planning is growing rapidly.

- The Internet facilitates retirement planning.

Planners can help bring discipline to the individual planning process. Technology can make implementation easier. As the nation becomes wired and as computers with Internet access are placed in public libraries and community centers, individuals at a variety of income levels will have greater Internet access. Access does not mean usage, but greater opportunity is good.

Cheap bookkeeping software to allow generation of income statements, balance sheets, and projections is now available from many vendors. This software easily allows individuals to determine possible retirement budgets. Books and guides in print and online set forth the major steps in determining the retirement lifestyle one wants, standard of living in income terms, the needed protection against medical expenses and insurance, and estate planning if real assets are expected to remain.

The ability to get detailed information on income sources is now a mouse click or phone call away. Social Security now sends annual statements to all; additional reports may be requested by calling an 800 number. The growth of defined-contribution plans means quarterly statements, most of which are available by phone or online. The biggest job for the planner or individual is to know what the individual has earned while moving from job to job. Even defined-benefit plans are getting better at providing regular information due to both the law and the desire of employers and unions that workers appreciate the plans.

For those with very low income, the explosion of information and planning sources will be an aid, as it will tell them that they cannot afford to retire and should continue working longer. Reality says that the income situation will not change radically for the better, but the opportunities for control will expand. Individuals' being driven to adverse action through lack of information needed for rational and informed decisions will decline.

Can We Return to "The Way We Were"?

Writing prior to the enactment of ERISA, one leading actuary noted:

> A defined benefit final pay pension plan may be selected precisely because it is the only type of plan which permits the employer to design a pension formula that takes both sources of retirement income, Social Security and company benefits, into account. By doing so, a firm can provide higher paid employees a proportionately greater company pension. This compensates for the fact that these individuals receive a lower percentage of final earnings from Social Security. (Peters 1982)

ERISA and subsequent legislation have limited the degree to which a plan sponsor can integrate a pension plan with Social Security (how much defined benefit can be offset and how much can be contributed to a defined-contribution plan above the Social Security wage base), and funding and benefit limits have shifted much of what is done for high-income workers outside the qualified plan. Thus, the integration incentive (as it related to higher-paid employees) is essentially gone.

The actuary continued:

> Such a plan may also be necessary to reward an employee whose salary has increased rapidly or whose service was relatively short. Additionally, only a pension can reward past as well as future service and base the total benefit on final average pay. Finally, some companies believe that they are better able to assume investment risk.

Taking these in order, new funding and liability rules tied to plan termination insurance have all but ended the consideration of past service due to the liabilities it creates and the difficulties the new funding limits place on setting aside funding. Employers and unions that believe they can better absorb risk have continued defined-benefit plan balances. The combination of the PBGC and tax funding limits, however, makes it unlikely that new defined-benefit pension plans will be formed by either single employers or multiemployer groups. Whether this is good or bad, right or wrong, matters little in light of the public policies that make it so.

The actuary concluded:

> The corporate viewpoint on the defined benefit versus defined contribution issue is formed by various competing factors: (1) whether its financial position can sustain the economic uncertainties posed by a defined benefit plan, (2) the extent to which competitive factors determine benefit levels and types, and (3) the corporation's perception of its responsibility to provide for employees' retirement and other financial needs.

Fewer employers are willing to assume that they can financially sustain a plan, as they may well be taken over or spun off tomorrow. Employers are inclined to respond to new-hire and retention competition with current cash and short-term incentives, not generous defined-benefit pensions. Increasingly, employers view their primary obligation to be survival so that they can provide work, leaving postwork planning to the individual.

The regulatory environment, the workforce, world economics, and technology have changed. Taken together, they suggest that we will not return to the defined-benefit design dominance of yesterday, regardless of the economic security consequences for the individual retiree, nor will we return even to the dominance of annuity payouts.

How 25 Years Have Changed Demands and Motivations

The government does influence action, and ERISA changed design drivers. The law went from no minimum vesting standard to immediate vesting in some cases, from use of plan assets for building the firm to arm's length transactions, from clear distinctions between *capital accumulation* and *retirement plan* to limited distinctions, from allowing selective provision of lump sums to an all-or-none requirement, from less tax revenue from lump sums to greater revenue from lump sums, from a retirement-income focus to a cash-portability focus, from a regulatory and tax-incentive bias toward defined-benefit plans to a strong regulatory and tax-incentive bias toward defined-contribution plans, from clear advantages for employer or union provision to an increased focus on individual self-determination and "retail delivery," from a paternalistic philosophy of social obligation and corporate identification to one of maximum satisfaction of individual workers (Holland 1966, 1970; Ture and Fields 1976; Salisbury and Jones 1994; Salisbury 1995).

As one expert has put it, movement from "golden handcuffs" to an employee–employer contract of partnership, personal accountability, and self-reliance moved the nation away from traditional defined-benefit plans and toward greater financial and psychological independence (Tharp 1998).

Plan design and recruitment strategy have moved from broad-based attraction to key-employee attraction, from delivery of fast-vested matches in short-term savings programs to vested matches for long-term savings programs, from delivery of final pay annuities to long-term workers to smaller accumulations for all workers (Vernon 1993), and from employers and unions bearing long-term risks to placing the burden of risk on individuals and families.

As one executive notes:

> While income security is an issue, it is increasingly being recognized that long-term security can best be achieved through personal development and professional growth. Ironically, the presence of high-cost "1950s, one-size-fits-all benefits" may, in fact, be a precursor to job insecurity as cost-cutting measures may be necessary for an organization to carry this heavy burden. . . .

There is a general question of whose responsibility it is to provide retirement income. There is increasing emphasis today on the notion that it is up to individuals to provide a greater portion of their own retirement security.

For the decades ahead, such views are likely to dominate pension decision making. Many of these views are now entering the debate over the future of Social Security. Proposals by both the Republican and Democratic candidates for president in 2000 included government-sponsored individual accounts to supplement traditional Social Security. In short, whatever one would like the pension world to be from a normative perspective, this descriptive review suggests that it will look more like the pension world of the 1990s than that of the 1950s. The individual will be king, and economic well-being once one is no longer working will increasingly rest on prior saving and consumption choices. The adage "choose to save" is taking on new meaning, as it will determine whether individuals can retire or must work forever.

Notes

[1] Employee Retirement Income Security Act. Public Law No. 93-406, 88 Stat. 829, 29 U.S.C. Sect. 1001–1381.

[2] See Employee Benefit Research Institute Education and Research Fund (1997) for additional references.

References

"Abstract of 1995, Form 5500 Annual Reports." 1999. *Private Pension Plan Bulletin*, no. 8 (Spring).

Allen, Everett T., Joseph J. Melone, Jerry S. Rosenbloom, and Jack L. VanDerhei. 1992. *Pension Planning: Pensions, Profit-Sharing, and Other Deferred Compensation Plans*, 7th ed. Homewood, IL: Richard D. Irwin.

Andrews, Emily S. 1989. *Pension Policy and Small Employers: At What Price Coverage?* Washington, DC: Employee Benefit Research Institute Education and Research Fund.

Copeland, Craig, and Jack VanDerhei. 2000. "Personal Account Retirement Plans: An Analysis of the Survey of Consumer Finances." *EBRI Issue Brief*, no. 223 (July).

Duzak, Thomas F. 1982. "Defined Benefit and Defined Contribution Plans: A Labor Perspective." In Dallas L. Salisbury, ed., *Economic Survival in Retirement: Which Pension Is for You?* Washington, DC: Employee Benefit Research Institute Education and Research Fund, pp. 67–75.

EBRI-ERF Pension Investment Report, 4th Quarter 1998. 1999 (May). Washington, DC: Employee Benefit Research Institute Education and Research Fund.

Employee Benefit Research Institute. 1995. *EBRI Databook on Employee Benefits*, 3rd ed. Washington, DC: Employee Benefit Research Institute.

Employee Benefit Research Institute Education and Research Fund. 1997. *Fundamentals of Employee Benefit Programs*, 5th ed. Washington, DC: Employee Benefit Research Institute Education and Research Fund.

"401(k) Plan Asset Allocation, Account Balances, and Loan Activity." 1999. *EBRI-ERF Issue Brief*, no. 205 (January).

Holland, Daniel M. 1966. *Private Pension Funds: Projected Growth*. Boston: National Bureau of Economic Research.

———. 1970. *Private Pensions and the Public Interest*. Washington, DC: American Enterprise Institute.

Ippolito, Richard A. 1986. *Pensions, Economics and Public Policy*. Homewood, IL: Irwin.

———. 1997. *Pension Plans and Employee Performance: Evidence, Analysis, and Policy*. Chicago: University of Chicago Press.

Olsen, Kelly, and Jack VanDerhei. 1997. "Defined Contribution Plan Dominance Grows across Sectors and Employer Sizes, While Mega Defined Benefit Plans Remain Strong: Where Are We and Where Are We Going?" *EBRI-ERF Issue Brief*, no. 190 (October).

Pension Benefit Guaranty Corporation. 1998. *Annual Report*. Washington, DC: Pension Benefit Guaranty Corporation. <http://www.pbgc.gov/publications/annual_repts/ANNREP.htm>.

Peters, Robert B. 1982. "Defined Benefit and Defined Contribution Plans: A Corporate Perspective." In Dallas L. Salisbury, ed., *Economic Survival in Retirement: Which Pension Is for You?* Washington, DC: Employee Benefit Research Institute Education and Research Fund, pp. 81–86.

"Projecting IRA Balances and Withdrawals." 1999. *EBRI Notes*, Vol. 20, no. 5 (May), pp. 1–3.

Quick, Carol. 1999. "Cash Balance Retirement Plans." *EBRI Notes*, Vol. 20, no. 7 (July), pp. 1–8.

Rosenbloom, Jerry S. 1996. *The Handbook of Employee Benefits: Design, Funding and Administration*. Homewood, IL: Dow Jones–Irwin.

Rosenbloom, Jerry S., and G. Victor Hallman. 1991. *Employee Benefit Planning*, 3rd ed. Englewood Cliffs, NJ: Prentice Hall.

Salisbury, Dallas L., ed. 1980. *Should Pension Assets Be Managed for Social/Political Purposes?* Washington, DC: Employee Benefit Research Institute.

———, ed. 1995. *When Workers Call the Shots: Can They Achieve Retirement Security?* Washington, DC: Employee Benefit Research Institute Education and Research Fund.

———, ed. 2000. *The Future of Private Retirement Plans*. Washington, DC: Employee Benefit Research Institute Education and Research Fund.

Salisbury, Dallas L., and Nora Super Jones, eds. 1994. *Pension Funding and Taxation: Implications for Tomorrow*. Washington, DC: Employee Benefit Research Institute Education and Research Fund.

Tharp, Charles G. 1998. "Yes." In Dallas L. Salisbury, ed., *Do Employers/Employees Still Need Employee Benefits?* Washington, DC: Employee Benefit Research Institute Education and Research Fund, pp. 11–13.

Ture, Norman B., with Barbara A. Fields. 1976. *The Future of Private Pension Plans*. Washington, DC: American Enterprise Institute.

U.S. Department of Labor. 1999. *Private Pension Plan Bulletin*, no. 8 (Spring).
Vernon, Steven G. 1993. *Employee Benefits: Valuation, Analysis and Strategies*. New York: Wiley.

CHAPTER 7

Rising Expectations: Women, Retirement Security, and Private Pensions

TERESA GHILARDUCCI
University of Notre Dame

Women's lives are getting better and worse. On one hand, women have made substantial gains in the labor force. Yet women stand alone in enduring high rates of poverty in old age. Why? The answer lies mostly in the labor market and, secondarily, in marriage. This chapter describes how the U.S. model of work-based and marriage-based retirement security, particularly employer-based pensions, poses special difficulties for women.

The first section examines the changing fortunes of elderly women, especially how their sources of income have changed since 1940. The economic, biological, and social roles of women come together to explain elderly women's poverty rates. Specifically, women work much less, are paid less, live longer, and spend more time out of the paid labor market caring for dependent children and older adults. These factors combined endanger old-age income security.

The second section reviews the empirical literature on women's private pension coverage. In the late 1980s and early 1990s, it looked as if women's pension coverage rates were improving and catching up to men's. Yet women workers are less likely to participate in pension plans, and when older women receive pensions from private employers, the pensions are half the amount of men's. The latest evidence indicates that the gap is closing only because men's coverage is falling faster than women's. This is a bitter path to equality.

The third section probes competing explanations of the persistently lower economic status of elderly women. According to neoclassical economists, women choose jobs that provide less in the way of pensions, they prefer other forms of benefits, and they lack commitment to employers because of their nonmarket responsibilities. Neoclassical economists infer that women are more cautious investors and thus earn lower returns by choice. On the other hand, feminist economists attribute the poorer fortunes of elderly women to labor market discrimination and to inequities in the Social Security formula.

The fourth section explores policy implications and the future. Employers offering pensions are increasingly adopting supplemental defined-contribution (DC) plans, and new pension plan coverage tends to be in primary DC plans. Defined-benefit (DB) principles are much more favorable to women. Women are better off having group-based annuities. Despite the complaints about gender inequities in Social Security, its defined benefit, price indexing, and redistributive role still keep large numbers of older women out of poverty.[1]

Elderly Women's Status

Where do older women get income? Except in a few industrialized nations (e.g., Denmark and the Netherlands) women's access to old-age income mainly comes from earnings-related pension programs (from their own or their husband's work), government welfare programs, their own wealth, and, primarily in developing nations, children (Rix, Rosenmann, and Schulz 1998). In the United States, older men and women are protected against age discrimination. A significant source of income to the U.S. elderly is paid employment, particularly for men.

The good news is that the relative status of the elderly, including women, among Americans is improving. The bad news is that even though women outnumber men among the 32 million elderly (58% of Americans over age 65 are women), older women's share of poverty far exceeds their share of the elderly population. Of the 11% of the elderly who are poor, 75% are women (Bajtelsmit and Bernasek 1999). Although work- and marriage-based pension systems are somewhat similar in industrialized nations, the United States' unique emphasis on voluntary retirement systems based on work before and after retirement determines women's inferior status. (International comparisons, though fascinating, are beyond the scope of this chapter.)

First, here is the good news. Bajtelsmit and Bernasek (1999) show that elderly married couples' income as a percentage of the median household income improved considerably since 1969—from 49% of the median household income to a whopping 83% in 1989. Single elderly women shared in this relative improvement; they had just 21% of the median household income in 1969 but reached 33% by 1998.

The bad news is that, despite the trends, nearly one out of five elderly women is still poor, and every elderly woman's chance of falling into poverty increases by 470% (22.8% compared to 4%) if she does not have a husband. The data in table 1 are startling because, despite the high rates of poverty among single older women, the rate for single women with young children is an appalling 45.9%. Moreover, though both groups experienced an increase in real income between 1969 and 1996, single women over 65 did much better, obtaining a 63% increase, compared with the much smaller 10.2% increase for unmarried women with children. The connection between the two rates is that single mothers' bleak economic status can affect their pensions.

TABLE 1
Poverty Rates in 1996 and Change in Income 1969–1996 for Certain U.S. Households

Household	Poverty rate	Change in real income 1969–1996 (%)
Elderly		
Couples over age 65	4.0	57.0
Single men over 65	13.4	63.2
Single women over 65	22.8	63.0
Families		
Couples with children under 18	9.1	25.3
Unmarried women with children under 18	45.9	10.2

In addition to the absence of husbands, women's living standards are also harmed by the deferred wage structure of pensions. When retirement income is based on deferred wages, the situational choices and limitations women face early in their lives, when they usually forgo work hours, cause them to suffer long-term consequences in low old-age income (Rix, Rosenmann, and Schulz 1998).

The U.S. pension system principally combines four sources of income to the elderly: (1) mandatory and nearly universal Social Security, (2) voluntary employer-based pensions, (3) private wealth, and (4) continued work. (The United States stands apart from other nations in its absence of a mandatory retirement age.) Welfare is a small part of retirement income: less than 2% for unmarried women and less than 0.5% for married couples (Grad 1996).

The U.S. Social Security system, like most others, is progressive: it provides higher replacement rates for lower-income workers. The program is not means-tested so that contributors with similar work histories get similar benefits even if one has a large amount of wealth. Unmarried older women received the majority (56%) of their retirement income from Social Security in 1996 (Grad 1996) because of the progressive formula, the subsidy to dependents, and the annual cost-of-living adjustments that help those who live longer than the average beneficiary. Couples, in contrast, receive less than 38% of their income from Social Security (Grad 1996).

The second source of income is voluntary employer-provided pensions. Coverage and generosity vary greatly among occupations, employers, and industries. Less than half of American workers have employer-based pensions, and women's pensions are half the value of men's. Women receive approximately $3,000 per year (Costello and Stone 1995). While almost one fifth of married couples' income comes from employer-based voluntary systems (Grad 1996), only 16% of single women's income comes from employer pensions. This low rate stems from low pension coverage, inferior pensions, and inadequate rules about survivorship and divorce.

Assets are the third source of income for older Americans. Elderly married couples obtain 16.6% of their income from assets; unmarried women receive 18.9% (Grad 1996).

Although the labor force participation of American women has increased rapidly, the rate for women over 65 has remained low. In 1996, a large 22.9% of income for elderly couples came from earnings, while only 8.8% of income for unmarried older women came from earnings. The large work-based share of old-age income is significant. Unlike other nations, older citizens in the United States may remain in the labor force to earn additional income. Having the option to work, ironically, may limit pressure for higher Social Security benefits and better pensions.

In sum, the idea that retirement income is based on a "three-legged stool" of Social Security income, employer-based pensions, and savings is inaccurate in describing older women's retirement income reality. The bulk of income, 56%, to single women comes from Social Security. Only one sixth of retirement income comes from employer pensions, less than 20% comes from assets (savings and home equity), and a small portion, 8.8%, comes from earnings. Sex differences in longevity and the fact that men and women have different labor market experiences produce a less than adequate pension contribution to the "three-legged stool" of retirement income for women.

Table 2 summarizes the major explanations for why women do more poorly under Social Security and employer pensions. Notice that work, longevity, and marriage are factors.

TABLE 2

Gap in Factors That Determine Ultimate Private Pension Income

	Women	Men
Women work less.		
Labor force participation rate of a 30- to 34-year-old in 1996 (reflects attachment to labor force; Devine 2000: table 2)	72%	92%
Age at which fully insured under Social Security (reflects attachment to paid work; Levine, Mitchell, and Phillips 2000: table 1x)	38.9 yr	30 yr
Women are paid less.		
Half earned less than this annually in 1998 (Devine 2000: table 4)	$18,000	$30,000
Women need more pensions.		
Life expectancy for 65-year-olds in 1997	19.2 yr	15.6 yr
Life expectancy for 65-year-olds in 2025 (Munnell 1999: table 1)	20.2 yr	16.8 yr
Husbands matter.		
Penalty for not being married (poverty rate when living alone after age 65; computed from Bajtelsmit and Bernasek 1999: table 1)	22.8%	13.8%

Women's pay is so much lower than men's because they are paid less and work fewer hours and years. A woman on average is almost 40 before she is fully insured under Social Security. Men are covered by age 30. Another way to look at a group's attachment to the labor force is the labor force participation during the group's prime working years. Fewer than three fourths (72%) of primary-age (30–34) women are working or looking for work, while almost all (92%) men are in the labor force.

Although women have made progress, they still earn far less than men do. Women's median annual earnings are only 60% of men's. Also, since women live longer, they need pension income more. In 1997, old women lived 23% longer than men, and in 2025 they will live 20% longer. Defined-contribution pensions do not favor those with long lives since the lump-sum accounts can run out and the annuities have unfavorable rates. Insurers worry about "moral hazard"; they project that it is healthy people who tend to buy annuities.

Last, rules about survivors' benefits and divorced women's benefits, as well as consumption norms, may cause the poverty rates for women without husbands to be higher than for couples or single men. Divorced women's access to pensions depends heavily on the prowess of their lawyers and the state where they obtained their divorces. Consequently, only 27% of divorced women collect pensions from former spouses. To collect, a woman must receive a qualified domestic relations order (QDRO), which women usually trade for the house. The poverty rate for single older men, though high at 14%, is far lower than the 23% poverty rate for older women without husbands.

Private Pensions and Women

There are three data sets that enable us to examine women's coverage under pension plans. The Current Population Survey (CPS) asks individual workers if they are covered by an employer-provided pension plan and whether they participate in that plan. The CPS data set does not ask about the "quality" of the pension and other fringe benefits.

The Survey of Consumer Finances (SCF) asks workers to evaluate the worth of their pension. Workers' evaluations are, however, almost always wrong (Ghilarducci 1992). Moreover, the SCF has a disproportionate share of high-income individuals. I use the IRS 5500 forms to describe various characteristics of the quality of pensions.

Bajtelsmit and Bernasek (1999) reproduced the Employee Benefits Research Institute's compilation of CPS data to show a mixed pattern of pension coverage rates among men and women. Using data up to 1993, they showed that women are actually more likely to have employers who offer pensions, although they are not more likely to be covered by them. This is a marked change from the situation in 1979 and 1983. However, workers need both employers' providing a pension plan and the eligibility to participate.

As mentioned earlier, there are gaps between two more meaningful rates. The first statistic to examine is the rate at which women participate in plans compared with the rate of all workers, the participation rate. The second is the rate at which women participate in the employer's plan compared with all workers whose employers offer plans. Every year, the sex gap in pensions is getting smaller because men's rates are getting worse.

Consider the sponsorship rate in table 3. From 1979 to 1993, women's employment with firms sponsoring pensions increased by 12%; men's declined by 5%. The participation rate for men fell 13% compared with women's increase of 11%. Women are slightly more likely to

TABLE 3
Rates of Pension Plan Coverage for Women and Men, 1979–1993

	Workers with employers who sponsor pensions (sponsorship rate)		Workers who participate in pensions (participation rate, % of all workers)		Workers who participate in pensions (% of all workers with employers who sponsor pensions)	
	Women	Men	Women	Men	Women	Men
1979	52%	59%	38%	51%	73%	87%
1983	50%	54%	38%	47%	76%	88%
1993	58%	56%	42%	45%	72%	81%
Change, 1979–1993	12%	–5%	11%	–13%	–1%	–7%
Women's rate as % of men's in 1993	104%		93%		89.5%	

Source: Bajtelsmit and Bernasek (1999: table 4).

work for employers who sponsor pensions (58% compared with 56% for men) but are less likely to participate in pension plans (42% versus the male rate of 45%). To probe the differences between men's and women's participation rates, a third statistic is added. Of all workers working for firms that sponsor pensions, women are 9 percentage points (72% compared to 81%) less likely than men to participate in the plans (see the last column of table 3).

So far we have been concerned with the "catch-up" question. The closing of the pension sex gap may cause us to lose sight of what is happening to men and the common goals of men and women. Women and men in all income categories suffered from a decline in pension coverage, considering both newer DC plans like 401(k)s and traditional DB plans. Table 4 has more recent data on coverage by income. Men's coverage under employer pensions is still falling faster than coverage for women, and the women's coverage rate is falling too.

TABLE 4
Percentage Covered by Employer or Union Pension Plans by Income Distribution, 1979–1996

	1979	1996	Change in coverage
Women in top third	65	61	–6
Women in middle third	46	40	–13
Women in bottom third	17	16	–6
Men in top third	76	71	–7
Men in middle third	60	53	–12
Men in bottom third	24	19	–21

Source: Ellwood (2000), derived from CPS data for all workers over age 18.

The decline is even more disturbing because the workers less likely to have other resources in retirement have experienced the steepest decline in coverage rates. The pattern of men's pension loss mimicked the distribution of income losses of this period: those at the bottom fell further. Men at the bottom third of the income scale in 1996 faced a whopping 21% lower rate of coverage than men in 1979. Those in the middle suffered a 12% loss.

Women who were at the top third of the income distribution in 1996 had 6% less pension coverage than in 1979. Men in the same position had 7% less. Oddly, unlike women's wage decrease, which is worse for those at the bottom, the loss in pensions for women is much worse for workers in the middle income range. (The bottom never had much coverage and therefore had less to lose.) Women who were in the middle third of the income distribution in 1996 had a 13% lower rate of coverage than similarly situated women in 1979 (see table 4).

Investigating the Sex Gap in Pension Coverage

In 1993, Janet Currie investigated whether the sex gap in pension coverage can be explained by sex differences in productivity or whether fringe-benefit discrimination is yet another manifestation of pay discrimination by sex. Another explanation is that women give housework more priority than market work and "most likely trade-off wages and other benefits for those benefits, which are of use in household production" (Currie 1993:3). This trade-off assumption depends highly on pensions and wages being substituted for one another. The idea is that if women trade away pensions, they get something for it: more "family-friendly" flexibility, higher pay, and so on. However, pensions and wages are complements. The higher paid the job, the more likely it will have fringe benefits attached.

Currie (1993), using the May supplement to the 1988 CPS (which can control for those who accept coverage under an offered benefit), found that previous research had overestimated the extent to which women lacked health insurance because they declined coverage (presumably because they were covered by their husbands' benefits). However, Currie discovered that women were 8% less likely to be offered a pension and that much of the difference in coverage was due to differences in job tenure. To control for job tenure, Currie examined men and women with 10 years of tenure with an employer and found that women were still 5% less likely to be in jobs with pension plans.

Women workers have fewer pensions than similarly situated men, even though they have all the signs of being committed workers. Currie concluded that women's lack of pensions is not due to personal choices:

> A comparison of married, university-educated women with children to similar women with only a high school education shows that for most individual benefits, the gender gap is just as large for women with the greater investment in human capital, even though these women presumably have a great commitment to market work. (p. 11)

Finally, Currie (1993) used regression analysis to predict whether the pension sex gap would disappear if women had earned the same wages as men. She found that nearly all the gap would disappear and concluded that pensions and wages are complementary, not substitutes, and that women do not make trade-offs.

Korczyk (1993) found that women had lower pension coverage because women have lower-paid jobs for the same levels of work experience and age: sex discrimination generates differential pension coverage. Improvements in women's pension coverage have come about because women are getting better jobs, which pay well and offer pensions, and because women are working more hours and choosing to stay longer with their employers.

Korczyk's optimism was based on data up to 1988. Full-time female workers increased their pension coverage from 38% in 1972 to 43% in 1988, a whopping 13% increase. Unfortunately, full-time male workers' coverage declined from 54% in 1972 to just 49% in 1988, a 9% decrease. The decline in male coverage is especially worrisome because the workforce has been aging. In 1998, men ages 25 to 34 constituted 26% of the male workforce, down from 30% in 1983. Instead of a fall, we would have expected male pension-coverage rates to increase as male workers got older. Perhaps employers are less apt to provide pensions and encourage men to leave their jobs because employer commitment to male workers is falling (Osterman 1999). Declines in median tenure for men occurred in every age group over the 1983–1998 period. For men ages 40 to 64, the proportion who had worked for their employer at least 10 years fell by about 10 percentage points in each five-year age group (Bureau of Labor Statistics 1999).

On the other hand, as female workers became older, their pension-coverage rates increased. According to Korczyk (1993), they earned more, got better jobs, and stayed with their employers longer. The percentage of women age 25 and over with 10 years or more of tenure with their current employers was 28.4% in February 1998, up by 3.5 percentage points from January 1983. The trend toward rising proportions of women with long tenure occurred mainly among 35- to 54-year-olds.

Korczyk (1993) also showed that female-dominated industries such as retail and services and female-dominated occupations such as clerical work and sales are less likely to be covered than male-dominated jobs. Women's integration into predominantly male occupations and industries helps expand their coverage. Though Korczyk (1993) and Currie (1993) probed the reasons for the pension sex gap and growing women's coverage, the last year they examined was 1988. The 1993 data cheered Bajtelsmit and Bernasek (1999) somewhat by showing that women's pension coverage is increasing. Yet Ellwood's 1996 data (Ellwood 2000) do not show that women are doing better; their pension coverage rates have been falling since the late 1980s.

Hinz and Turner (1998) examined why an employer may not sponsor pensions. The rise of DC plans and the decline of collective bargaining have made pensions more voluntary for both the worker and the employer. Most employers who offer participation in a 401(k) do not make participation mandatory for everyone. Also, of course, employers do not have to provide pensions and are under considerably less institutional pressure to do so now that unions have declined. Hinz and Turner (1998) found three basic nonoptimal pension situations in which workers might find themselves.

The first situation is that a worker may not want a pension but is covered anyway. The Hinz and Turner (1998) study's innovative methodology defined workers who do not want pension coverage (but are covered anyway) to be those who are similar to workers who decline pension coverage when offered. Minority, female, and low-income workers are more likely to decline coverage when it is voluntary. Hinz and Turner found that members of these groups who had pensions (despite expectations) work for large firms.

Second, workers could choose not to work for firms with pensions because they do not want them. Alternatively, workers may refuse plans that are offered (this group is more likely to be workers with short tenure or who work part-time). Women and young people are often thought to fall in this category.

In the third situation, the worker wants a pension, but the firm does not offer one. Sometimes employers find the administrative costs prohibitive.

This is often true for small employers. Other employers who clearly have the resources to offer pensions choose not to do so (such as Microsoft and Time Warner, who have classified many full-time employees as temporary to avoid paying benefits). A worker who desires a pension may be employed at a firm where most of the other workers do not want one. This may apply to firms with many young and part-time workers.

Hinz and Turner (1998) concluded that many women fall in the first category. Many women have pensions because their employers cover people in male-dominated occupations and IRS nondiscrimination rules and union contracts force the employers to include even lower-paid workers in the pension plans.

Evidence for the second reason that people are not covered can be found in the coverage rate versus the "uptake" rate, that is, the rate at which workers take pensions when they are offered. The uptake rate for 401(k)s is quite low for all workers. In 1993, only 65% of workers in firms offering 401(k)s reported that they chose to participate. Uptake is assumed to be the worker's choice. More women turn down coverage than men. Fifty one percent of "turndowns" are female (women constitute 49% of the pension-covered and 41% of the pension non-covered private sector work forces (Hinz and Turner 1998:25)).

Hinz and Turner (1998) cite a federal worker survey that probed why women and men do not participate in the voluntary Federal Thrift Savings Plan. The most often cited reason for nonparticipation was the same for women and men: that there was no money to spare. Thirty-five percent of the women and 29% of the men responded that way. One fourth of the men and one fifth of the women said they preferred other investments. We find the largest sex gap in these two answers. Sex gaps also appeared with respect to confidence in the plan: 10% of men but only 6% of women did not have confidence that they would receive promised benefits. Based on the answers, the lack of disposable income for savings seems to be the most important reason that women are not participating.

Hinz and Turner concluded that the supply problem—workers want pensions but firms don't offer them—is a significant reason that pension coverage has stagnated. Twenty percent of the uncovered workers have the same characteristics as workers who choose pensions when they can. Hinz and Turner downplayed the administrative cost argument; costs have fallen and there are low-cost alternatives, such as the simplified employee pension (SEP).

The Quality of Women's Pensions

This section compares the quality of women's and men's pensions. The data are indirect but are the best available. IRS Form 5500 is required annually from pension sponsors and contains useful financial data about each plan and the three-digit SIC code of the sponsors. I assume that the plan participants and the firm are typical of the industry in terms of the concentration of female workers. I have gleaned the differences in pension plan characteristics over time for what I call female-majority industries (more than 50% women) and male-dominated industries (fewer than 20% female employees).

In 1981 and 1996, female-majority industries were less likely than male-dominated industries to offer only DC pension plans (see table 5a). In 1981, 5.9% of the female-majority industries compared with 13.3% of male-dominated industries offered only DC plans. In 1996, 14.3% of the female-majority industries compared with 18.8% of the male-dominated industries offered only DC plans.

However, when we compare female-majority industries with male-majority industries (those in which men constitute over 50% of the workforce), there is no clear pattern in the types of plans offered. In 1981, workers in female-majority industries were less likely to have only DC plans; in 1996, female-majority industries were more likely to have only a DC pension plan than male-majority industries.

On the other hand, there is a very clear pattern with regard to DB generosity (defined as the actuarial normal cost divided by the number of active participants) and average employer contributions by the sex majority of the industry. Female-majority industries have worse pension plans. Women's DB plans are only 66% to 90% (depending on year and comparisons) as generous as plans in industries dominated by men and industries that employ mostly men.

There are important sex differences in funding ratios (assets to liabilities) of DB pension plans in female-majority industries and in male-majority industries. The plans are not as well funded for women. In 1996, female-majority industry plans had a funding ratio of 0.706. In comparison, the average 1996 male-dominated plan ratio of assets to liabilities was 0.762, and for male-majority plans it was a much larger 0.974.

Male-dominated industries have more participants in collectively bargained plans than do female-majority industries. Only 18.2% of participants in female-majority industries were unionized in 1996, while

TABLE 5a
Pensions in Female-Majority Industries Compared with Pensions in Male-Dominated Industries

Pension structure and characteristics	Female majority (>50% female) 1981 (n = 17)	1996 (n = 21)	Male dominated (>80% male) 1981 (n = 14)	1996 (n = 15)	Ratio of female-majority plans to male-dominated plans 1981	1996
Firms with a DC-only pension structure	5.90%	14.30%	13.30%	18.80%	0.44	0.76
Generosity (normal cost per active participant)	$367.75	$1,217.35	$505.86	$1,440.4	0.73	0.85
Total participants	240,132	85,307	43,426	61,517	5.53	1.39
Funding ratio	0.926	0.706	0.846	0.762	1.09	0.93
Average employer contribution	$857.85	$1,206.42	$1,045.05	$1,371.92	0.82	0.88
Unionization	N/A	18.2%	N/A	50%	N/A	0.364

TABLE 5b
Pensions in Female-Majority Industries Compared with Pensions in Male-Majority Industries

Pension structure and characteristics	Female majority 1981 (n = 17)	1996 (n = 21)	Male majority 1981 (n = 71)	1996 (n = 76)	Ratio of female-majority plans to male-majority plans 1981	1996
DC only	5.90%	14.30%	9.90%	11.80%	0.60	1.21
Generosity	$367.75	$1,217.35	$555.77	$1,345.24	0.66	0.90
Total participants	240,132	85,307	120,926	84,906	1.99	1.00
Funding ratio	0.926	0.706	0.876	0.974	1.06	0.72
Average employer contribution	$857.85	$1,206.42	1,154.12	$1,544.94	0.74	0.78
Unionization	N/A	18.2%	N/A	36.80%	N/A	0.49

36.8% and 50% of participants in male-majority and male-dominated industries, respectively, were in union-bargained pension plans. (The collectively bargained status of the pension plans on Form 5500 is available only after 1990.) Union plans are more generous and have higher employer contributions than non–collectively bargained plans (Ghilarducci 2001).

Last, female-majority industry plans were much larger in 1981 and 1996 than plans in the male-majority and male-dominated industries. These findings confirm Hinz and Turner's (1998) conclusion that women are likely to be covered by a pension plan when they are swept up in a large pool of workers.

Unionization Effects on Women's Pension Coverage

The union effect needs more study. Most of the researchers cited earlier observed that unionization raises the level of women's coverage. Table 6 shows the advantage of unionization for pension coverage for both men and women. The union advantage is higher for men: 63% versus 57%.

TABLE 6
Full-Time Workers Covered by Pensions, by Union Status

	Women	Men
Union	74%	78%
Nonunion	47%	48%
Union advantage (increase in coverage rate when workers are unionized)	57%	63%

Source: U.S. Department of Labor et al. (1994: table B12).

Currie (1993) found that unionization does what fringe benefit coverage was expected to do: equalizes compensation among workers in the same firm because everyone has the same coverage. Likewise, by including all workers in a bargaining unit, a union contract compresses the compensation for members precisely because fringe benefits are a major part of the contract.

Unionization also explains the sex variance in coverage after controlling for industry, occupation, pay, and other factors thought to affect pension coverage. One reason could be that union workers tend to value fringe benefits more than nonunion workers. The rate of increase in unit labor costs going to nonwage compensation is much higher for union workers than nonunion workers (Ghilarducci 2001). This union effect on "saving for retirement" could be due to the union leadership's encouragement of delayed gratification. Alternatively, the process of planning one's economic future (which happens during collective bargaining when workers are asked to construct and vote for contract demands) could make people less myopic.

Pension trends based on employers' commitment to workers are changing, and these changes will affect both women and men. In the next section, I focus on the impact on women.

Theories about Why Older Women Have Low Incomes

Why do old women have worse pensions and higher rates of poverty than men? Feminist economists blame a number of factors for older women's low economic status. They concentrate on Social Security and not, for the most part, on employer pension policy. They accuse the system of providing a "housewife bonus" that subsidizes nonworking wives and, therefore, strengthens patriarchal systems (Bergmann 1986; Holden 1996).[2] When a working wife receives benefits on her spouse's record, which is more likely because men's pay is so much higher, she is, in effect, receiving a "zero return" on her own contributions. Recent work suggests that a woman's earnings would have to increase substantially over 20% for her to "earn a benefit of her own" under Social Security (Levine, Mitchell, and Phillips 2000).

Nancy Folbre's (1994) arguments relate to Social Security and employer pensions. She notes that men struggled for "retirement" by striking for pensions at the workplace and forming political coalitions for increased Social Security benefits.[3] A patriarchal bias developed that allows fathers to abandon children and yet garner a decent Social Security benefit. She argues further that the Social Security system, as the major U.S. policy for income support, does not make women's and children's income security a priority. Employer pensions as deferred wage systems also do not give women and children automatic entitlement to adequate income.

Olson (1982) examined how Social Security and employer pensions redistribute income from some workers to other workers. Olson emphasized that "capital" does not pay for pensions because Social Security and employer pensions are paid for by workers either directly through a deferred wage or through rules that redistribute benefits among workers. Ghilarducci (1992) showed, using an institutional bargaining model, that employer pensions may reduce the overall compensation to workers that otherwise would have been paid.

These studies reflect a common concern about whether pensions (and Social Security) are fair to women. Knowing how well employer pensions cover women is a key first step in assessing whether women are entitled to more pensions or will obtain more coverage in the future.

Historical case studies of the treatment of women workers during the time that employers were developing pension plans emphasize the behavior of employers in the exclusion of women. Sanford Jacoby (1997) described the strategic use of women workers that precluded their participation in Sears, Roebuck and Company's and Kodak's emerging pension plans. In 1916, social reformers had attacked Sears for paying women poverty wages and forcing them into prostitution. In response to the bad publicity, Sears created "one of the nation's most generous and publicized profit sharing plans" (Jacoby 1997:97). Ironically, because only full-time workers with one year of service could participate, "the plan's prime beneficiaries were not women but men" (Jacoby 1997:68). Sears's only concession to women was that if women left to get married, they could take the company contributions after 5 years of service rather than the usual 10 (assuming they were covered; Jacoby 1997:98).

I have already shown that working for a company with a pension plan, but not participating in it, is more common for women than men. ERISA has been modified to reproduce some aspects of the Social Security rules for spousal entitlement in private plans. The 1984 Retirement Equity Act, sponsored by Congresswoman Geraldine Ferraro, gives spouses more rights to claim their partners' pensions earned at work.

Institutional labor economists see family dynamics and employer behavior as intertwined. Segmented labor market theory suggests that women are used as buffers, complements, and cheaper substitutes for men's labor (Blau and Ferber 1998; Rubery 1978). When labor market demand is high, women are brought into jobs, and they are fired in recessions. Women are also hired in so-called women's jobs to complement the better primary-sector jobs that go to men. Last, employers can hire women to "flip" a male-dominated occupation into a female occupation and pay those jobs less (Blau and Ferber 1998). Sexist social norms and corresponding family choices can facilitate these transformations; bus driving, residential real estate, bank telling, and bartending are all examples of occupations that changed from "male" to "female" jobs. All these factors mean that women have more marginal labor market roles. Benefit coverage is expected to be lower, especially benefits such as DB pensions that aim to create long-term relationships with employees.

Employer Pensions
and the Future of Women's Retirement Security

Devine (2000) emphasized an essential point: there is no such thing as a bundle of reforms that are "good for women" or "bad for women" because there is no such thing as a representative woman. Socioeconomic position is as important as sex in explaining retirement income security. But sex inequality in security and living standards persists into retirement. Despite the difficulty in generalizing, I propose the following new policies for women's pensions. Each would go a long way to help women gain retirement income security.

The growth in DC and 401(k) plans poses special challenges to women's retirement income security. First, employers are more likely to offer all types of pensions to higher-income workers. Workers whose employers offer DB plans cannot opt out of participation, whereas the choice to participate is the hallmark of 401(k) plans. Low-income workers are less likely to voluntarily contribute to pension or savings plans, and as shown earlier, women earn less than men.

Recommendation 1: Modify 401(k) rules so that the tax advantage applies only if the employer enrolls all eligible employees in the plan and provides a minimum contribution (perhaps 1% to 3%) for all employees. Employees may opt out only if they sign an informed consent form. This would give workers an incentive to save and would overcome the natural inclination to be shortsighted, to value the present more than the future. McDonald's Corporation has default enrollment, and participation is much higher than it is at the average food service firm.

Recommendation 2: 401(k) rules should be updated to include the same spousal protections that are in DB and DC rules. The Retirement Equity Act of 1984 requires spousal consent for pension distributions other than joint and survivor options.

Currently, pensions enter into divorce settlements as property. Because women more often than men face financial difficulties in divorce, wives are likely to choose cash over pensions in the settlement. If there is no deal and a qualified domestic order issued, the pension is not divided. Moreover, valuing pensions is difficult for most lawyers and having them do so is expensive.

Recommendation 3: If one half of the marital share of a participant's accrued benefit were given to the former spouse by default in all divorce decrees, more ex-wives would likely collect. In a closely related proposal, the Department of Treasury could publish model spousal consent forms for 401(k)s and qualified domestic orders in order to spare individuals expensive lawyer time to determine the value.

Some intriguing proposals draw analogies between childcare and military service.

Recommendation 4: Workers on parental leave should be able to make up missed pension contributions and service by being able to buy back service credit. (More boldly, employers could be required to maintain contributions to pension and health plans while workers are on leave for parental duties.)

However, this proposal could very well be regressive since higher-income individuals would be more likely to have the extra cash, especially around the financially stressful time of a child's birth, to buy back service. Moreover, higher-income individuals are more likely to take unpaid leave to care for children.

Many joint and survivor options mimic the Social Security survivor formula. Social Security pensions are reduced by 33% when a worker dies. (Social Security provides the couple 150% of the worker's pension, and the survivor gets 100% of the worker's pension.) One can live more cheaply than two, but only 12% to 25% less, not 33%.

Recommendation 5: Default joint and survivor options and the Social Security formula should redistribute the pension and Social Security benefits so that a couple gets a little less and the survivor more.

Many problems particular to women have not elicited remedies. DC-type pensions are not adjusted to make up for losses due to inflation (employers do not have a relationship with the annuity or worker after retirement as they do in most DB cases). Since women live longer, inflation takes a bigger bite.

Since workers choose their own DC plan investments and women invest more conservatively than men, their yields are significantly less for the same amount of contributions (up to 16% less in one study; Ross 1997). Higher incomes would make up for the gender differences in risk aversion. It is important to note that the problems with individual accounts cited earlier—low levels of pensions, women's greater longevity, and disputes over marital property—would be exacerbated if Social Security was transformed into individual accounts.

Why do women have less income in retirement? Is it patriarchy or women's free choice? The answer is probably both. However, women can help themselves by obtaining pensions, protecting pensions in divorce, and planning for widowhood by being in a stronger bargaining position vis-à-vis their spouses and employers during their working and married lives.

The studies cited in this chapter show that being in a union and getting equal pay will also help women get better pensions. But the stark reality is that employers are providing fewer pensions. Those workers with the least income are hardest hit by the fall in pension coverage. Since 401(k) plans have grown relative to DB plans, the pensions offered are riskier. It would probably take Social Security reform targeted at the poorest of the elderly poor to significantly improve the lives of elderly widows and divorced women.

Acknowledgments

I wish to acknowledge support from the Retirement Research Foundation and the Higgins Labor Research Center at the University of Notre Dame and the research assistantship of Wei Sun and Anne Geggie. I also benefited from comments from Ruth Ghilarducci and Steve Nyce.

Notes

[1] The idea that human nature and optimism about mortality, pension rules, Social Security benefit structures, and family relations cause "young" older couples to take on debt, travel, and buy consumption goods over and above the "life-cycle" consumption of the longest-living spouse requires more research.

[2] All workers earn a Social Security pension based on their own earnings records. If the Social Security benefit earned on a spouse's own work history is higher than the dependent benefit (50% of the spouse's benefit) then the spouse receives her or his own benefit. (The United States has had gender-neutral dependent benefits since 1975; the European integration treaty required gender neutrality by 1999.) Even though most married women in 1994 will be eligible for retired worker's benefits, their spouse's benefits will be higher. Only 29% of women have a worker benefit higher than their spouse's benefit and thus receive credit for their work (Holden 1996). Even when the early baby-boom cohort starts to retire in 2009, most women will receive wives' benefits because their own benefits will be smaller.

[3] Folbre (1994) noted that the pay-as-you-go system exploits women's labor since the older man's benefit is based on the current and future productivity of children. Since children's ability to work is linked to the amount and quality of undervalued female labor, patriarchy is enhanced as men exploit women.

References

Bajtelsmit, Vickie, and Alexandra Bernasek. 1999. "Women and Retirement." *Research Dialogues* (TIAA-CREF), no. 61.

Bergmann, Barbara. 1986. *The Economic Emergence of Women*. New York: Basic Books.

Blau, Francine, and Marianne Ferber. 1998. *Women and Men and the Economics of Work*. New York: Prentice Hall.

Bureau of Labor Statistics. 1999. "Labor Force Statistics from the Current Population Survey." <http://stats.gov/news.release/tenure>.

Costello, Cynthia, and Anne J. Stone, eds. 1995. *The American Woman, 1994–1995: Where We Stand: Women and Health*. New York: W.W. Norton.

Currie, Janet. 1993. *Gender Gaps in Benefit Coverage*. NBER Working Paper Series No. 4265 (January). Boston, MA: National Bureau of Economic Research.

Devine, Theresa. 2000. "Women and Social Security Reform." Paper presented at the American Economics Association Meetings, January 8, Boston.

Ellwood, David. 2000. "Winners and Losers in America: Taking New Measures of Economic Realities." In David Ellwood et al., eds., *Working Nation: Workers, Work and Government in the New Economy*. New York: Russell Sage Foundation.

Folbre, Nancy. 1994. *Who Pays for the Kids? Gender and the Structures of Constraints*. London: Routledge.

Ghilarducci, Teresa. 1992. *Labor's Capital: The Economics and the Politics of Private Pensions*. Cambridge, MA: MIT Press.

———. 2001. "Small Benefits, Big Pension Funds." In Tessa Hebb, Archon Fung, and Joel Rogers, eds., *Working Capital: The Power of Labor's Pensions*. Ithaca, NY: Cornell University Press, pp. 158–72.

Grad, Susan. 1996. *Income of the Population 55 or Older 1994*. SSA Publications No. 13-11871. Washington, DC: U.S. Government Printing Office.

Hinz, Richard P., and John A. Turner. 1998. "Pension Coverage Initiatives: Why Don't Workers Participate?" In Olivia S. Mitchell and Sylvester J. Schieber, eds., *Living with Defined Contribution Plans*. Philadelphia: Pension Research Council, Wharton School of the University of Pennsylvania, and University of Pennsylvania Press, pp. 17–37.

Holden, Karen. 1996. "Social Security and the Economic Security of Women: Is It Fair?" In Eric Kingson and James H. Schultz, eds., *Social Security in the 21st Century*. New York: Oxford University Press, pp. 91–104.

Jacoby, Sanford M. 1997. *Modern Manors: Welfare Capitalism Since the New Deal*. Princeton, NJ: Princeton University Press.

Korczyk, Sophie. 1993. "Are Women's Jobs Getting Better or Women Getting Better Jobs?" In Dallas Salisbury and Richard B. Burkhauser, eds., *Pensions in a Changing Economy*. Washington, DC: Employee Benefit Research Institute, pp. 59–67.

Levine, Phillip, Olivia Mitchell, and John Phillips. 2000. "A Benefit of One's Own: Older Women's Retirement Entitlements under Social Security." Paper presented at the American Economics Association Meetings, January 8, Boston.

Munnell, Alicia. 1999. "Why Social Security Privatization Would Hurt Women." <http://www.socsec.org/library/mun_women.htm>.

Olson, Laura Katz. 1982. *The Political Economy of Aging: The State, Private Power, and Social Welfare*. New York: Columbia University Press.

Osterman, Paul. 1999. *Securing Employment*. Princeton, NJ: Princeton University.

Rix, Sara, Linda Rosenmann, and James H. Schulz. 1998. "Privatization and Older Women's Financial Needs: Gender Differences in Public and Private Targeting." Paper presented at the Second International Social Security Association Conference on Social Security, January 25–28, Jerusalem.

Ross, Jane. 1997. "Testimony before the Social Security Subcommittee of the House Ways and Means Committee on Social Security Reform: Implications for the Financial Well-Being of Women." GAO/T-HEH-97 112, April 10. Washington, DC: General Accounting Office.

Rubery, Jill. 1978. "Structured Labor Markets, Workers Organizations and Low Pay." *Cambridge Journal of Economics,* Vol. 2, no. 1 (March), pp. 17–36.

U.S. Department of Labor, Social Security Administration, U.S. Small Business Administration, and Pension Benefit Guaranty Corporation. 1994. *Pension and Health Benefits of American Workers: New Findings from the April 1993 Current Population Survey*. Washington, DC: U.S. Government Printing Office.

CHAPTER 8

Prospects for National Health Insurance in the United States

DAVID C. JACOBS
American University

Former Labor Secretary Robert Reich wrote a piece for the *Los Angeles Times* in the early months of the George W. Bush administration in which he challenged the political odds. "What better time than now," he wrote, "to revive the idea of universal health care?" He provided the reasons:

> There's a huge budget surplus. Meanwhile, the number of Americans lacking health insurance continues to rise (now almost 43 million, up from 38 million 10 years ago). And those who have it are paying more than ever in co-payments, deductibles and premiums. As the economy sinks, working families will have an even harder time. If they lose their jobs, their health insurance may disappear. (Reich 2001)

National health insurance (NHI) represents the last unfulfilled plank of the New Deal agenda for social security. President Franklin Delano Roosevelt's Committee on Economic Security called for health insurance as a part of social security, but the president omitted it in order to facilitate enactment of the program. He recognized that the opposition of the American Medical Association (AMA) to NHI would otherwise doom the larger social security initiative.

NHI is, most simply stated, a means to guarantee all citizens access to an adequate, perhaps even equal, standard of health care. Advocates of NHI reject the notion that health care is a commodity, a product that one chooses to buy in a marketplace differentiated by price and quality. Health care is unlike traditional commodities because it is essential for survival, it is a precondition for family welfare and economic success, and it requires decisions beyond the capacity of ordinary "rational" consumers.

One very important feature of health care is the partial management of demand by providers. Diagnosis by doctors (under the constraints set by cost accountants in insurance companies and health maintenance organizations) determines the scope, and ultimately the expense, of treatment. Consumers may decide when to visit physicians, but such visits in themselves determine cost far less than the treatments that doctors prescribe. This, combined with the severe imbalance between doctor and patient in medical knowledge, ensures that the health care industry violates the assumptions of neoclassical economics. Prices cannot serve as the allocative mechanism as neoclassical economics would have it (D. Jacobs 1987).

Private insurance companies boost the cost of health care access for a few reasons. The costs of advertising in pursuit of market share and profit maximizing add to premiums. Overhead costs are likely to be higher than for a public enterprise that lacks the need to advertise and comparable profit pressures. Moreover, a single national health insurance system has the market power to negotiate lower drug prices with the pharmaceutical industry (Fauber and Manning 2001).

The United States is the only industrialized nation without NHI. (Outside the United States there is wide acceptance of the principle that health access should not be determined by income.) The United Kingdom and Spain have national health services, government enterprises that directly provide health care. Canada, Denmark, Norway, and Sweden guarantee access to health care through governmental insurance systems, combined with a mix of private and public hospitals and clinics. Germany and France rely on sickness funds, paying hospitals and physicians uniform rates to ensure that no citizen lacks health insurance. Developed nations with universal health insurance tend to report lower infant mortality, longer life expectancy, and a smaller percentage of the gross domestic product invested in health care than the United States (Guyer et al. 1998; Miringoff and Miringoff 1999).

The three tables illustrate the United States' mediocre performance with respect to infant mortality and life expectancy, despite high investments in health care as a proportion of gross domestic product. The absence of a national health insurance system is likely to be a factor.

TABLE 1

Life Expectancy at Birth in Selected Industrial Nations, 1996

Japan	80
Canada	79
France	79
Sweden	78
Switzerland	78
Spain	78
Greece	78
Netherlands	78
Italy	78
Australia	78
United Kingdom	77
Austria	77
Norway	77
Israel	77
Belgium	77
New Zealand	77
United States	76

Note: The U.S. value masks great disparities. Native American males on some reservations average 56.5 years' life expectancy, while Asian women in affluent New York and Massachusetts counties live into their mid-90s (Miringoff and Miringoff 1999:69).
Source: UNICEF statistics (Miringoff and Miringoff 1999:71).

TABLE 2

Infant Mortality in Selected Industrial Nations, 1995–1996

Sweden	3.5
Finland	3.9
Norway	4.1
Japan	4.3
Switzerland	4.8
Slovenia	4.8
France	4.9
Austria	5.0
Netherlands	5.1
Germany	5.3
Spain	5.6
Belgium	5.6
Denmark	5.7
Australia	5.7
United Kingdom	6.1
Italy	6.1
Canada	6.3
Ireland	6.4
Portugal	6.5
New Zealand	6.7
United States	7.3

Note: Deaths in first year of life per 1,000 births.
Source: United Nations statistics (Miringoff and Miringoff 1999:53).

TABLE 3
Total Expenditure on Health Care as a Share of Gross Domestic Product, 1999

Australia	8.5
Austria	8.2
Belgium	8.8
Canada	9.5
Czech Republic	7.2
Denmark	8.3
Finland	6.9
France	9.6
Germany	10.6
Greece	8.3
Hungary	6.8
Iceland	8.3
Ireland	6.4
Italy	8.4
Japan	7.6
Korea	5.0
Luxembourg	5.9
Netherlands	8.6
New Zealand	8.1
Norway	8.9
Poland	6.4
Portugal	7.8
Spain	7.1
Sweden	8.4
Switzerland	10.4
United Kingdom	6.7
United States	13.6

Source: Organisation for Economic Co-operation and Development (2000).

Public Support for National Health Insurance

There is considerable evidence that the majority of Americans favor universal health insurance. The National Election Studies of the University of Michigan show consistent majorities since World War II for the concept of a government guarantee of access to health care. Opinion analysts Robert Blendon and Karen Donelan wrote in 1991 that support for NHI had reached a 40-year high. Harris Wofford's upset victory in his 1991 campaign for the Senate from Pennsylvania seemed to hinge on his appeal for NHI. L. Jacobs and Shapiro (1994) reported increasing support for government activism. Despite evidence of broad support, opponents have thus far been able to defeat the varied movements for health care reform, most recently the Clinton administration's efforts in 1994.

The campaign for NHI has been marked by significant steps but many failed efforts. Early in the 20th century, progressive reformers sought unsuccessfully to build state programs. At the time, the AMA was sympathetic to this goal. As I have noted, President Roosevelt chose not to undertake the battle on NHI in the 1930s. Labor and public health groups proposed NHI under social security in the 1940s. Although NHI was popular and the Truman administration announced its support, the right-wing opposition successfully used the charge of socialism to derail reform. Democrats settled on the less ambitious goal of health care for the elderly under social security. This was finally achieved, along with health care assistance for the poor, under Johnson's Great Society. The opposition was intense and could hardly have been greater if the goal had been universal health insurance (Marmor 1994).

The United Auto Workers founded the Committee for National Health Insurance (CNHI) to lead the campaign for NHI in the late 1960s. Liberal social insurance and health care specialists devised a set of principles to guide lobbying. They emphasized a single standard of care for all citizens (single payer) under an expanded social security system, comprehensiveness of benefits, access to preventive care, and controls on costs. The principle-driven approach of CNHI was an intelligent approach to policy making, but it was a barrier to compromise. The advocates of NHI were already exhausted by the long trail of defeat and compromise. They opposed half measures that would leave citizens disillusioned with incomplete coverage. When the Nixon administration advanced a proposal for NHI through employer mandate, CNHI and its allies in Congress were opposed.

An opportunity to enact a skeletal framework for NHI may have been lost. However, it is not clear that the Nixon administration would have made good on its initial support for health care reform. President Nixon's enthusiasm cooled; perhaps he became distracted by other political developments. Ironically, the reformers' inability to win active support from the Carter administration and Carter's own defeat in 1980 stimulated the search for a new strategy, culminating in a turn toward the once-spurned employer mandate model in the late 1980s (D. Jacobs 1987, 1989). (CNHI disbanded during this period.)

The 1992 election of President Bill Clinton accompanied by Democratic majorities in Congress led to considerable optimism about the prospects for NHI. Clinton had endorsed universal health care in the 1992 campaign. However, the Democratic sweep was not sufficient to bring NHI to pass. The defeat of the Clinton health care plan occurred for a number of reasons. Some of the obstacles were new, but most were familiar.

Problems with the Clinton Plan

As a "New Democrat," Clinton considered the traditional liberal approach, universal health insurance under social security, suspect. The administration sought to fashion a plan that would elide conventional ideological categories. One element of the Clinton plan, an employer mandate to offer health insurance that satisfied minimum criteria, resembled the legislation that the Nixon administration had proposed and had won support from former Presidents Ford and Carter. The concept of purchasing cooperatives or health alliances in the Clinton plan was a means to negotiate with but not displace private health insurers. Unfortunately, this complicated synthesis of employer mandate and purchasing cooperatives mystified much of the population and failed to mobilize voters.

As Robert Reich (2001) has explained, "The Clinton health plan sank because it was too complicated for the public to understand, which made it a perfect foil for right-wing demagogues." The Clinton approach was very easy for the opposition to caricature. Despite the concessions to market logic, conservative opponents were still able to charge that the administration sought to impose "big government" on unwilling consumers. President Clinton was under the illusion that his complicated version of health care reform would win the support of swing senators and a sizable subset of employers, but he underestimated the opposition of conservative ideologues.

Blendon, Brodie, and Benson (1995) found that public support for the Clinton plan dropped precipitously as opponents mobilized and took advantage of public confusion about the plan. Many in the middle class came to believe that they would lose benefits they already enjoyed.

The Power of Ideology

Republican conservatives aggressively fought universal health insurance because it would, in their eyes, legitimize government solutions to social problems and advance the interests of the Democratic party. Republican strategist William Kristol, then affiliated with the Project on the Republican Future, regarded the defeat of fundamental health care reform as crucial to Republican fortunes. He counseled Congressional Republicans to deny any crisis in access to health care and to cease efforts to compromise with Democrats. Kristol's strategy derived impetus from the greater propensity of the affluent, who possess health insurance, to vote. The defeat of health care reform contributed to the demobilization of lower-income Democratic constituencies and the Republican conquest of Congress in 1994 ("Health Reform" 1994).

A number of Republicans, most notably Senator John Chafee of Rhode Island, were originally prepared to work toward compromise on NHI. Chafee's enthusiasm cooled after a Kristol memo crystallized Republican opposition to compromise with the Clinton plan. Robert Packwood of Oregon had in the early 1970s been the leading advocate of extending social benefits through employer mandate. By the 1990s he was fighting censure because of allegations of sexual misconduct. Now dependent on the support of fellow Republicans for his political survival, Packwood abandoned his former views (Seelye 1994). The Republican party settled on a strategy of noncooperation with regard to most of the Democratic program. Republican party leaders were able to maintain solidarity within their ranks to a greater degree than the Democrats.

Compounding problems for NHI advocates, several Democrats were subject to influence from the business lobbies. For example, John Breaux from Louisiana, an advocate of Medicare vouchers, worked with other conservative Democrats to fashion legislation more solicitous of insurance companies.

Shaky Business Support

One promising development in the 1990s was that there was now significant employer support for health care reform as a result of the cost pressures of the existing system of employer-provided benefits. Unfortunately, private health care interests, fast-food chains, and strong opponents in the business community isolated the advocates. Those favoring reform in the mainstream business lobbies (e.g., within the Business Roundtable and Chamber of Commerce) were outmaneuvered by the health care industry and sharply criticized by the Republican hierarchy in Congress.

Major business lobbies had historically been hostile to NHI, fearing that government activism of all kinds would follow. Labor had regularly pressed employers for endorsement of NHI, arguing that they would benefit from socialization of health care costs. In the late 1980s, some employers providing generous health plans did respond to rising premiums by reconsidering their doubts about governmental solutions (D. Jacobs 1987, 1989).

Discussions among leaders of business and labor led to the formation of the National Leadership Coalition for Health Care Reform, including executives from Chrysler Corporation, Bethlehem Steel, Cincinnati Bell, Dayton-Hudson, Georgia-Pacific, International Paper, Lockheed, Safeway, and Xerox. They endorsed a plan according to which employers would be required either to provide health insurance to their employees or pay a payroll tax for a government plan. With the support of Senator Jay Rockefeller, American Airlines, Chrysler Corporation, and Southern California Edison, the Health Care Reform Project, which specifically endorsed the Clinton health care reform initiative, was organized in 1994. Reform-oriented small-business groups, including the American Booksellers Association, National Farmers Union, National Farmers Organization, and the National Retail Druggists Association, joined the Small Business Health Care Reform Coalition (D. Jacobs 1998; Toner 1994).

Despite apparently increasing business support for health care reform, the Business Roundtable deferred to the interests of health-related companies and chose to oppose the Clinton administration bill. The CEOs of General Motors, Ford Motor, Chrysler Corporation, Bethlehem Steel, American Airlines, Southern California Edison, and other firms voted in favor of the Clinton plan within a Business Roundtable committee. Seventeen of the 65 companies participating in the vote represented health-related businesses (Judis 1995).

When the Chamber of Commerce showed some openness to Clinton administration proposals early in 1994, Republican party leaders in Congress reacted sharply, revealing their expectations of Chamber loyalty. The Republican party placed pressure on the Chamber leadership and helped mobilize grassroots members of the Chamber. In apparent response, the Chamber withdrew conciliatory testimony prepared for a Congressional committee considering the Clinton plan (Rich and Devroy 1994; Weisskopf 1994a, 1994b).

Ameritech executives were rebuked by the Republican leadership for their endorsement of health care reform. Michael Weisskopf (1994b) noted in the *Washington Post*, "Four Republicans on the [House] Energy and Commerce subcommittee on telecommunications and finance, including the ranking minority member, wrote Ameritech President Richard C. Notebaert registering 'strong displeasure' with the endorsement and pointedly referring to pending industry legislation vital to the company." Firms supporting the Health Care Reform Project faced informal pressure from other businesses.

No Important Left-Wing Alternative

There was no credible left-wing alternative to increase pressure for compromise. Labor unions and allied groups failed to rally for the single-payer option, thereby surrendering terrain to the conservative opposition. Reformers chose to support the Clinton initiative despite reservations. (The popularity of radical alternatives to social security had increased the odds for the enactment of a social security system in the 1930s.)

Political scientist Marie Gottschalk (2000) argued that labor's increasing investment in a private health care system, particularly its reliance on health and welfare funds jointly administered with employers, has dulled its appetite for fundamental health care reform: a single-payer, government health insurance system. While labor movements around the world traditionally support socialized medicine, the AFL-CIO and many affiliated unions had turned toward the strategy of an employer mandate, rather than single-payer, in the 1980s. Gottschalk submitted that the employer-mandate strategy was poorly suited to the task of popular mobilization, that it relied too much on the favor of the business community.

Perhaps unions should have joined public interest groups in a campaign for a single-payer system rather than endorse the Clinton plan. Especially in an era in which enterprises offer increasingly unstable employment and declining prospects for careers, it seems particularly inappropriate to base health care access on place of employment.

On the other hand, challenging Clinton's health care plan would have been a difficult course politically. The more liberal industrial and public-sector unions have long been advocates of a single-payer system. The United Auto Workers Union led the campaign for single-payer national health insurance from the 1960s into the 1980s. The American Federation of State, County, and Municipal Employees was a leading backer of the single-payer approach more recently. For these unions, endorsement of the Clinton plan seemed like a reasonable compromise given the political resources of the presidency. With the defeat of the Clinton approach, some in the leadership of these unions have returned to vocal advocacy of a single-payer system.

Given the many obstacles to reform in the United States, the defeat of NHI (at least in 1994) should not be attributed to the strategic choices of labor and other advocates of reform.

Why Social Reform Is Difficult in the United States

The federal structure of government in the United States gave (and continues to give) the opposition to universal health insurance the advantage. There are significant hurdles to reform. Concurrent majorities and sometimes supermajorities are required for enactment of legislation. Majority support in the House requires majorities in a majority of Congressional districts. This is probably the easiest step.

The Senate poses a larger obstacle. Majority support for NHI does not ensure victory in the Senate. The even distribution of seats in the Senate gives small, sparsely populated states equal power with the most populous. Small, conservative states have as many senators as the most populous and labor-friendly ones. A majority of senators can be assembled only if many rural states are represented by senators with pro-NHI views. This is rendered somewhat more difficult by the persistently conservative politics of many such states. The persistent conservatism is a function of elite power as well as a reflection of local attitudes (Lee and Oppenheimer 1999; Lazare 2000).

The filibuster reinforces the advantage of business opponents of NHI. Even assuming that a Senate majority (representing a diverse collection of states) favors NHI, opponents can employ the strategy of prolonged debate. There may be a vote on the proposed legislation only if 60 votes, a supermajority, are available for cloture. Even individual senators can secure a hold on votes.

Winning enactment of new legislation depends on a multistate campaign. States differ in their hospitality to labor and other social groups who tend to favor NHI. However, the Chamber of Commerce is well organized everywhere, and well-heeled groups are capable of advancing their messages in the mass media with near-universal penetration.

James Madison's (1961) Federalist Paper Number 10 reveals his preference for a republican model that would contain majoritarian movements. His cure for the "mischief of faction" was a political structure inviting the proliferation of faction. This, he hoped, would lead one faction to check another. He noted that the uneven distribution of property was a likely source of faction and worried about the possible tyranny of the majority, particularly the majority who were lacking in property (Madison 1961).

As Madison predicted, it is difficult to assemble a majority across a geographically expansive and decentralized nation. It is particularly difficult to build an effective movement in the interest of the majority who desire health security in the face of the entrenched interests of the health care industry.

Voter Participation

Even given the superior resources of the health care industry, the ballot box is in the long run decisive. Unfortunately, voter participation rarely exceeds 50% of eligible voters in the United States. Nonvoters are disproportionately poor, and many are uninsured or underinsured. Those who vote on the whole have somewhat less reason to worry about health insurance.

Lani Guinier (2001) has written:

> We are a democracy that supposedly believes in universal suffrage, and yet the [difference in] turnout rates between high-income and low-income voters [is] far greater than in Europe, where they range from 5 percent to 10 percent. More than two-thirds of people in America with incomes greater than $50,000 voted [in 2000], compared with one-third of those with incomes under $10,000.

Success on NHI could give nonvoters a clearer sense of what might be accomplished in electoral politics, but it may be impossible in the absence of an expanded electorate.

Money and Politics

Insurance companies sought to influence the debate over health care reform through two lobbies: the Health Insurance Association of America (representing smaller insurers) and the Alliance for Managed Competition (for the larger firms). They were able to amass substantial fortunes for an advertising campaign against NHI. The so-called "Harry and Louise" ads played a critical role in persuading many in the public that the Clinton plan would result in a dangerous expansion of governmental power. (In prior years, it was the American Medical Association that led and financed the public relations crusade in opposition to reform.) The Health Care Reform Project also mounted a grassroots campaign, but reform forces were no match for the very wealthy insurance industry and its allies in the broader business community (Skocpol 1995).

The Current Political Environment

Prospects for the enactment of national health insurance are close to nil early in the George W. Bush administration. President Bush is likely to propose the "voucherization" of Medicare, which would attenuate guarantees with regard to health care for the elderly. He is an advocate of the privatization of Social Security. He is unlikely to acquiesce in any new mandates on employers (though he may be compelled to sign legislation for an increase in the minimum wage). As Texas governor, Bush failed to take advantage of a Clinton initiative to expand health insurance to children (the State Children's Health Insurance Program).

There is, however, a surprising new initiative on health care reform—a rather modest effort, to be sure. Families USA, which supports NHI, has joined with the AFL-CIO, the Health Insurance Association of America, and the American Hospital Association to push tax concessions for employers who pay a larger share of medical premiums for their low-wage workers than for more affluent employees. The program would also expand Medicaid and the State Children's Health Insurance Program. A loosely connected newspaper advertisement campaign has been mounted by the AFL-CIO, Families USA, Health Insurance Association of America, American Hospital Association, and the Chamber of Commerce (Eliopoulis 2001).

This initiative attests to the persistence of vexing problems in health care, to the tenacity of health care reformers, as well as to the worries of entrenched interests. The participating health care industry lobbyists want to forestall more meaningful reform, and conservative Republicans want new allies for tax cuts. Conservative strategists at the Heritage Foundation and Cato Institute would like to use tax credits to remake all governmental health programs as inducements to do business with private insurers rather than as any kind of right to health care. Tax breaks also limit the financial resources of government; conservatives see this as an effective means to limit government activism.

Universal health insurance remains a distant hope until and unless the necessary voter mobilization and Congressional supermajorities emerge. A grand coalition of trade unions, public health, and public interest groups committed to a common program stated in clear language and active in most or all of the 50 states would be necessary. There will be little progress without organizing.

In the meantime, there may be further action with regard to children's health insurance, although it may be a matter of tax credits of dubious value. Individual states may follow the path of Hawaii and Massachusetts and experiment with universal health care on the state level. Tens of millions of Americans will remain uninsured.

References

Blendon, Robert J., Mollyann Brodie, and John Benson. 1995. "What Happened to Americans' Support for the Clinton Health Plan?" *Health Affairs*, Vol. 14, no. 2, p. 7.

Blendon, Robert J., and Karen Donelan. 1991. "Public Opinion and Efforts to Reform the U.S. Health Care System: Confronting Issues of Cost-Containment and Access to Care." *Stanford Law and Policy Review*, Fall, p. 146.

Eliopoulis, Phoebe. 2001. "A Shot in the Arm for America's Uninsured." *Business Week*, March 5, p. 98.

Fauber, John, and Joe Manning. 2001. "Hard to Swallow: As U.S. Foots World's Drug Bill, Seniors Cross Borders." *Milwaukee Journal Sentinel*, March 31. <http://www.jsonline.com/news/state/mar01/drug01033101.asp>.

Gottschalk, Marie. 2000. *The Shadow Welfare State: Labor, Business, and the Politics of Health Care in the United States*. Ithaca, NY: Cornell University Press.

Guinier, Lani. 2001. "What We Must Overcome." *American Prospect*, Vol. 12, no. 5, pp. 26–31.

Guyer, Bernard, Marian F. MacDorman, Joyce A. Martin, Kimberley D. Peters, and Donna M. Strobino. 1998. "Annual Summary of Vital Statistics—1997." *Pediatrics*, Vol. 102, no. 6, pp. 1333–49.

"Health Reform Played a Substantial Role in Republican Victory." 1994. *Business and Health*, Vol. 12, no. 12 (December), pp. 11–12.

Jacobs, David C. 1987. "The UAW and the Committee for National Health Insurance: The Contours of Social Unionism." In D. Lewin, D. B. Lipsky, and D. Sockell, eds., *Advances in Industrial and Labor Relations*, Vol. 4. Greenwich, CT: JAI Press Inc's, pp. 119–40.

———. 1989. "Labor and the Strategy of Mandated Health Benefits." *Labor Studies Journal*, Vol. 14, no. 3, pp. 23–33.

———. 1998. "Labor and Social Legislation in the United States: Business Obstructionism and Accommodation." *Labor Studies Journal*, Vol. 23, no. 2, p. 52.

Jacobs, Lawrence R., and Robert Y. Shapiro. 1994. "Questioning the Conventional Wisdom on Public Opinion toward Health Reform." *PS, Political Science and Politics*, Vol. 27, no. 2, p. 208.

Judis, John B. 1995. "Abandoned Surgery: Business and the Failure of Health Care Reform." *American Prospect*, Vol. 21 (Spring), pp. 65–73.

Lazare, D. 2000. "Senatorial Privilege." *American Prospect*, Vol. 11 (September 25), pp. 77–79.

Lee, F. E., and B. I. Oppenheimer. 1999. *Sizing Up the Senate: The Unequal Consequences of Equal Representation*. Chicago: University of Chicago Press.

Madison, James. 1961. "Federalist Paper Number 10." In Clinton Rossiter, ed., *The Federalist Papers*. New York: Penguin.

Marmor, Theodore. 1994. "The Politics of Universal Health Insurance: Lessons from Past Administrations?" *PS, Political Science and Politics*, Vol. 27, no. 2, pp. 194–200.

Miringoff, Marc, and Marque-Luisa Miringoff. 1999. *The Social Health of the Nation: How America Is Really Doing*. New York: Oxford University Press.

Organisation for Economic Co-operation and Development. 2000. "Frequently Asked Data: Total Expenditure on Health—% Gross Domestic Product." <http://www.oecd.org/els/health/software/fad16.htm>.

Reich, Robert. 2001. "If Not Now, When, for Universal Care." *Los Angeles Times*, April 2. <http://www.commondreams.org/views01/0402-03.htm>.

Rich, S., and A. Devroy. 1994. "Chamber of Commerce Opposes Clinton Health Plan." *Washington Post*, February 4, p. A12.

Seelye, Katherine Q. 1994. "The Fall and Amazing Rise of Senator Bob Packwood." *New York Times*, July 10, p. E3.

Skocpol, Theta. 1995. "The Rise and the Resounding Demise of the Clinton Plan." *Health Affairs*, Vol. 14, no. 1, pp. 66–81.

Toner, Robin. 1994. "Small Business Is Big Foe of Clinton's Health Plan." New York Times, April 26, p. A1.

Weisskopf, Michael. 1994a. "Health Care Lobbies Lobby Each Other." *Washington Post*, March 1, p. A8.

———. 1994b. "Lobbyists Shift into Reverse." *Washington Post*, May 13, p. A3.

Chapter 9

Medicare: Past, Present, and Future

Edith Rasell

Economic Policy Institute

The Medicare program, the federal health insurance program created in 1965, provides health insurance to 39 million people, about one out of every seven Americans. Prior to Medicare in 1963, just 56% of people age 65 and above had hospital insurance, while 75% of the population under age 65, who were less in need, had health insurance (Andersen, Lion, and Anderson 1976, cited in Gornick et al. 1996). In 1998, the 39 million Medicare beneficiaries included 34 million elderly (age 65 and above) and about 5 million people below age 65 with physical disabilities or kidney failure (Social Security Administration [SSA] 1999: 313, 314, 318). In 1998, Medicare spent about $217 billion for health care services, 12% of the federal budget.

Medicare is composed of two separate programs. The hospital insurance program (HI, also called Part A) covers hospital services, treatments received in skilled nursing facilities following hospital discharge, home health care, and hospice care. From its inception, the HI program has been closely tied to Social Security Old Age and Survivors Insurance (OASI). Eligibility for OASI, either as a primary beneficiary or spouse, also confers eligibility for HI. Starting in 1972, disabled workers covered by Social Security Disability Insurance (DI) and people with kidney failure (on dialysis or with a transplant) became eligible for HI.

Supplementary Medicare Insurance (SMI, also called Part B) is an optional program that provides coverage for outpatient health care, including visits to doctors and other professionals, outpatient hospital services, and laboratory and diagnostic tests including X-rays. Anyone over age 65 or eligible for HI may also obtain Part B coverage by paying a monthly premium ($45.50 in 2000). By law, Part B premiums are adjusted annually to cover 25% of SMI costs. About 97% of HI beneficiaries also have SMI coverage.

Financing

The two parts of Medicare have different revenue sources. HI is funded with a 1.45% payroll tax assessed on all earnings and paid by both workers and their employers. Unlike Social Security, there is no cap on earnings subject to the payroll tax. The tax rate has not been increased since 1986. However, the earnings cap was eliminated in 1994.[1] In large part, Part A is a pay-as-you-go program; most of the payroll tax revenues are spent in the same year they are collected. In years when tax revenues exceed expenditures, the surplus is used to buy special nonmarketable Treasury securities that are credited to the Medicare Trust Fund.[2] In 1999, the HI surplus of $21 billion boosted the total assets held by the HI trust fund to $141 billion. The bonds paid an average of 7.6% interest, earning $9.8 billion for the trust fund in 1999.

In other years, when expenditures exceed tax revenues, bonds in the trust fund are sold to raise the additional funds. From 1995 to 1997, Medicare ran a deficit, but during the other years of the 1990s, including 1998 and 1999, Medicare had a surplus and increased the stock of treasury bonds in the trust fund.

While Part A is funded with a payroll tax, three quarters of Part B funding comes from general federal revenues. The other quarter of the costs is covered by the insurance premiums paid by beneficiaries. Strictly speaking, concerns about trust fund solvency are pertinent to the HI trust fund only.

Containing Costs

The Health Care Financing Administration (HCFA), the federal agency that administers Medicare and Medicaid, has been a leader in cost containment for over 15 years. Faced with rising costs for hospital care, in 1983 Medicare moved from traditional cost-based reimbursement to a prospective payment system (PPS) for acute-care hospital treatment. To construct these payment rates, the average cost of efficiently treating over 500 medical conditions or diagnosis-related groups (DRGs) was determined. Each Medicare patient admitted to a hospital is categorized into a DRG based on the medical diagnosis and treatment plan. Medicare pays the hospital the prospectively determined reimbursement associated with the DRG. (DRG payments also vary by geographic location and other hospital characteristics.) The system is credited with slowing the growth of Part A expenditures by 20% between 1983 and 1990. One third of this slowdown is attributed to declines in admissions, but there is little evidence that DRGs resulted in arbitrary denial of hospitalization or reductions in quality (Gold et al. 1993).

Since the late 1960s (when the Medicare program was fully implemented) until 1997 (the most recent year for which we have data), the growth in spending per Medicare beneficiary has been slower than in the private health insurance system, where most people under age 65 obtain coverage (Moon 1999a).[3] See chart 1. The Balanced Budget Act (BBA) of 1997 made a number of changes to further reduce the growth of Medicare expenditures. These included a slowdown in the growth in

CHART 1
Spending by Medicare and Private Health Insurance
for Consistently Covered Services, 1970–97

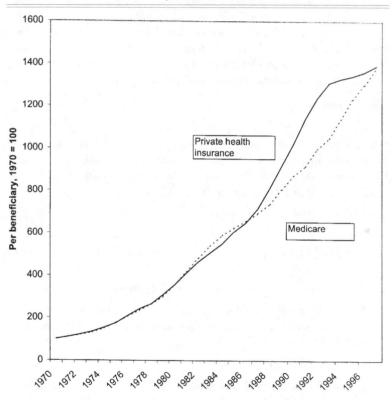

Source: Moon. 1999a.

payments to hospitals, establishing a date to implement a PPS system for skilled nursing facilities and home health care, and changing the way fees for managed care plans are determined.

In 1998, total nominal Medicare expenditures grew by 1.5%; real per capita expenditures declined. In 1999, total nominal expenditures *fell* by 1%, a historically unprecedented change (Love 2000). While the BBA may have too severely restrained payments to some hospitals and home health providers, even if modifications raised some providers' fees, the savings would still be very large.

Between 1999 and 2008, total Medicare spending is projected to grow more slowly than private health insurance expenditures, even though the number of people covered by Medicare will grow more rapidly than will enrollments in private insurance (S. Smith et al. 1999).

In addition to being a leader in cost containment, Medicare is also very efficiently run. Expenses for overhead and administration are less than 2% of benefits paid out. Private insurance companies are estimated to have overhead rates of 12% to 14% or more. Overhead in managed care organizations such as HMOs is often even higher.

Inadequate Benefits

The Medicare benefit package has changed little since 1965. As was typical of most health insurance policies in the mid-1960s, outpatient prescription medicines, dental care, eye exams and glasses, hearing aids, most preventive care, and long-term care are not covered. Some of the required cost-sharing amounts in 2000 include

- $776 deductible per hospital stay,

- 20% co-insurance for most outpatient services, including doctors' visits and outpatient surgery (laboratory tests and X-rays are covered at 100%),

- 50% co-insurance for outpatient mental health services,

- $97 per day copayment for days 21–100 in a skilled nursing facility (stays are covered only when they immediately follow a hospital stay), and

- $100 deductible for SMI services.

In 1997, Medicare paid 86.4% of the costs incurred by beneficiaries for covered services; beneficiaries' cost-sharing liability funded the other 13.6% (Health Care Financing Administration 1999:124). However, since many services are not covered, Medicare pays for about

53% of all the health care used by beneficiaries (National Bipartisan Commission on the Future of Medicare 1999, cited in B. Smith and Rosenbaum 1999).

About 15% of Medicare beneficiaries (called dual eligibles) have Medicaid assistance to help with cost-sharing obligations, the Part B premium, or coverage of services not included in the Medicare benefit package. About 14% of Medicare beneficiaries receive Supplemental Security Income (SSI)[4] or have very large medical expenses and are eligible for full Medicaid benefits, including payment of all cost sharing and premiums. Other beneficiaries with incomes below the federal poverty level (FPL) for the elderly ($8,592 for one person, $11,496 for two in 2000) and assets of less than $4,000 per individual or $6,000 per couple are eligible for Medicaid assistance in paying the SMI premium and Medicare cost-sharing amounts. (These dual-eligible beneficiaries are called qualified Medicare beneficiaries, or QMBs.) Other beneficiaries (called specified low-income Medicare beneficiaries, or SLMBs) with incomes up to 120% of the FPL and assets within the QMB limits are eligible for assistance with their Part B premium but not cost-sharing requirements. In 1998, just 78% of the estimated 5.7 million beneficiaries eligible for the QMB program and 16% of the 1.6 million eligible for SLMB were enrolled (Moon, Brennan, and Segal 1998).

Beneficiaries with incomes between 120% and 175% of the FPL are eligible for assistance in paying all (incomes up to 135% of the FPL) or part (135% to 175% of the FPL) of their SMI premium under a new block grant established under the BBA (which also raised the Part B premium). However, unlike the QMB or SLMB programs, this assistance is not an entitlement but depends on federal appropriations. When this program was established in 1997, the funding provided was sufficient to pay the premiums of just one fourth of beneficiaries with incomes between 120% and 135% of FPL (Moon, Gage, and Evans 1997).

In 1999, out-of-pocket spending on health care by noninstitutionalized, elderly beneficiaries averaged 19% of income, 33% of income for those with incomes below poverty, and 24% to 25% of income for those between 100% and 200% of poverty (Gross and Brangan 1999). In 1995, fully 25% of beneficiaries spent 24% or more of their income for health care, and 10% spent 40% or more (Medicare Payment Advisory Commission 1999:11).

While dual eligibles receive assistance through the Medicaid program, most higher-income beneficiaries also augment their Medicare coverage with supplemental insurance. Slightly more than one third of beneficiaries have additional coverage through a retiree health plan from a former employer, a nearly equal share purchase a private "Medigap" policy, and 8% are enrolled in HMOs that provide extra benefits. But 9% of beneficiaries, generally those too poor to afford a Medigap plan but with too high an income to qualify for Medicaid, have no supplemental coverage. They pay their additional costs out of pocket or forgo care.

Even with supplemental insurance, beneficiaries may not have the coverage they need. For example, only about one third of beneficiaries with Medigap policies have drug coverage. In total, 35% of all Medicare beneficiaries have no insurance to cover prescription medicines. Among Medicare beneficiaries in 1995, slightly more than half of all expenditures for prescription drugs were made out of pocket (Poisal et al. 1999:18). See table 1.

TABLE 1
Supplemental Insurance and Prescription Drug Coverage, 1995

| | Of those with this insurance, | |
	Share of all beneficiaries	Share without drug coverage
All beneficiaries[a]	100%	35%
Source of supplemental coverage		
From a former employer	37	14
Medigap (individually purchased)	32	64
Medicaid (dual eligibles)	15	10
HMO	8	5
No supplemental coverage	9	100

[a]Not in a nursing home.
Source: Davis et al. (1999).

The share of firms offering health benefits to retirees is fairly small and declining. In 2000, just 9% of firms with 3 to 199 employees offered retiree benefits, while 52% of firms with 5,000 or more workers provide these benefits (Kaiser Family Foundation and Health Research and Educational Trust 2000). See table 2. Between 1988 and 2000, the share of all firms with 200 or more employees that provided retiree health insurance declined from 66% to 37%.

The Financial Future

Each year, the trustees of the Medicare program[5] are required by law to report to Congress on the financial and actuarial status of the HI trust fund over the next 75 years.[6]

In their most recent report issued in 2000, the trustees' intermediate projections show that spending for HI is projected to rise from 1.39% of GDP in 2000 to 2.92% in 2075. At the same time, SMI expenditures will rise from 0.94% of GDP in 2000 to 2.36% in 2075 (see table 3).

TABLE 2
Share of Firms Offering Retiree Health Insurance, 2000[a]

Firm size (number of employees)	
3–199	9%
200–999	35
1,000–4,999	44
5,000 or more	52[b]

[a]Either to early retirees below age 65 or to Medicare eligibles.
[b]Statistically different from all firms.
Source: Kaiser Family Foundation and Health Research and Educational Trust (2000: 142, 143).

TABLE 3
Medicare Disbursements as a Share of GDP, Selected Years, 2000–2075

	HI	SMI	Total
2000	1.39%	0.94%	2.33%
2015	1.63	1.47	3.09
2035	2.42	2.22	4.64
2075	2.92	2.36	5.28

Source: Board of Trustees of the Federal Hospital Insurance Trust Fund (2000:82).

The trustees project that income received by the HI trust fund will exceed outgo through 2014. From 2015 through 2022, the shortfall in income will be filled by redeeming trust fund assets. By 2023, the trust fund will be exhausted, and tax revenue will cover just 80% of costs. (In last year's report, the exhaustion year was 2015, eight years earlier.) See chart 2. In subsequent years, assuming no change in the tax rate, payroll taxes will cover a declining share of Medicare Part A costs: 66% in 2030 and 51% in 2075 (Board of Trustees of the Federal Old-Age and Survivors Insurance and Disability Insurance [OASID] Trust Funds 2000: table III.B4). SMI, funded primarily through general federal revenues, does not face the issue of trust fund insolvency. To provide 75 years of actuarial balance, the payroll tax for HI would need to rise by 1.21 percentage points in 2000; to cover its rising costs, SMI will need a similar amount of additional money.

Despite the gloom and doom with which this projection is received on Capitol Hill and in the media, the current estimate of 23 years of

CHART 2
Portion of Part A Costs Able to Be Paid
under Existing Program

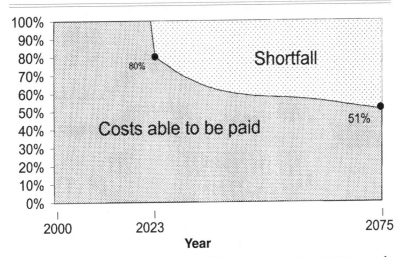

trust fund solvency is a historic record *for longevity*. Since 1970, in only two years have the trustees projected more than 15 years of solvency: "about 20" years in 1975 and 17 years in 1988 (cited in Aaron and Reischauer 1995:18).

The trustees' projections rely on three types of estimates about the future: economic, demographic, and health care costs. There are serious problems with each of these.

Economic Projections

The Medicare trustees rely on economic projections made by actuaries in the Social Security Administration that are quite pessimistic. For example, the intermediate projections show GDP rising at an average annual rate of 2.3% between 1999 and 2009, substantially below the 3.0% of the 1989–1999 business cycle,[7] then declining to 1.5% to 2.1% for the rest of the 75-year period. Labor productivity is expected to average 1.5% over the next 75 years. Over the 20th century, productivity growth averaged 2% (Council of Economic Advisors 2000:59). Even with this pessimistic forecast, GDP will be 75% larger in 2035 than in 2000 and more than three times greater in 2070, after adjusting for inflation. Average real wages[8] will be about 40% higher in 2035 and more than double today's level in 2075. See table 4.

TABLE 4

Projected Economic Variables (Intermediate Projections)

	GDP (billions, 2000 $)	Share of 2000 GDP	Wages (2000 $)	Share of 2000 wages
2000	9,781	100%	31,685	100%
2015	12,810	131	36,610	116
2035	17,161	175	44,387	140
2075	29,965	306	65,256	206

Source: Board of Trustees of the Federal OASID Trust Funds (2000:177).

Cost and Demographic Projections

When HCFA calculates for the trustees the per capita health costs of future beneficiaries, the costs are age adjusted. That is, an upward shift in the age distribution of beneficiaries would drive up expenditures, even if the total number of beneficiaries were unchanged. But this method is flawed. This rise in costs with age is primarily driven by the costs of care given to the dying. Some 27% to 30% of Medicare expenditures are devoted to caring for beneficiaries in their last year of life (Emanuel 1996; Lubitz and Riley 1993). But with rising life expectancies, fewer seniors die in each age group. So an average 80-year-old will cost less in the future than today, all else equal, since her chance of dying will be lower. Research has also shown that, once someone reaches age 65, average health expenditure at any given age is not related to chronological age but to years remaining before death (see White 1999). Moreover, Medicare payments associated with an additional year of life and average annual payments over a Medicare enrollee's lifetime both decrease as the age at death increases (Lubitz, Beebe, and Baker 1995). By not including these cost adjustments, health cost projections are overstated.

On the other hand, there are sound arguments for projecting larger declines in mortality than are currently considered in the trustees' models (Technical Panel of Assumptions and Methods 1999; Lee and Skinner 1999). In other words, life expectancy may rise more rapidly than projected, increasing the number of Medicare beneficiaries and costs.

There are two demographic trends occurring. The first is the demographic bulge of baby boomers. The second is an ongoing increase in longevity. This means that average seniors, pre–baby boomers as well as boomers, will be spending more years in the Medicare program. The increase in longevity translates into rising enrollments and a long-term rise in Medicare expenditures, although smaller than is generally thought for the reasons given earlier. Overlying this gradual long-term trend is a more rapid but also shorter-term increase in costs due to the number of baby boomers. The boomers' effect on Medicare expenditures is more dramatic than their effect on national health expenditures. The costs for employer-sponsored health insurance will actually *fall* as the average age of the workforce *declines*. For the nation as a whole, the increase in Medicare costs associated with the baby boomers will be partially offset by the decline in non-Medicare health expenditures.

75-Year Projections

Despite anyone's best efforts, it is essentially impossible to make accurate 75-year projections, the equivalent of assessing the world in 2000 from the perspective of 1925. Just in the past five years, as a result of changes instituted under the Balanced Budget Act of 1997 and, to a much lesser degree, improvements in the economy, the Medicare trustees' projections of the 75-year HI funding shortfall *declined by 73%*. The shortfall is commonly assessed with regard to the increase in the payroll tax (remaining in place for 75 years) needed to eliminate it. In 1996, this increase was estimated to be 4.52 percentage points. By 2000, it had fallen to 1.21 percentage points. In other words, in 2000, the current tax of 2.9% (divided between employers and employees) would need to rise to 4.11% to eliminate the 75-year shortfall. See table 5. Put another way, in 1996, the trustees estimated the HI program would cost $18,921 billion in 2070 (current dollars), or 5.04% of GDP (Board of Trustees of the Federal OASID Trust Fund 1999:182, 187). In 2000, HI expenditures in 2070 were projected to be $7,656 billion, or 2.84% of GDP (Board of Trustees of the Federal OASID Trust Fund 2000:183, 189). These large shifts over just a few years illustrate the impossibility of making accurate projections 75 years into the future.

TABLE 5
Trustees' Assessment of the Medicare Part A Trust Fund

Year of report	Year begin using trust fund	Year of trust fund depletion	Payroll tax increase needed for 75-year solvency (percentage points)
1996	1996	2001	4.52
1997	1996	2001	4.32
1998	2003	2008	2.10
1999	2007	2015	1.46
2000	2015	2023	1.21

Source: Board of Trustees of the Federal Hospital Insurance Trust Fund (various years).

Not only are 75-year projections impossible to make with any accuracy, they are inherently biased against the incremental but successful cost-containment efforts implemented in the past. HCFA's cost-containment methods involve fine-tuning payments and fees to providers. However, to specify the fine adjustments that must be made in fees and payments 75 years into the future requires a level of detail and precision that is impossible to attain. It is this care and specificity that have made these methods successful in containing costs with a minimal amount of disruption of the Medicare system.

These multiple small changes are very difficult to incorporate into 75-year projections, and their effects are very difficult to quantify. On the other hand, radical (and disruptive) changes in the Medicare program, such as raising the eligibility age or instituting vouchers for beneficiaries to use to purchase a private insurance plan, can more readily show a large effect on the 75-year cost trajectory. In a policy debate where the goal (often the only goal) is reducing the 75-year shortfall, there is an inherent bias against fine-tuning in favor of radical approaches (see White 1999).

Medicare and HMOs

In 1997, 14.2% of Medicare beneficiaries were enrolled in HMOs (HCFA 1999:94), up from just 6.6% in 1994 (Committee on Ways and Means 1998:174). Since HMOs and other managed care organizations appear to have slowed the growth of health costs in the private health insurance sector, it is often assumed that this has occurred in Medicare as well. Just the opposite is true. The average HMO enrollee costs Medicare more than he would have if he had remained in the traditional fee-for-service program where Medicare pays only for costs incurred when beneficiaries use health care services. The reason is that healthier-than-average Medicare beneficiaries enroll in HMOs, and when they get sick, they tend to return to traditional Medicare.

Like all people, Medicare beneficiaries vary greatly in their need for health care. In any year, most are healthy and use very few services, while a small share of people are very ill, use many services, and incur huge health care bills. For example, in 1997, about 20% of enrollees used no Medicare services. Of beneficiaries with medical expenses covered by Medicare, 36.0% used less than $500 in Medicare services, and another 26.4% used between $500 and $1,999 (HCFA 1999:30). Just 6.3% incurred costs of $25,000 or more, but these few people were responsible for half of all Medicare expenditures over the year. This concentration of health expenses occurs not just among Medicare beneficiaries but also among populations in other countries and people of all ages (Berk and Monheit 1992; Aaron 1991).

Selection bias in HMO enrollments has been shown repeatedly. The savings to HMOs are likely very large. One study by the Congressionally established Physician Payment Review Commission examined risk-bearing HMO enrollees and disenrollees between 1989 and 1994. Researchers first examined health expenditures for new HMO enrollees in the six months prior to their HMO enrollment while they were still in the traditional Medicare plan. Use of health care services by these beneficiaries was 37% lower than by the average beneficiary in the traditional plan. Moreover, beneficiaries who disenrolled from HMOs and returned to the traditional Medicare plan had expenditures in the following six months that were 60% higher than the average for the traditional plan (Physician Payment Review Commission 1996:260–61). Other studies report similar findings. Even before this research was done, HCFA was aware of the potential for selection bias in HMO enrollments and had instituted a discounted rate for HMO reimbursement, paying just 95% of the average per capita cost of a fee-for-service beneficiary in the same geographic area.[9] Research demonstrated that the fees were not sufficiently discounted, and further changes were then instituted with the Balanced Budget Act of 1997. As excess fees were reduced, HMOs found they could no longer afford to provide enrollees with extra benefits such as prescription drugs and reduced cost sharing that Medicare does not cover and for which HMOs are not reimbursed. Some HMOs have found that their Medicare business is no longer financially viable, and they have left the market. (Congress could respond most effectively by expanding the benefits for all covered by the Medicare program rather than by boosting reimbursements to HMOs. The former strategy would still raise fees to HMOs but would not force seniors to join HMOs for the additional benefits that excess reimbursements would finance.)

In addition to concerns about appropriate fee adjustments, there is also some doubt whether enrollees' health outcomes in HMOs are as good as in traditional fee-for-service Medicare. In a four-year study of people age 65 and above with chronic disease (high blood pressure, diabetes not requiring insulin, recent heart attack, or congestive heart failure), researchers found that seniors enrolled in HMOs had worse outcomes than those in fee-for-service Medicare. Over the four-year period, 54% of the study population in HMOs had a deterioration in health compared with 28% in fee-for-service, while 37% in the HMOs but 63% in fee-for-service maintained the same quality of health (p = .001; Ware et al. 1996).

Premium Support (Vouchers)

Projections of a funding shortfall beginning in 2023, expectations of growing costs due to the aging of the baby boomers, rising longevity, and, in some quarters, long-standing opposition to a federal health insurance program have led some people to call for fundamental restructuring of the Medicare program. The most popular option among federal policy makers and many health economists is to replace the Medicare entitlement to insurance with an annual "premium support" or voucher that beneficiaries would use to purchase traditional Medicare or a private fee-for-service or managed care plan. Any difference between the amount of the voucher and the cost of a beneficiary's chosen plan would be paid out of pocket. Because Congress would determine the amount of the voucher, federal Medicare outlays could be controlled. Proponents envision that savvy seniors, made newly conscious of the cost of their health care, would carefully search out the most cost-efficient plan that met their health care preferences. Health plans, to attract seniors' business, would be forced to hold their prices down. Those that provided the best value would thrive, while less efficient plans would have few enrollees and might eventually go out of business. There are a number of serious problems with this proposal.

Protecting Seniors' Pocketbooks

An immediate concern is whether the vouchers would provide beneficiaries with sufficient funds to purchase either traditional Medicare coverage or a good private health plan. Congress could set the value of the voucher at any level. This would put seniors at risk since they would need to pay any difference between the cost of the health coverage they selected and the value of the voucher. If the cost of health care rose faster than the amount provided in the voucher, Medicare beneficiaries would need to make up the growing difference with their own money or switch into a lower-cost plan if one were available. The federal budget would be protected, but seniors' budgets would be at risk.

Shopping Around to Contain Costs

For competition to lower costs, seniors would need to leave high-cost plans and enroll in lower-cost ones. In other words, a senior would need to compare plans and (during an annual enrollment period) switch to a less expensive one that appeared to offer care of equal quality. Health care quality is very difficult and expensive to measure. Moreover, seniors do not readily change plans to save money since switching plans often also means switching doctors (Buchmueller, forthcoming). In addition, many seniors are physically unable to shop around and determine which plan might give the best value for their dollar. Fully one third of Medicare beneficiaries have physical or mental health problems so severe as to limit their ability to properly evaluate plans (Moon 1999b). Even prime-age adults without obvious physical or mental limitations have difficulty evaluating insurance policies.

These imperfections in the operation of the market for health insurance would reduce the ability of competition to set the optimum price. This would be exacerbated by the oligopoly in health care services that is developing. Health care is notorious for market imperfections. This is the reason many countries and the U.S. Medicare and Medicaid programs set prices through an administrative process. Moving toward greater reliance on markets to control prices seems at odds with the evidence from the United States and abroad about the relative effectiveness of cost containment in market-based and administered systems.

Getting Prices Right

Establishing a level playing field so that competition can reward the best plans will be very difficult. It will depend on the currently impossible task of determining the proper amount of each person's voucher. Not everyone will be able to buy health insurance for the same price. Health expenditures are concentrated. The average per-beneficiary Medicare expenditure in 1997 was over $4,500, but more than half of all beneficiaries used less than $500 in services. Six percent used more than $25,000. The easiest way for health plans to hold down costs and attract more business is to "cherry-pick," to use a variety of subtle and not-so-subtle techniques to avoid enrolling sick people who are much more expensive to treat than generally healthy people.

To be sure that everyone will be able to find insurance, people with chronic illnesses will need to have larger vouchers than healthy ones. To avoid overpaying the plans (as has been occurring with HMOs), the value of each person's voucher would need to be carefully calculated to just offset the health costs she would likely incur over the next 12 months. This is difficult to get right. If the amount is too low, then sick people may find that health plans do not want to enroll them. If the amounts are too high, then the plans will make excess profits and Medicare will not be saving money but wasting it. If the amount of the vouchers is incorrect, then the price signals will also be incorrect. Plans that are overpaid will be able to charge lower prices and attract more business, while plans that are mistakenly underpaid will need to raise fees, losing business. A plan's efficiency in delivering care and keeping people healthy will be a less important factor in determining success.

Some progress has been made in the theoretical and practical understanding of risk adjustment, in the determination of the value of a voucher that would correspond with the Medicare beneficiary's need for health care services. However, a recent assessment by three Harvard researchers concluded that risk adjustment was "not likely to be adequate for many years" (Newhouse, Buntin, and Chapman 1999). An alternative proposal to base the voucher amount on a mix of a flat, per-person fee (capitated rate) and a risk-adjustment factor does not eliminate health plans' incentives to cherry-pick or the numerous other problems associated with vouchers.

Sorting into Plans

In a voucher system, any Medicare beneficiary may enroll in any plan. The beneficiary would most likely select a plan based on personal income and the price of the plan. Low-income individuals would be likely to enroll in lower-cost plans, modest-income beneficiaries would enroll in the moderately expensive plans, and the affluent would choose high-cost plans. This informal sorting into plans based on income would be a departure from today's Medicare program in which all beneficiaries (except those in HMOs) see the same doctors and use the same hospitals.

This sorting could result in reduced health care quality for people in the lower- and mid-cost plans. There is a fairly extensive literature documenting the variances in care associated with race and class, holding constant insurance type (see Kahn et al. 1994; Ayanian et al. 1993; Whittle et al. 1993). Consider the current public education system in the United States, where schools in poor neighborhoods tend to be of lower quality than schools in middle-income neighborhoods, which tend to be of lower quality than schools in high-income ones. In a school or a health plan where people from all walks of life are served, quality is often higher than in an institution that serves primarily people of low or moderate income. Preserving a single Medicare plan is important for maintaining high quality for all beneficiaries.

Raising the Age of Eligibility

Another proposal for saving money is to raise from 65 to 67 the age at which people become eligible for Medicare. This would not save much money and would increase the number of uninsured people. In 1992, 13.3% of Medicare beneficiaries were age 65 or 66. Even if the eligibility age were increased, the disabled, people with kidney failure, and those on Medicaid would still be covered with public insurance. Just 11.3% of beneficiaries would actually lose coverage, and since younger beneficiaries tend to be the healthiest, total Medicare expenditures would decline by only 6.2% (Waidmann 1998). Spending under Part A would decline by 5.8%. Among seniors age 65 and 66 in 1992, 12% had incomes below $25,000 and had not purchased supplemental insurance. In 1997, about half a million people would have likely been underinsured or uninsured if the age of eligibility were 67. If we add to this group 65- and 66-year-olds whose only supplemental coverage is a privately purchased Medigap policy (which would become much more expensive, possibly unaffordable, if Medicare were not the primary insurer), the total uninsured and underinsured would have been an estimated 1.75 million people in 1997.

Delaying eligibility is inconsistent with the recent trend toward earlier retirement. Many seniors would be forced to continue working, particularly given recent declines in retiree health insurance coverage. Current employment patterns among 61- to 64-year-olds can shed light on what might occur among 65- to 66-year-olds if the age of Medicare eligibility were raised. In 1997 among adults ages 61 to 64, just 31.4% worked full-time, 11.4% were employed part-time, and 57.2% were not working. Among nonworkers in this age group, just 49.7% had health insurance coverage in 1997, down from 57.9% in 1989. If current trends continue, by 2005, the number of uninsured people ages 61 to 64 will rise by an estimated 42% (Glied and Stabile 1999). If the decline in employer-sponsored retiree coverage also continues in the future and affects 65- and 66-year-olds, an increase in the age of eligibility would result in millions of uninsured seniors.

Not everyone can easily work until age 67. Even in a high-tech world, many occupations continue to be physically demanding, such as mechanic, machine operator, truck driver, childcare or health care worker, waiter and waitress, retail salesperson, construction worker, miner, farmer, fisher, and forester. A recent study found that older blue-collar workers are at greater risk for health problems (e.g., muscu-loskeletal, respiratory, and emotional disorders and diabetes) than are older white-collar workers (U.S. General Accounting Office 1998). People in strenuous jobs that often also pay relatively low wages and lack retiree health insurance would be much more likely to become uninsured.

A Better Solution

While a system of vouchers or premium support is not the answer for Medicare, some changes are necessary both to enhance the benefits and to strengthen the finances in the future.

Better Benefits

As a start on improving the benefit package, Medicare must cover prescription drugs with just a minimal copayment requirement. This would bring Medicare more in line with standard employer-sponsored plans. In addition, Medicare must obtain the price reductions from pharmaceutical companies that other insurers already receive. In the future, additional expansions of coverage will be needed to reduce out-of-pocket spending and to cover dental services, glasses and hearing aids, preventive care, and nursing homes.

These additional benefits could be financed in a variety of ways. Part of the federal budget surplus should be devoted to Medicare. The pay-roll tax could also be increased in the future when additional money is needed. The Medicare trustees' current 75-year projections incorporate no increase in the payroll tax over this entire period. While tax increases are never popular, they may be warranted. Since people are living longer and will spend more years with Medicare coverage, it is reason-able that they pay more for it.

If the payroll tax were increased in 2000 to cover the projected increase in Part A costs over the next 75 years, it would need to rise by 1.21 percentage points, from the current level of 2.9% to 4.11%. For a worker making $30,000, this increase would total $182; the worker's employer would pay a similar amount. Even though Part B is not funded with a payroll tax, the necessary increase in funding for the 75-year period, expressed as a share of GDP, is similar to that needed for Part A.

Another way to view the funding options is to look at 25-year increments (see table 6). To pay all the costs of Part A incurred during the first period, 2000–2024, payroll tax rates would need to rise by 0.12 percentage points, from 2.9% to 3.02% (Board of Trustees of the Federal Hospital Insurance Trust Funds 2000: table II.E3). Average real wages are projected to rise by 29.64% over this period (Board of Trustees of the Federal OASID Trust Fund 2000: table II.D1). At the end of the period, the net increase in real wages would be 29.52%. (Note that these projections of wage gains have been criticized for being too pessimistic.)

TABLE 6
Financing Option for Medicare Part A

25-year period	Needed payroll tax increase (percentage points)	Increase in average real wages by end of period (%)	Increase in wages after deducting payroll tax increase (%)
2000–2024	0.12	29.64	29.52
2025–2049	1.71	28.88	27.17
2050–2075	0.90	29.53	28.63
Total change by end of period			
2000–2049	1.83	67.08	65.25
2000–2075	2.73	116.42	113.69

Source: Board of Trustees of the Federal OASID Trust Fund (2000: table II.D1) and Board of Trustees of the Federal Hospital Insurance Trust Funds (2000: table II.E3).

Over the next 25 years, 2025–2049, payroll tax rates would need to go up another 1.71 percentage points to a total of 5.82%. During this period, real wages are projected to rise another 28.88%. So in 2049, despite the increases in the payroll tax, real wages would be 27.17% higher than in 2025 and 65.25% larger than in 2000. In the third period, 2050–2075, the payroll tax would need to rise another 0.9 percentage points, while real wages rise 29.53%. The net gain in wages would be 28.63% over the 25-year period. Wage gains since the year 2000, despite the tax increases, would be 113.69%.

In each period, the wage increases would accumulate over the period. The payroll tax increases would occur in the first year, reducing after-tax wages. Nonetheless, wages are rising far faster than taxes, and even in the early years of each period, real wages would be far above levels in 2000.

Enhanced Cost Containment

Medicare must continue to refine the adjustments made in fees paid to doctors, hospitals, and other providers. Relatively small changes in these fees can have a large effect on Medicare expenditures. By adjusting fees, closing loopholes that permit excessive billing, and discouraging providers from providing excess services (and billing for them), significant savings can be achieved. Medicare can also do more to regulate the purchase of new expensive equipment and construction of excess facilities. An ongoing series of adjustments can keep Medicare strong for many years. Eventually, however, more will need to be done to contain costs both in Medicare and in the health care system as a whole. In addition, many of the fee adjustments enacted in the BBA are due to expire in 2002. Most of these should be extended indefinitely.

The Long-Term Future of Health Care in the United States

Even though Medicare is not in crisis and will be affordable for many years to come, high health care expenditures in the United States have been a problem for many years and will continue to be. While Medicare has played a leading role in showing the way costs can be contained, even this large program (some 20% of the nation's health care dollars flow through Medicare) cannot by itself solve the problem of high health care costs. In the long run, cost containment in Medicare requires cost containment in the whole health care system.

One attractive option that could provide insurance to the uninsured while also maintaining high-quality care for those who are insured is to expand Medicare to the entire population. The Medicare benefit package of covered services would first need to be fully modernized to include prescription drugs, preventive care, improved mental health and substance abuse services, and better cost sharing. In addition to providing universal coverage and high-quality care, there are other advantages of a universal Medicare program. Having a single insurer, Medicare, pay the bills for all medically necessary health care services (a "single payer") would greatly streamline the paperwork done by physicians, hospitals, and other providers. Multiple investigators, from the U.S. General Accounting Office (1991) to Harvard-based researchers (Woolhandler and Himmelstein 1991), have estimated that these savings would be sufficient to pay all the costs of providing insurance to the 44 million people currently uninsured. In addition to being more efficient, such a system would allow enhanced cost containment that would slow the growth in health care spending. An enhanced Medicare program covering all Americans (Medicare-for-All) is the best way to provide universal, high-quality, affordable health care.

Notes

[1] Since 1986, the trust fund has had one other new source of revenue. In 1993, the share of Social Security benefits included in the definition of adjusted gross income rose from 50% to 85%. The additional income tax revenue resulting from this change is credited to the Part A trust fund.

[2] The trust fund buys these special nonmarketable securities because the Treasury has agreed to promptly exchange them for cash whenever Medicare needs to do this; the trust fund need not wait until the bonds reach maturity to redeem them.

[3] The comparison is for consistently covered services only, that is, services that are covered under both Medicare and private insurance policies and used by both population groups. Therefore, the data omit prescription drug coverage that Medicare does not provide and home health and skilled nursing care, which are seldom used by private insurance beneficiaries.

[4] To qualify for SSI, a program for the elderly and disabled, an individual must have income of no more than $500 per month and assets of $2,000 or less; a couple must have income of $751 per month or less and a maximum of $3,000 in assets.

[5] By law, the six trustees include the Secretary of the Treasury, Secretary of Labor, Secretary of Health and Human Services, and the Commissioner of Social Security. In 1999, the other two members, appointed by the president and confirmed by the Senate, were Marilyn Moon, an economist at the Urban Institute, and actuary Stephen G. Kellison. These trustees oversee both the Social Security and Medicare programs.

[6] They also report on Part B, but since it is funded by transfers from the general fund of the U.S. Treasury and beneficiaries' premiums, income is projected to equal expenditures for all future years.

[7] The growth over the 1990s was already far lower than the 4.1% average annual rate of the 1980s and the 5.0% of the early 1970s, and even below the 3.6% of the bad old days of stagflation in the late 1970s.

[8] In the 96% of all jobs covered by Social Security (Social Security Administration 1999:31).

[9] These fees were also adjusted by a number of other factors including age, sex, institutional status, presence of disability, and Medicaid eligibility.

References

Aaron, Henry. 1991. *Serious and Unstable Condition: Financing America's Health Care*. Washington, DC: Brookings Institution.
Aaron, Henry, and Robert Reischauer. 1995. "The Medicare Reform Debate: What Is the Next Step?" *Health Affairs*, Vol. 14, no. 4, pp. 8–30.

Andersen, R., J. Lion, and O. Anderson. 1976. *Two Decades of Health Services: Social Survey Trends in Use and Expenditures*. Cambridge, MA: Ballinger.

Ayanian, J. Z., I. S. Udvarhelyi, C. A. Gatsonis, C. L. Pashos, and A. M. Epstein. 1993. "Racial Differences in the Use of Revascularization Procedures after Coronary Angiography." *Journal of the American Medical Association*, Vol. 269, pp. 2642–46.

Berk, Marc, and Alan Monheit. 1992. "The Concentration of Health Expenditures: An Update." *Health Affairs*, Vol. 11, no. 4, pp. 145–49.

Board of Trustees of the Federal Hospital Insurance Trust Fund. Various years. *Annual Report*. Washington, DC: Board of Trustees of the Federal Hospital Insurance Trust Fund.

Board of Trustees of the Federal Old-Age and Survivors Insurance and Disability Insurance Trust Funds. 1999. *Annual Report*. Washington, DC: Board of Trustees of the Federal Old-Age and Survivors Insurance and Disability Insurance Trust Funds.

———. 2000. *Annual Report*. Washington, DC: Board of Trustees of the Federal Old-Age and Survivors Insurance and Disability Insurance Trust Funds.

Buchmueller, Thomas. Forthcoming. "Price Sensitivity of Medicare Beneficiaries in a Premium Support Setting." In Marilyn Moon, ed., *Competition with Constraints: Challenges Facing Medicare Reform*. Washington, DC: Urban Institute.

Committee on Ways and Means, U.S. House of Representatives. 1998. *1998 Green Book*. Washington, DC: U.S. Government Printing Office.

Council of Economic Advisors. 2000. *Economic Report of the President*. Washington, DC: U.S. Government Printing Office.

Davis, Margaret, John Poisal, George Chulis, Carlos Zarabozo, and Barbara Cooper. 1999. "Prescription Drug Coverage, Utilization, and Spending among Medicare Beneficiaries." *Health Affairs*, Vol. 18, no. 1, pp. 231–43.

Emanuel, Ezekiel. 1996. "Cost Savings at the End of Life: What Do the Data Show?" *Journal of the American Medical Association*, Vol. 275, no. 24, pp. 1907–14.

Glied, Sherry, and Mark Stabile. 1999. "Covering Older Americans: Forecast for the Next Decade." *Health Affairs*, Vol. 18, no. 1, pp. 208–13.

Gold, Marsha, Karyen Chu, Suzanne Felt, Mary Harrington, and Timothy Lake. 1993. "Effects of Selected Cost-Containment Efforts: 1971–1993." *Health Care Financing Review*, Vol. 14, no. 3, pp. 183–225.

Gornick, Marian, Joan Warren, Paul Eggers, James Lubitz, Nancy De Lew, Margaret Davis, and Barbara Cooper. 1996. "Thirty Years of Medicare: Impact on the Covered Population." *Health Care Financing Review*, Vol. 18, no. 2, pp. 179–237.

Gross, David, and Normandy Brangan. 1999. *Out-of-Pocket Spending on Health Care by Medicare Beneficiaries Age 65 and Older: 1999 Projections*. Washington, DC: American Association of Retired Persons.

Health Care Financing Administration. 1999. *Medicare and Medicaid Statistical Supplement to the Health Care Financing Review*. Washington, DC: Health Care Financing Administration.

Kahn, K. L., M. L. Pearson, E. R. Harrison, K. A. Desmond, W. H. Rogers, L. V. Rubenstein, R. H. Brook, and E. B. Keeler. 1994. "Health Care for Black and Poor Hospitalized Medicare Patients." *Journal of the American Medical Association*, Vol. 271, pp. 1169–74.

Kaiser Family Foundation and Health Research and Educational Trust. 2000. *Employer Health Benefits*. Menlo Park, CA: Kaiser Family Foundation.

Lee, Ronald, and Jonathan Skinner. 1999. "Will Aging Baby Boomers Bust the Federal Budget?" *Journal of Economic Perspectives*, Vol. 13, no. 1, pp. 117–40.

Love, Alice Ann. 2000. "Health Care Bill up 5.6% on Higher Drug Costs." *Washington Post*, January 10, p. A2.

Lubitz, James, James Beebe, and Colin Baker. 1995. "Longevity and Medicare Expenditures." *New England Journal of Medicine*, Vol. 332, pp. 999–1003.

Lubitz, James, and Gerald Riley. 1993. "Trends in Medicare Payments in the Last Year of Life." *New England Journal of Medicine*, Vol. 328, pp. 1092–96.

Medicare Payment Advisory Commission. 1999. *Report to Congress: Selected Medicare Issues* (June). Washington, DC: MedPAC.

Moon, Marilyn. 1999a. *Beneath the Averages: An Analysis of Medicare and Private Expenditures*. Menlo Park, CA: Kaiser Family Foundation.

———. 1999b. "Will the Care Be There? Vulnerable Beneficiaries and Medicare Reform." *Health Affairs*, Vol. 18, no. 1, pp. 107–17.

Moon, Marilyn, N. Brennan, and M. Segal. 1998. "Options for Aiding Low-Income Medicare Beneficiaries." *Inquiry*, Vol. 35 (Fall), pp. 346–56.

Moon, Marilyn, B. Gage, and A. Evans. 1997. *An Examination of the Key Medicare Provisions in the Balanced Budget Act of 1997*. Washington, DC: Urban Institute.

National Bipartisan Commission on the Future of Medicare. 1999. *Draft Working Document*. January 22. Washington, DC: U.S. Government Printing Office.

Newhouse, Joseph, Melinda Beeuwkes Buntin, and John Chapman. 1999. *Risk Adjustment and Medicare*. New York: Commonwealth Fund.

Physician Payment Review Commission. 1996. *Annual Report to Congress, 1996*. Washington, DC: Physician Payment Review Commission.

Poisal, John A., Lauren Murray, George Chulis, and Barbara Cooper. 1999. "Prescription Drug Coverage and Spending for Medicare Beneficiaries." *Health Care Financing Review*, Vol. 20, no. 3, pp. 15–27.

Smith, Barbara M., and Sara Rosenbaum. 1999. "Potential Effects of the Premium Support Proposal on the Security of Medicare." *Journal of the American Medical Association*, Vol. 282, no. 18, pp. 1760–63.

Smith, Sheila, Stephen Heffler, Mark Freeland, and the National Health Expenditures Projection Team. 1999. "The Next Decade of Health Spending: A New Outlook." *Health Affairs*, Vol. 18, no. 4, pp. 86–95.

Social Security Administration. 1999. *Annual Statistical Supplement to the Social Security Bulletin*. Washington, DC: U.S. Government Printing Office.

Technical Panel of Assumptions and Methods. 1999. *Report to the Social Security Advisory Board*. Washington, DC: Social Security Administration.

U.S. General Accounting Office. 1991. *Canadian Health Insurance: Lessons for the United States*. GAO/HRD-91-90. Washington, DC: U.S. General Accounting Office.

————. 1998. *Social Security Reform: Raising Retirement Ages Improves Solvency but May Cause Hardship for Some.* GAO/T-HEHS-98-207. Washington, DC: U.S. General Accounting Office.

Waidmann, Timothy. 1998. "Potential Effects of Raising Medicare's Eligibility Age." *Health Affairs*, Vol. 17, no. 2, pp. 156–64.

Ware, John E., Jr., Martha Bayliss, William Rogers, Mark Kosinski, and Alvin Tarlov. 1996. "Differences in 4-Year Health Outcomes for Elderly and Poor, Chronically Ill Patients Treated in HMO and Fee-for-Service Systems." *Journal of the American Medical Association*, Vol. 276, no. 13, pp. 1039–47.

White, Joseph. 1999. "Uses and Abuses of Long-Term Medicare Cost Estimates." *Health Affairs*, Vol. 18, no. 1, pp. 63–79.

Whittle, J., J. Conigliaro, C. B. Good, and R. P. Lofgren. 1993. "Racial Differences in the Use of Invasive Cardiovascular Procedures in the Department of Veterans Affairs Medical System." *New England Journal of Medicine*, Vol. 329, pp. 621–27.

Woolhandler, Steffie, and David Himmelstein. 1991. "The Deteriorating Administrative Efficiency of the U.S. Health Care System." *New England Journal of Medicine*, Vol. 324, pp. 1253–58.

Chapter 10

Contingent Workers: Health and Pension Security

Helene J. Jorgensen
Center for Economic and Policy Research

Robert E. McGarrah, Jr.
AFL-CIO

Beginning in the 1980s, downsizing put an end to permanent employment for many workers. As companies restructured and downsized, contingent work arrangements—temporary, contracted, and leased workers and independent contracting—blossomed. The use of contingent workers by U.S. businesses has become a widespread business practice in today's economy. By some estimates (Belous 1997; Houseman and Polivka 1998; Hudson 1999; Jorgensen 1999), the contingent workforce now makes up almost one third of the total workforce.

The rise in contingent work has coincided with a more general shift toward greater flexibility and lower costs for employers. But it also means *less* economic security for employees. A recent report by the U.S. Department of Labor (U.S. DOL 1999b) finds that demand for just-in-time labor has increased as expenditures for labor are determined more by the bottom line than by norms and traditions. For companies concerned only with the bottom line, contingent workers can be an effective strategy to increase flexibility, cut labor costs, and increase profits.

Most types of contingent work arrangements have grown over the last decade. Bureau of Labor Statistics (BLS) surveys (Levine 1999; BLS 1995, 1997, 1999) find that contingent work not only has grown in total numbers but makes up an increasing share of the overall workforce. The use of temps, probably more than of other contingent work arrangements, has shown an explosive growth. Today, about 3.5 million temp workers are employed by temp agencies that supply labor services to other companies for a fee.[1] There has been a doubling of temp jobs since 1993. Who are these temp workers? The "Kelly girls" were once considered to be the prototypical temps: young women with high school degrees, working as receptionists or secretaries through a temp agency before marrying. While this stereotyping was never accurate, it is even less so today. Women and men of all races and ethnicities work as temps, and they have varied educational backgrounds. Some have not graduated from high school, while others have Ph.D. degrees. This development probably inspired the U.S. Department of Labor, in its recent report on the new workforce (1999a), to rename the "Kelly girls" the "Kelly chemists." Never mind that the data show that Kelly chemists is an even less accurate description of today's temps. Only a minority of the temp workforce in fact have college degrees—and the ones with college degrees often end up in jobs that do not utilize their skills and knowledge.

There are significant labor-cost savings for a company using subcontracted labor. Although the client company pays a substantial fee to the temporary agency for temporary labor services, leasing fees are often outweighed by cost savings in terms of payroll taxes, benefits, applicant search, screening and training, and payroll paperwork.[2] These savings arise because temp workers are not considered employees of the company, and thus they can be—and often are—paid substandard wages and benefits. Many temporary workers do not receive health insurance and pensions. Other benefits—such as paid vacation; paid sick leave; bonuses; and subsidized transportation, parking, and lunch—are practically unheard of. Employers further save on administrative costs, federal and state payroll taxes, and, of course, workers' compensation by not having these workers on their payrolls. Search and hiring costs are transferred to the temp agency, which conducts the interviewing and screening of potential job candidates.

A survey of U.S. firms by the American Management Association (1999) confirms that reductions in payroll, health insurance, and pension costs are important factors for companies using contingent workers: 51% of surveyed firms said that health insurance cost reduction was an important or somewhat important reason for using contingent workers, and 36% said that pension cost reduction mattered. This is further supported by a 1997 study conducted by the W. E. Upjohn Institute (Houseman 1997) that found labor-cost savings were an important reason for using temp agency workers. Twelve percent of surveyed businesses revealed that they use temporary agency workers to cut wage or benefit costs or both, and an additional 5% to reduce training costs. As benefit costs have risen sharply in the 1990s, particularly health insurance costs, it is increasingly desirable for employers to provide benefits to only part of their workforce and shed their responsibilities to other workers.

Another business advantage in using temps, according to Peter Cappelli (2000), professor of management at the Wharton School of Business, is the flexibility managers gain when they limit company operations to core functions, relying on just-in-time workers for everything else. Businesses can meet constantly fluctuating needs of production, customer demand, and Wall Street's insatiable appetite for greater earnings. Cappelli and others go so far as to say that companies that employ only regular, full-time staff are needlessly doomed to failure. Cappelli (2000:104) writes: "There is an alternative: a market-driven retention strategy that begins with the assumption that long-term, across-the-board employee loyalty is neither possible nor desirable. . . . It requires executives to take a hard-headed, analytical approach to what has long been viewed as a soft side of business: the management of people."

Tax and benefit laws have been designed to discourage employers from providing different benefit packages to different groups of their own workers. Securing workers through temporary agencies or similar arrangements provides an avenue for companies to avoid benefit laws and *not* provide health insurance and pension coverage to all who actually work for them. The W. E. Upjohn Institute's study found that companies that provide health and pension benefits to their permanent employees were, in fact, *more* likely to use temporary agency workers than other companies. According to the study's author (Houseman 1997:51): "One possible explanation . . . is that employers want to offer different benefit levels to different groups of workers, but cannot legally discriminate among regular full-time workers in benefits provisions. Thus, the firm may use alternative work arrangements to fill certain positions in order to avoid providing certain workers with costly benefits."

The flexibility to circumvent labor and employment laws is probably the greatest benefit for companies that adopt contingent work arrangements as an employment strategy. Since the client company is often not considered the legal employer of temp workers and independent contractors, it does not hold the same responsibilities for these workers as for its permanent workforce. When temporary workers become ill, sick days typically are unpaid and doctor visits often have to be paid out of their own pockets. Further, a temp worker who is injured should not expect to be automatically compensated by the company for which he or she works because it is not the employer under the law. This gives companies that use temps little incentive to provide a safe workplace or to spend money on safety training and safety equipment that would diminish injury risk. Even when courts have found corporate negligence on the part of the client company, the "exclusive remedy" limitation in state workers' compensation statutes shields the client company from liability: the injured temp may seek compensation only from his or her "employer." Finally, workers who try to improve their pay, benefits, and working conditions by seeking union representation can quickly end up without work because a client company legally can end the assignment of any temporary agency worker who expresses an interest in union membership. If the client company were the employer, on the other hand, this would be illegal.

Health Insurance

While some workers benefit from contingent work arrangements, the vast majority lose out. Contingent work generally pays less than regular work and is much less likely to provide benefits. The result is that many contingent workers go without health insurance and pension coverage. In particular, workers with little educational attainment are the big losers in the contingent labor market. Almost no temporary workers with less than a college degree have health insurance or a pension through their employer (the temp agency), and the few that do end up paying for most of these benefits.

Young adults, ages 19–23, are particularly vulnerable: a study by the Commonwealth Fund (Quinn, Schoen, and Buatti 2000) reported:

> Taking into account those who are in the workforce and no longer in school and those still in school but working part-time or summer jobs, we see that four-fifths of people ages 19 to 23 work during the year but just one-third work full-time, all year. Only one-fifth have insurance coverage through their own employer. . . . The health of uninsured young adults is at risk, especially for those with low incomes. Half of uninsured adults ages 19 to 29 whose income puts them below 200% of the poverty level (about $17,000 a year for an individual) went without needed medical care during the past year. Two-thirds

reported not being able to pay a medical bill or being contacted by a collection agency in this time.

Today, 44.3 million Americans are without health insurance according to the Bureau of the Census (1999). Further, a growing number of Americans have inadequate health insurance and are unable to properly meet their medical needs. The Bureau of Labor Statistics (1999) study compared health insurance coverage of regular full-time workers with that of contingent workers and found that regular full-time workers are much more likely to have health insurance, with 58% of wage and salary workers in traditional work arrangements having coverage through their employer and an additional 25% having coverage through an alternative source. For workers employed in contingent arrangements, the situation is very different. The employer-based health insurance system completely failed these workers. Last year, three in five (59%) temporary workers did not have any form of health insurance coverage, and workers fortunate enough to have insurance usually obtained coverage outside the workplace.

TABLE 1

Health Insurance Coverage among Temporary Agency Workers and Independent Contractors, February 1999

	Temporary agency workers	Independent contractors	Workers in regular jobs
No health insurance coverage	59.0%	26.7%	17.2%
Coverage through employer	8.5%	N/A	57.9%
Fully paid by the employer	1.3%	N/A	16.3%
Coverage from other source	32.5%	73.3%	24.9%
Total number of employees	1,188,000	8,247,000	119,109,000

Note: The CPS household survey finds a much lower number of workers employed through temporary help agencies than the BLS establishment survey's report of 3.5 million temporary help workers.
Sources: Bureau of Labor Statistics (1999: table 9) and authors' analysis of CPS February 1999 Supplement on Contingent and Alternative Work.

According to a 1999 Bureau of Labor Statistics survey, less than 9% of all temporary agency workers had health insurance coverage through the temp agency for which they were working. Many staffing agencies do not offer health insurance to their employees, and the ones that do offer insurance contribute little if any amount toward the premium, making coverage unaffordable to many workers. A Henry J. Kaiser Family Foundation study (Glied 1999:7) found that unless employees' premium levels are below $50.00 per month, few employees, particularly those at lower income levels, will take up the offered health insurance coverage. Over half (52%) of all temps were employed by temporary agencies that did not offer any form of health insurance plan. An additional 8% of temps were not covered by the plan offered because they had not worked long enough or enough hours to qualify for the agency's health plan.

According to the BLS 1999 survey, temp agencies that do offer health insurance to their temp workforce often pass the cost on to the workers. In fact, three out of four (75%) temp agency workers with health insurance had to pay some or all of their insurance premium. All in all, only 1.3% of temp agency workers have health insurance paid by the agency. Given already low wages, health insurance is unaffordable to many temps. Our analysis of the BLS survey finds that 45% said that they did not have health insurance through their temporary agency even though it was offered because they could not afford the premium.

College graduates were more likely to have employment-based health insurance than other workers employed through temporary agencies. About 1 in 6 college graduates had insurance through the temp agency, compared with only 1 in every 15 workers with just a high school degree. Moreover, workers with higher educational attainment were more likely to have their health insurance premium paid by the temp agency. On the other hand, workers with low educational attainment often ended up paying the whole insurance bill out of their own pocket. Surprisingly, temp workers without a high school degree appeared to be more likely to have health insurance than high school graduates with no higher education. One plausible explanation may be that temp workers who have not graduated from high school are less likely to have a spouse or other family members on whom they can rely for insurance coverage, and they therefore have to buy it from the temp agency.

While some temporary workers have health insurance coverage from sources other than employment (most often another family member), many are uninsured. It has been argued that temporary agency workers are young and healthy and thus do not want health insurance. But the data do not support this argument. Only 0.5% of temporary agency workers said they did not have health insurance because they felt they did not need it. Temporary workers without health insurance are of all ages, many with families and children to support.[3] Their demand for health insurance coverage is great, but the demand often goes unmet because temporary help agencies do not offer affordable coverage.

TABLE 2

Educational Levels of Temporary Agency Workers with Health Insurance Coverage,
February 1999

	With coverage	Through employer
Less than high school	32.9%	12.2%
High school degree, no college	39.3%	6.6%
Some college	41.4%	6.1%
College degree and more	54.4%	16.3%
All	41.0%	8.5%

Source: Authors' analysis of CPS February 1999 Supplement on Contingent and
Alternative Work.

In fact, it is often workers who need affordable employer-provided
insurance the most who end up without it. They are often low-wage
workers who cannot afford to pay the high insurance premium, and
their spouses, parents, or other family members in many cases do not
have health insurance coverage either. Only 33% of temps without a
high school degree and 39% with a high school degree had health insurance coverage, compared with 54.4% of college graduates. The most
common source of health insurance was through a spouse. Many workers with a college degree purchased health insurance in the private market. Individual coverage is now available only through a dwindling number of insurance companies because its costs are prohibitive (Robert
Wood Johnson Foundation 1999). Even this, however, is not an option
for low-wage workers who cannot afford the high premium. Instead,
many low-wage workers with or without a high school degree relied on
Medicaid for health insurance—or went without insurance altogether.

Another group of contingent workers who have been left behind by
the employer-based health insurance system is independent contractors.
Because independent contractors are classified as self-employed, they
have, by definition, no access to health insurance through an employer.
Instead, many turn to the private insurance market to buy an often very
expensive insurance policy. Others have to rely on their spouse or other
family members for health insurance coverage. As with temporary workers, independent contractors with a college degree have greater access
and are better able to afford health insurance from alternative sources
than workers with lower educational attainment.

Pension Provision

As a greater share of the workforce is employed through staffing
agencies or classified as independent contractors, more and more
workers go without pension coverage. Fewer and fewer workers have

pension coverage through their employer, and again, workers in alternative arrangements are the least likely to have any pension or personal savings for retirement. The BLS (1999) survey finds that only 5.8% of workers employed through a temporary agency had pension coverage, compared with 48.3% of workers in regular jobs. Instead, temporary help workers and other contingent workers have to rely on their private retirement savings. In fact, our analysis of the CPS data shows that more temporary help workers (10% vs. 5.8%) set up and pay for their own retirement, by means such as IRAs and other tax-deferred plans, than receive pension coverage from their employer.

TABLE 3

Pension Coverage among Temporary Agency Workers and Independent Contractors, February 1999

	Temporary agency workers	Independent contractors	Workers in regular jobs
No pension coverage	83.3%	63.4%	45.8%
Pension coverage through the employer	5.8%	1.9%	48.3%
Pension coverage from other source	10.9%	34.7%	5.9%
Total number of employees	1,188,000	8,247,000	119,109,000

Note: The CPS household survey finds a much lower number of workers employed through temporary help agencies than the BLS establishment survey's report of 3.5 million temporary help workers.
Sources: Bureau of Labor Statistics (1999: table 9) and authors' analysis of CPS February 1999 Supplement on Contingent and Alternative Work.

The most common reason mentioned by temporary agency workers for *not* having employer-provided pension coverage is that the temp agency does not offer a retirement plan. According to the BLS contingent worker survey, two thirds (65%) of workers in temp agencies said that the agency did not offer any retirement coverage. In cases where temp workers were not covered even though the agency offered a plan (about two out of three workers in such circumstances), the most common reason for noncoverage was that workers had worked too few hours to qualify. Many, however, simply could not afford to participate.

Independent contractors do not fare much better than other contingent workers. Two thirds of all independent contractors did not have pension coverage or tax-deferred retirement accounts. Only about a third of independent contractors were able to put money aside for their retirement. Finally, a small number of independent contractors were covered under the 401(k) plan of the company for which they contract, but this was the exception rather than the rule.

The disadvantages facing independent contractors and other contingent workers follow them into retirement. Few contingent workers have pension coverage or the ability to save for retirement. Moreover, because of their more sporadic work history and lower pay due to their contingent status, many contingent workers face penalties in Social Security benefits and are unable to accumulate personal savings.

The lack of health insurance and pension coverage for workers in temporary agencies and independent contractors further exacerbates the high level of economic insecurity these workers face. Job insecurity for temporary agency workers in particular is very high. Agencies or client firms can terminate assignments without notice and without guarantees of new assignments. Because pay is often low and work hours are often erratic, earnings provide little room for saving for the future or for emergencies. Personal illness or the need to care for a sick relative or friend can be a setback that quickly becomes a crisis: not only does the worker not get paid for time not worked, but because health insurance coverage is unlikely, medical expenses have to be paid out of pocket. For low-wage workers with limited savings and limited alternative income sources, staying healthy or catching the flu can mean the difference between getting by or living in poverty.

Solutions

Health insurance and pension coverage are basic necessities. Without them, job, family, and employment security are all in jeopardy. When President Clinton began his campaign for Health Security in 1993, 33 million Americans had no health insurance, and 60 million more had inadequate insurance coverage. Today, 45 million Americans have no health insurance, and nearly 60% of them have been uninsured for at least two years. Most of the uninsured are working (Wellstone 2000).

When Franklin D. Roosevelt signed Social Security into law in 1935, he commented that he had put "that [payroll trust fund] tax in there so no politician could ever take it out." In 2000, after the longest economic boom in U.S. history, the Republican presidential candidate proposed that individuals have the right to invest at least part of their Social Security payroll taxes in the stock market. Although advocates of the Bush plan maintain that no one would lose any money as the result of unsuccessful stock market investments of Social Security funds, at least one respected analyst concludes that the consequences could well mean benefit cuts as large as 40%. At the same time, the U.S. General

Accounting Office (2000) reports that the growth of contingent work has resulted in significant underpayment of Social Security and federal income taxes. In 1984, the last time it estimated the losses to the Social Security Trust Fund from employers who deliberately misclassify their employees as independent contractors to avoid paying the tax, the Internal Revenue Service calculated a one-year loss of $1.6 billion. The figure would certainly exceed $10 billion now, given the growth of contingent work and inflation.

Another cause of declining health care coverage, of course, is the decline of unions. At their peak, strong unions persuaded business and government to expand tax-preferred, employer-paid health insurance. Today, however, a study sponsored by the Federal Reserve Bank of San Francisco (Buchmueller, DiNardo, and Valletta 1999) attributes roughly 17% to 20% of the decrease in employer-provided health insurance among private-sector workers during the period 1983–1997 to the decline of labor unions.

Much of the business community opposed the Clinton Health Security plan's requirement that each employer contribute at least a portion of the premium for comprehensive coverage for every worker and his or her children. Business successfully lobbied against the Clinton plan on the grounds that it would cost too much and destroy corporate profits. The "Harry and Louise" television commercial campaign was deliberately designed to frighten Americans who had health insurance into thinking that "big government" would take it away.

Seven years later, corporate profits have never been higher, contingent employment has expanded throughout the old and the new economy, and more people are working—yet more Americans go without necessary medical care and insurance than ever before. Where liberal advocates of a tax-financed, single-payer health plan argued to replace an inefficient, employment-based health insurance system in 1993, conservatives in 2000 call for tax vouchers, a private market, and an end to the employer-based health insurance system. Both are correct in the following sense: the current employer-based health insurance system is clearly unable to meet the health care needs of working Americans.

Since unions were largely responsible for the postwar growth of employment-based health insurance, it comes as no surprise that their decline, coupled with the growth of temporary and contingent work, has significantly contributed to the rising numbers of uninsured workers and families. Not surprisingly, unions cite the growth of nonstandard work as a major cause of their declining membership. Thus, the interaction of a growing nonstandard workforce and the decline in unionization, both practices and policy objectives of American business over the past quarter century, brings the issue of health insurance to the center of the public policy debate. But the conservative solution, to provide tax vouchers to needy citizens so that they can purchase health insurance on the private market, has little merit when one examines the blatant failure of the individual health insurance market.

Some version of the liberal solution, favored by Democrats since Harry S. Truman, is probably inevitable. Truman attempted to expand Social Security to include universal health insurance in 1948. But an alliance of businesses and physicians managed to kill the plan. They banded together to kill universal coverage in 1974, 1979, and, of course, 1994. Today, however, there are signs that the alliance may be breaking down under the pressures of managed care.

Not only has managed care failed to hold down costs, it has alienated physicians and consumers by substituting market priorities for clinical decision making in the best interests of the patient. At the same time, low-wage, nonunion jobs continue to grow, while business continues to find new ways to add nonstandard, nonunion jobs. Ironically, those who oppose a government-run financing system, to be consistent, should favor greater unionization of the workplace, since unions and private health insurance are so nearly inseparable. Yet a global economy that demands ever leaner and cheaper means of production and contingent work inexorably forces businesses to cut costs, particularly health care costs. Lacking health insurance, these workers, when sick, have no choice but to turn to government.

Creating a government-financed, universal health insurance system would seem to have obvious advantages in the era of contingent work. No longer would employees have to worry whether an employer offered health insurance; they could move from job to job without fear of losing coverage. Employers would be freed from the needless expense of administering their own health plans. Administrative costs and insurance company profits from the current system would instead go to pay for coverage of every uninsured American. In 1994, the General Accounting Office estimated that a universal system would generate cost savings of $122 billion, enough to cover the health insurance needs of every uninsured American. In 2000, cost-savings estimates for universal state insurance plans in Maryland and Massachusetts fell within the same per capita range.

Social Security has a proven track record of providing retirement protection for all Americans. The same would be true of a universal health security plan. The American accident of tying health insurance to employment worked better when employers were willing to bargain for labor peace. In a global economy, that bargain appears to be out of reach. Today's workers, full-time and contingent, need comprehensive health and retirement security. Today's businesses need to compete in a global market that is free from the costs and administrative nightmares of managed care.

Winston Churchill once remarked that Americans could always be counted upon to do the right thing—after they had tried everything else. This is certainly true of health care. No other modern economy on earth lacks universal health insurance. It is long past time for the creation of a government-run financing system that covers people irrespective of their work status. Business would do a great public service by offering its support.

Interim measures, however, continue to proliferate: Senator Edward Kennedy now proposes an expansion of the Children's Health Insurance Plan (CHIP) and a Family Insurance Plan. Each would add several million workers and their dependents to the ranks of the privately insured. States continue to experiment with managed-care alternatives for their poorest citizens and with pooled coverage for small businesses. No state has attempted to cover part-time or contingent workers. Unions continue to press the matter at the bargaining table, with some success. Part-time grocery store workers at Safeway, Kroger's, and Giant Food all receive a prorated benefit package, as do the newly organized janitors in the Los Angeles metropolitan area. The problem, of course, is that prorated coverage means a lower take-up rate, unless the employer is willing to assume the majority of the premium cost.

Senator Paul Wellstone (Democrat from Minnesota), drawing on the lessons of the 1994 campaign, recently introduced the Health Security for All Americans Act. His proposal would require each state to enact its own system of universal coverage by 2007. All workers would receive full coverage. According to Wellstone (2000:4): "A family of four with an annual income of $25,000 would be responsible for no more than $11 a month in total health care costs." Massachusetts, Washington, California, and Maryland all have proposals that move in the direction of the Wellstone proposal.

The 2000 presidential campaign, however, was unlikely to provide much assistance to contingent workers. Both of the major parties limited their health insurance initiatives to incremental reforms that would, at best, cover the children of contingent workers. As for pensions, contingent workers can at least count on Social Security, since it covers all workers.

The New Economy has an Achilles' heel: it ignores the contingent worker's basic need for health security, yet it demands more hours of work from everyone. Whether the American worker can attain health security—despite work status as a full-time, part-time, or contingent employee—is the first true test of the New Economy. Few would dispute the New Economy's ability to generate unparalleled wealth. Its success, however, depends on its ability to invest that wealth for the benefit of future growth—and all Americans.

Notes

[1] The BLS establishment survey (BLS 2001) finds a larger number of workers employed by temporary help agencies than estimated by the BLS household survey (the Current Population Survey [CPS], Supplement on Contingent and Alternative Work Arrangements). The household survey estimates a total of 1.2 million temporary help agency workers, compared with 3.5 million by the establishment survey. The establishment survey is generally considered a more reliable estimate of employment than the household survey.

[2] The fee can be quite substantial, normally ranging from 25% to 40% of wages, but much higher fees are not unheard of.

[3] Temporary agency workers ages 35 to 55 are more likely than workers younger than 35 to have health insurance through the temporary agency. Still only about 10% of workers ages 35 to 55 have employer-provided health insurance.

References

American Management Association. 1999. "1999 AMA Survey: Contingent Workers." <http://www.amanet.org/research/pdfs/cngmtwrk.pdf>.

Belous, Richard S. 1997. "The Rise in the Contingent Workforce: Growth of Temporary, Part-Time, and Subcontracted Employment." *Looking Ahead* (National Policy Association), Vol. 19, no. 1, pp. 1–25.

Buchmueller, Thomas, John DiNardo, and Robert Valletta. 1999. *Union Effects on Health Insurance Provision and Coverage in the United States.* San Francisco Federal Reserve Working Paper. San Francisco: San Francisco Federal Reserve.

Bureau of Labor Statistics. 1995. "New Data on Contingent and Alternative Employment Examined by BLS." News release, August 17. Washington, DC: Bureau of Labor Statistics.

———. 1997. "Contingent and Alternative Employment Arrangements, February 1997." News release, December 2. Washington, DC: Bureau of Labor Statistics.

———. 1999. "Contingent and Alternative Employment Arrangements, February 1999." News release, December 21. Washington, DC: Bureau of Labor Statistics.

————. 2001. "Establishment Data Series from the Monthly B Tables." <http://www.bls.gov/cesbtabs.htm>.

Bureau of the Census. 1999. "Increase of 1 Million Uninsured People, Census Bureau Says." Press release, October 4. Washington, DC: Bureau of the Census.

Cappelli, Peter. 2000. "A Market-Driven Approach to Retaining Talent." *Harvard Business Review*, January–February.

Glied, Sherry. 1999. *An Assessment of the Strategies for Expanding Health Insurance Coverage*. Washington, DC: Henry J. Kaiser Family Foundation.

Houseman, Susan N. 1997. *Temporary, Part-Time, and Contract Employment in the United States: A Report on the W. E. Upjohn Institute's Employer Survey on Flexible Staffing Policies*. Working Paper, W. E. Upjohn Institute (June). Kalamazoo, MI: W. E. Upjohn Institute.

Houseman, Susan N., and Anne E. Polivka. 1998. *The Implications of Flexible Staffing Arrangements for Job Security*. Working Paper, Bureau of Labor Statistics (April). Washington, DC: Bureau of Labor Statistics.

Hudson, Ken. 1999. *No Shortage of "Nonstandard" Jobs: Nearly 30% of Workers Employed in Part-Time, Temping, and Other Alternative Arrangements*. Economic Policy Institute Briefing Paper (December). Washington, DC: Economic Policy Institute.

Jorgensen, Helene J. 1999. *When Good Jobs Go Bad*. Washington, DC: 2030 Center.

Levine, Linda. 1999. *Temporary Workers as Members of the Contingent Labor Force*. CRS Report for Congress (February 16). Washington, DC: Library of Congress, Congressional Research Service.

Quinn, Kevin, Cathy Schoen, and Louisa Buatti. 2000. *On Their Own: Young Adults Living without Health Insurance*. New York: Commonwealth Fund. <http://www.cmwf.org/programs/insurance/quinn_ya_391.asp>.

Robert Wood Johnson Foundation. 1999. Conference on the Evolution of the Individual Insurance Market: Now and the Future. Washington, DC.

U.S. Department of Labor. 1999a. *Future Work: Trends and Challenges for Work in the 21st Century*. Washington, DC: U.S. Department of Labor.

————. 1999b. *Report on the American Workforce, 1999* (September). Washington, DC: Department of Labor.

U.S. General Accounting Office. 2000. *Contingent Workers: Incomes and Benefits Lag Behind Those of Rest of Workforce*. Report GAO/HEHS-00-76. Washington, DC: GPO.

Wellstone, Paul. 2000. Health Security for All Americans Act. *Congressional Record*, July 19.

Chapter 11

Benefits for Same-Sex Partners

Nancy J. Sedmak
Bureau of National Affairs

Gay and lesbian employees who do not receive employer-provided benefits for their same-sex partners as do married employees are being paid at least 5% less than their married co-workers. This calculation is based on a 1990 Chamber of Commerce study that reported that the average American worker receives about 40% of his or her total compensation in the form of benefits (of which about three fourths of the value is direct benefits to the individual employee in the form of paid time off, life insurance, retirement, unemployment and workers' compensation benefits, and other benefits), attributing roughly 5% to health benefits for spouses and dependents (Mickens 1994).

> It didn't seem fair that those of us who had relationships that looked like a marriage, felt like a marriage, talked like a marriage, worked like a marriage, cost like a marriage, gave emotional support like a marriage, and involved stress like a marriage could be told we didn't have a marriage because we're denied a piece of paper that says we're married. That's long been true. But to realize that we're being paid five percent less than our colleagues whose lives are almost identical to our own, except that they have access to a certificate—well, that's just plain galling. . . . The motivation behind the push for domestic-partnership benefits is the desire for something symbolic as well as economic. . . . The economic side, for gay men and lesbians, could be described in simple and familiar terms: equal pay for equal work. (Mickens 1994)

The 5% pay differential is based on lack of access to health insurance benefits for the gay or lesbian employee's domestic partner. But health insurance, although a significant benefit, is not the only benefit denied to a domestic partner: bereavement leave, assumption of the employee's pension, sick leave to care for the partner, and access to employees' family discounts are among other employer-provided benefits not available to domestic partners.

Social Security and other federal and state benefits, including tax benefits, also are denied to domestic partners.

As of late 1999, according to the Human Rights Campaign, a lesbian and gay advocacy organization, over 2,500 private companies, colleges and universities, and state and local governments offered domestic-partnership health benefits (Mills and Herrschaft 1999). In the early 1990s, a number of major companies began to offer these benefits, but almost three quarters of these employers began offering domestic-partnership benefits as a direct result of a San Francisco Equal Benefits Ordinance that, as of 1997, required any company doing business with the city or county of San Francisco to offer the same benefits to the domestic partners of its employees as it offers to employees' legal spouses. While many of these employers are small, California-based employers, the ordinance has played a major role in effecting change in workplaces across the nation because large, nationwide employers who do business in San Francisco have had to tackle how to offer domestic-partnership benefits. Airlines flying into San Francisco airport challenged the ordinance, and the litigation is continuing (*Air Transport Association v. San Francisco*, 76 FEP Cases 1109 [DC N. Calif. 1998]). However, most of the airlines have offered benefits to their employees' same-sex partners.

Although domestic partners can be both heterosexual and homosexual, the growth of the issue of domestic partnership benefits is tied to the increasing attention to the discrimination against gay men and lesbians. As an equal rights issue, discrimination against homosexuals gained momentum generally in the 1990s. The election of President Clinton and his attempt to eliminate the ban on homosexuals in the military helped put this issue on the table. Attempts to prohibit discrimination against homosexuals have met with fierce resistance from groups with deeply held religious beliefs that homosexuality is evil and not an immutable characteristic, like race or sex. The future growth of domestic-partnership benefits is part of the struggle—should homosexuals have equal rights?

This chapter, in addressing domestic-partnership benefits, discusses the attempts to eliminate discrimination based on sexual orientation. The success or failure of these attempts will affect the future of domestic-partnership benefits. If the tide continues to go toward tolerance and even acceptance of human relationships that do not fit the traditional model, domestic-partnership benefits will slowly but inexorably become part of the American workplace. The rights of homosexuals in the global workplace are also briefly compared.

Background

About 4 million American opposite-sex couples cohabit, which is about 7% of couples sharing households (Tolson 2000). There has been a sharp rise over the last 30 years in unmarried cohabitation—from 523,000 households in 1970 to 1.6 million in 1980 to 2.7 million in 1990 (Bureau of National Affairs [BNA] 1991). Some of these numbers are estimates, however, since an "unmarried partner" box on the census form was introduced only in 1990. That census showed that more than 145,000 households reported themselves as same-sex unmarried partners—81,000 male and 64,000 female (Ly 2000).

Although most potential recipients of domestic-partner rights and benefits are heterosexuals, homosexual advocacy groups and individuals have undertaken most of the lobbying, demonstrations, and legal action on behalf of domestic partners and nontraditional families. This is because homosexuals do not have the option to get married. Some human resource professionals argue that employee benefits should be extended to nontraditional families because employees who are members of them are affected by the same work-and-family considerations as workers who are members of traditional families and because these benefits can help employers recruit and retain qualified workers (BNA 1991).

Early in the 1990s, the idea of extending health insurance to nontraditional family members created perhaps the most controversy because such a move cost employers more than any other benefit extension. With health care costs rising at a record rate, few employers wanted to expand their coverage to include employees' domestic partners and their dependents. Some employers feared that such an extension would increase their health insurance costs sharply and expose them to the catastrophic costs of caring for AIDS victims. In addition, some employers feared that their public image and morale among other employees would be damaged if they started providing benefits for unmarried homosexual and heterosexual domestic partners—that other workers and the public would think the employer sanctioned lifestyles that they believed are immoral and that in many states were illegal. And some company executives considered such benefit extensions "an onslaught on the family. Benefits in this country are for employees and their families" (BNA 1991:5). Even though the idea of providing domestic-partner benefits was being widely discussed in 1991, few employers were doing so. In 1990, 50% of survey respondents did not expect the number of employers that offer health insurance coverage to employees' domestic partners to grow (BNA 1991).

The Village Voice, in 1982, was the first U.S. employer to offer health insurance benefits to domestic partners of gay and lesbian employees (Mills and Herrschaft 1999). This was achieved through a collective bargaining request from UAW Local 65; the wage offer was low in that bargaining round, and the union requested health insurance coverage for all unmarried couples, homosexual and heterosexual. The stereotypical concern about promiscuity among gays was addressed by requiring a one-year waiting period after application before coverage would begin. In the decade following, a total of 20 couples were covered; only two requested a switch of partners, and both were heterosexual (Mickens 1994).

In 1996, an Oregon university was required to provide health and other benefits to its employees' domestic partners. *Tanner v. Oregon Health Sciences Univ.* (1996 WL 585547 [Ore. Cir. Ct. 1996]) was the first court case requiring public agencies to give same-sex partners the benefits of marriage. The court decided that the state health sciences university discriminated against homosexual employees by not extending health and other benefits to their domestic partners. The state's employee benefits provisions violated Oregon's statute prohibiting employment discrimination and its constitutional guarantee of equal privileges and immunities. The court ordered the state and university to make their insurance benefits equally available to the domestic partners of homosexual employees.

The city of Boston, however, was precluded from extending health insurance coverage to the domestic partners of city employees because it was found to be prohibited by state law (*Connors v. Boston*, 714 N.E. 2d 335 [Mass. Sup. Jud. Ct. 1999]). The Massachusetts Supreme Judicial Court struck down an executive order issued by Democratic Boston Mayor Thomas Menino extending health insurance to domestic partners. The decision said that the state's "home rule" law forbids municipalities from adopting policies that are inconsistent with state laws. State law governing group health insurance restricts coverage to public employees and their dependents and defines "dependents" as spouses and children. Cities and other governmental units are not free to expand the category. Domestic partners and their dependents fall outside the statutory definition of those who may claim an insurable interest through the employee and are therefore precluded from obtaining coverage. The legislature defined "dependents" of public employees in 1955. "Our decision is mandated only because, in the context of group health insurance provided by governmental units for their employees, the Legislature has defined precisely the scope of the term dependent to exclude all but spouses, unmarried children under [19] years of age, and older children in limited circumstances" (*Connors*, 714 N.E. 2d at 342). In 1998, state lawmakers passed a bill authorizing the city to extend health insurance to domestic partners, but the measure was vetoed by the governor, who objected to allowing coverage for heterosexuals who have the option of marriage. Some local governments in Massachusetts and other states have met with similar limitations.

Legal Battleground

The law on the rights of homosexuals and the understanding of gender identity and sexuality are evolving. About half the states have laws making sodomy, often defined to include oral as well as anal intercourse, a crime (Posner 1992).[1]

It appears that the battle for equal rights for homosexual Americans may have better success in the courts than in the voting booths. Several significant court decisions have found that depriving homosexuals of rights equal to heterosexuals violates the rights of homosexuals to equal protection under the U.S. or state constitutions. Meanwhile, attempting to legislate equal rights for homosexuals has often met defeat in public referenda on the issue.

The majority of Americans believe that homosexuality is unacceptable, according to a 1998 poll conducted by the *Washington Post*, the Henry J. Kaiser Family Foundation, and Harvard University (Rosin and Morin 1998). Despite this view, the poll also reported that 87% of respondents said homosexuals should have equal rights in terms of job opportunities. Only 23% support gay marriage, however. The poll also showed that opinions differed greatly according to the age of the respondent, with younger people overwhelmingly in favor of the statement that homosexual relations should be legal (71% of people ages 18–29 and 61% of people ages 30–49).

Employment Discrimination

Title VII of the Civil Rights Act of 1964 [42 U.S.C. 2000e-2(a)], which prohibits discrimination based on sex, does not encompass discrimination based on sexual orientation.[2] Homosexuality, bisexuality, and "gender identity disorders" are expressly excluded from the protections of the Americans with Disabilities Act (42 U.S.C. Sec. 12211). State laws that prohibit "sex discrimination" have also been found not to encompass homosexuality.[3] "Most federal and state anti-discrimination laws do not protect homosexuals against discrimination on the basis of their sexual preference, although a number of municipalities do, which is not surprising when we recall that homosexuals tend to be concentrated in cities," Judge Posner (1992) stated. But he also queried whether laws against racial and sexual and related forms of discrimination perceived as invidious should be extended to cover homosexuals. He asks, Is there any reason to exclude homosexuals from a protected category that already includes not only racial, religious, and ethnic groups but also women, the physically and mentally handicapped, all workers aged 40 and older, and, in some cases, even young, healthy, male WASPs? Is there less, less harmful, or less irrational discrimination against homosexuals than against the members of *any* of these groups (Posner 1992)?

Recognizing that Title VII and state laws patterned after it do not prohibit discrimination because of sexual orientation, some cities and counties (e.g., Montgomery County, Maryland;[4] New York City;[5] the cities of Aspen, Boulder, and Denver and the County of Denver, Colorado[6]) have added "sexual orientation" as a proscribed basis of discrimination. The District of Columbia and several states, including California, Connecticut, Hawaii, Massachusetts, Minnesota, New Jersey, Rhode Island, Vermont, and Wisconsin, prohibit employment discrimination on the basis of sexual orientation (*Fair Employment Practice Manual* n.d.).

Equal Protection under the U.S. Constitution

The U.S. Supreme Court ruled in *Romer v. Evans* (517 U.S. 620, 70 FEP Cases 1180 [1996]) that homosexuals cannot be denied protection against discrimination available to all others. The dispute that made its way to the Court was an amendment to the constitution of the state of Colorado, adopted in a 1992 statewide referendum, that (1) repealed local ordinances to the extent that they prohibited discrimination on the basis of homosexuality and (2) prohibited all legislative, executive, or judicial action at any level of state or local government designed to protect homosexuals. The Court stated that it could not accept the view that the amendment's prohibition on specific legal protections did no more than deprive homosexuals of special rights. The amendment imposed a special disability upon homosexuals alone in that they were forbidden the safeguards that others enjoy or may seek without constraint, the Court said. Reviewing the 14th Amendment's promise that no person shall be denied the equal protection of the laws and noting that most legislation classifies for one purpose or another, the Court said that it reconciles this conflict, if a law neither burdens a fundamental right nor targets a suspect class, by upholding the legislative classification so long as it bears a rational relation to some legitimate end.

The amendment failed this inquiry, the Court found, since it imposed a broad and undifferentiated disability on a single named group. Its breadth is so discontinuous with the reasons offered for it that the amendment "seems inexplicable by anything but animus toward the class it affects," the Court stated. The Court concluded that the amendment classified homosexuals not to further a proper legislative end but to make them unequal to everyone else.

The dissent, written by Justice Scalia and joined by Chief Justice Rehnquist and Justice Thomas, bitterly attacked the majority and claimed that the majority is reflecting the views and morality of the "lawyer class," which is in contrast to the more "plebeian attitudes" that still prevail in the United States and which have been unresponsive to attempts to extend to homosexuals the protections of federal civil rights laws. The dissent argued that the majority did not dispute the potential effect of the amendment on general antidiscrimination laws but assumed it to be true and argued that the real effect of the amendment was to prohibit giving homosexuals favored status. Coloradans are entitled to be hostile toward homosexual conduct, the dissent argued, but the majority portrayal of Coloradans as "gay-bashers" was false. The dissent pointed out that Colorado was one of the first states to repeal its antisodomy law. The majority invented a novel and extravagant constitutional doctrine to take victory away from the traditional forces, the dissent asserted, and it verbally disparaged as bigotry adherence to traditional attitudes. The amendment did not disfavor homosexuals, the dissent stated, but merely denied them preferential treatment. It was designed to prevent piecemeal deterioration of the sexual morality favored by the majority of Coloradans and is an appropriate means to that legitimate end, the dissent concluded.

The U.S. Supreme Court in *Oncale v. Sundowner Offshore Services, Inc.* (76 FEP Cases 221 [U.S. Sup. Ct. 1998]) ruled that Title VII's prohibition of sexual harassment covers same-sex harassment. Other courts also have noted that homosexuals are not excluded from protection under laws that protect "all persons."[7]

Right to Marry and Equal Protection under State Constitutions

The Vermont Supreme Court in December 1999 ruled that it violated the state constitution to deny same-sex couples the statutory benefits and protections afforded persons of the opposite sex who choose to marry and that the state is constitutionally required to extend to same-sex couples the common benefits and protections that flow from marriage under Vermont law (*Baker v. State of Vermont*, 744 A. 2d 864 [Vt. Sup. Ct. 1999]). The court left it to the legislature to determine whether to include same-sex relationships within the marriage law or within a parallel domestic-partnership or equivalent system.

In early 2000, Vermont enacted historic legislation allowing gay couples to form "civil unions" that carry many of the benefits and responsibilities of traditional marriages. The law stops just short of legalizing gay marriage, instead setting up a network of state benefits for gay couples, covering everything from hospital visits to inheritance rights to state taxes. Vermont has gone much further than any other state in sanctioning same-sex unions. Under the law, gay partners may apply for a license from a town clerk and get their civil union certified by a justice of the peace, a judge, or a member of the clergy. Partners in a civil union are eligible for 300 state benefits given to married couples, covering every phase of life. They can transfer property, make medical decisions for each other, inherit estates, and oversee one another's burials. Such couples can also file a joint state income tax return. The federal government still does not recognize such unions with regard to such things as immigration rights, Social Security benefits, and federal taxes. Vermont gay couples in civil unions are subject to burdens similar to those of married couples. Partners who want to end their civil union have to go through a dissolution proceeding in family court, similar to divorce proceedings. They also assume each other's debts. Although the law comes close to recognizing gay marriage, it reserved the term "marriage" for the union of a man and a woman.

It remains unclear whether couples from outside the state can apply for civil unions in Vermont and force their home state to recognize them. Gay advocates expressed the hope that states would be hard-pressed to deny partners in a civil union, for example, rights to make medical decisions should they find themselves in another state's hospital (Rosin and Ferdinand 2000).

A challenge to Hawaii's marriage statute, after homosexual couples were denied the right to obtain a marriage license, led that state's Supreme Court to rule that denying homosexuals the right to marry deprived them of equal protection under Hawaii's constitution.[8] The furor caused by that ruling led to a public referendum that amended the state constitution to prohibit the recognition of same-sex marriages. It also led to enactment by the U.S. Congress in 1996 of the Defense of Marriage Act (Pub. L. No. 104-199 [1996]), which clarified that all federal laws apply only to heterosexual marriages and specified that no state shall be required to give effect to same-sex relationships treated as a marriage, or any right or claim arising from such relationship, under the laws of any other state.

More and more states are passing laws, or referenda are being approved by the voters, to limit marriage to the union between a man and a woman (thereby excluding gay couples). California's Proposition 22 won by 61% to 39% in March 2000. The opponents of the antigay measure, however, say that they fear that this is only the first step in a nationwide attempt to roll back the gains of gays in such areas as domestic-partner benefits. Gay groups were disappointed at the margin of victory and are worried that its passage in California means the likelihood that similar initiatives will be tried in other states (Sanchez and Booth 2000).

Achieving Domestic-Partnership Benefits

The most popular benefit being pursued for domestic partners is health benefits (Mickens 1994). But the whole array of benefits offered employees are being pursued, including pension benefits, life insurance, stock and stock options, bereavement and family leave, travel benefits, child care, education, and employee discounts.

Survivor benefits were denied to a lesbian partner in *Rovira v. AT&T* (16 EBC 1888 [DC S. N.Y. 1993]) because the benefit went only to a "legal spouse." It was argued that the real issue is whether a company that holds itself out as nondiscriminatory can refuse to provide a death benefit under its pension plan to the surviving member of a gay couple (BNA 1991).

Life insurance can be assigned to any beneficiary, but "more and more" instances arise of life insurance companies requiring "blood relatives" as beneficiaries (Mickens 1994). Stock and stock options can be converted into joint ownership or transferred under the terms of a will (Mickens 1994).

Parental leave and bereavement leave (plus Family and Medical Leave Act leave) should be the first benefit sought, it is recommended, since they will make it much easier for union negotiators later to secure health coverage and ultimately pension benefits for domestic partners. Health coverage and pension benefits become the logical extension of family leave benefits (Pride At Work 1999). Companies' program and facility offerings to spouses vary widely but may include fitness facilities, courses and lectures, libraries, travel to conferences (and spousal programs while there), or psychological counseling. (Interestingly, many Employee Assistance Programs [EAPs] for counseling have long included domestic partners, on the theory that if there is trouble at home, both partners need to be brought into the solution. The decision is made confidentially and on the recommendation of a mental health professional, which is rarely questioned.)

Discounts figure prominently here. Many companies offer spousal or family discounts for their products or services, but few as of yet include domestic partners. Sometimes, companies offer domestic-partner benefits as the result of lawsuits. Woodward and Lothrop, a Washington, D.C., department store, lost a lawsuit brought by a gay employee in the 1980s and was forced to offer domestic-partner discounts equal to those provided spouses. Similar battles for discount flying privileges are being fought within the major airlines. Perhaps a sensible attitude comes from Levi Strauss, which operates a discounted "company store" open to employees and whatever guests the employee invites. As a spokesperson once pointed out, their business is selling and promoting their clothing. As long as they are not subsidizing somebody else's retail operation, why not let the employees make the determination?

Other family benefits include relocation expenses, including mortgage assistance, which should apply the same to partners as to spouses (Mickens 1994).

Collective Bargaining Considerations

Pride At Work (1999), a new constituency group of the AFL-CIO whose purpose is to mobilize support between organized labor and the lesbian and gay community, has put together a list of considerations in pursuing domestic-partnership benefits and provides a recommended approach:

1. Union bargainers should ensure that the contract includes strong nondiscrimination language and antiharassment protections.
2. "Lesbians, gays, bisexuals, and transgender employees" should be recognized and included in leave (parental, bereavement, family, and medical) clauses and policies. Additionally, union bargainers are encouraged to make sure to include all categories of domestic partners, not just same-sex couples, since a broad-based coalition will help win these rights.
3. After the protections in steps 1 and 2 are secured, union bargainers can move forward to secure health and ultimately pension benefits for domestic partners. During bargaining, the negotiators must be fully prepared for the employer's arguments and questions, such as reasons to offer benefits, costs, and ways to address employer's fear of negative publicity. The negotiators also must research which other employers in the area offer domestic-partnership benefits, the costs of the package, and sample contract language.

Probably the most direct way to secure benefits coverage for gay and lesbian couples is to expand the already existing contractual definition of "spouse" or to introduce alternative appropriately defined words such as "partner." There are a number of issues when choosing to redefine "spouse and family" in the collective bargaining contract:

- *Clear and consistent language.* Language should be very explicit. General phrases may seem attractive, but they invite different interpretations. Words such as "spouse," "partner," "life partner," "significant other," and "unspecified by sex" are all open to be interpreted as applying to opposite-sex relationships only. Consistency is another important consideration. Ideally, any definition in the contract should be the same as in any insured benefit policy or plan. If negotiators insert a definition of "spouse" or "partner," they should ensure that the defined word is used throughout the contract.

- *Remember other family members.* It is important to explicitly ensure that the definition extends to other relationships. Most employment benefits such as bereavement leave and leave for family illness specify a list of people who are legally related to the employee, such as through marriage or adoption. For example, if a domestic partner is considered a spouse for the purposes of the contract, an employee is entitled to bereavement leave in the event of the partner's death. But this will not necessarily be so in the case of the partner's mother's death unless the contract explicitly says so. Equally important is the designation "child." Negotiators should ensure that parental and adoption leaves, insured benefits coverage, and the like recognize the children of all domestic partners. The contract should expand the word "child" with the additional description such as "partner's child," "spouse's child," "child to whom the employee acts as a parent," and so on.

- *Ensure employer responsibility.* Make sure that it is the employer's responsibility to provide the benefit. This makes it grievable! It is the employer's responsibility to contract with the insurer for the agreed-upon benefits and to enforce eligibility based on the agreed definitions. It is also important to get the employer to take responsibility for finding the insurance carrier who will provide the agreed benefit. This is not an easy task, and many carriers continue to balk. The union is not precluded from advising the employer of insurance companies that may be likely to provide coverage. But the ultimate responsibility must rest with the employer. It is the employer who contracts with the carrier, and the employer can, if necessary, threaten to take its business elsewhere (Pride At Work 1999).

Expense of Benefits

Health coverage for domestic partners costs no more than coverage for spouses, according to the experience of the city of Seattle (Mickens 1994). Most employers report no significant increase in costs. A survey by the Society of Human Resource Management released in January 1997 found that 85% of respondents with domestic-partner benefits experienced no increase in their health care costs as a result of adding them (Pride At Work 1999).

AIDS as an obstacle to domestic-partner benefits has proved not to be as problematic as feared. Lesbians have the lowest incidence of any group, and in 1993 heterosexuals took over as the majority of new cases; insurers themselves say the costs they fear most are for neonatal care of premature babies and problem pregnancies ($250,000 to $1,000,000 per birth) and accidents among teenage dependents (Mickens 1994). Employers have not reported any spiking of insurance costs due to

HIV/AIDS. In 1994, the U.S. government estimated the lifetime cost of caring for someone with AIDS was $119,000. The cost of a kidney transplant can run as high as $200,000, while the cost of caring for a premature infant can run between $50,000 and $1 million. Maternity and cancers continue to be among the most expensive, insurable, treatable conditions (Pride At Work 1999).

The number of employees who avail themselves of domestic-partnership benefits has not been burdensome. Companies that offer domestic-partnership benefits to both same-sex and opposite-sex partners get more applicants for benefits but only about 2% to 3% of total employees more. Levi Strauss estimates that 60% of those who receive domestic-partnership benefits are heterosexuals (49% are women bringing in male partners, many of whom are self-employed or work for small companies unable to carry decent health coverage); among city of Seattle employees, about 70% who receive benefits are not gay.

Companies where domestic-partner benefits are offered to gay and lesbian employees only, such as Lotus, report that only 1% of employees have taken advantage of the program. Average enrollment in a domestic-partner benefit plan will probably not exceed 1% of the eligible population in any organization that employs between 100 and 100,000 employees. Likewise, average total cost increases will also not exceed 1%. These figures are based on offering domestic-partner benefits to all employees, not just same-sex couples. Many lesbian, gay, bisexual, and transgender couples are two-earner families in which both partners receive health care benefits where they work. In workplaces without nondiscrimination policies covering sexual orientation, some workers might not feel safe enough to "come out" and ask for such benefits. Most important, these benefits are counted as taxable income to the employee—unlike the same benefits given to the families of married couples (Pride At Work 1999).

Eligibility Issues

Most employers who extend benefits to domestic partners have defined a partnership in terms of a committed relationship of shared responsibilities and expenses. Most have established a registration procedure for domestic partners. Registration normally involves filing an affidavit attesting to the relationship's existence and the fact that the partners have lived together for a particular period of time (Pride At Work 1999).

Many employers that provide domestic-partnership benefits require the employee and his or her domestic partner to sign an "affidavit of domestic partnership" to obtain coverage, although they do not require this from married employees. Many companies require that domestic partners demonstrate that they

- have lived together for a specified period (generally, at least six months),

- are responsible for each other's financial welfare,

- are not blood relatives,

- are at least 18 years of age,

- are mentally competent,

- are life partners and would get legally married should the option become available,

- are registered as domestic partners if there is a local domestic partner registry,

- are not legally married to anyone, and

- agree to inform the company in the event that the domestic partnership terminates (Human Rights Campaign n.d.).

In addition to the affidavit, a company may require proof of financial interdependence or common residence. For example, an employer might stipulate that the employee present proof of a joint checking account, mortgage or rent agreements, utility bills, or drivers' licenses. Some employers require that the domestic partner sign a "termination of domestic partnership" form if the partnership ends (Human Rights Campaign n.d.).

Employees who sign the affidavits should be aware that doing so might have legal consequences. In the event that the employee violates any portion of the affidavit, he or she may be required to repay the company for the cost of the benefits. However, to date there is no evidence of fraud on the part of employees (Human Rights Campaign n.d.).

Employers should ensure that the process for registering for domestic-partner benefits is kept strictly confidential to respect employees who may not wish to publicly disclose their relationships (Human Rights Campaign n.d.).

Insurers

When domestic-partner benefits were first offered, the few insurance carriers that wrote such policies usually added a charge to cover any unexpected cost increase. Today, many insurance companies cover domestic partners. Most have stopped adding a surcharge, or the surcharge is often reduced or eliminated after the cost of the additional coverage is shown to be minimal.

For companies that are self-insured, adding domestic-partner benefits is a relatively simple process since it does not require state regulatory approval. Companies that offer insurance through an outside insurance carrier usually need to negotiate the specifics of the additional coverage with their insurer and get their plan approved by state insurance regulators. Some employers have had difficulty negotiating the coverage with their insurer. Furthermore, some state insurance commissioners have refused to approve plans that include domestic-partner coverage. Health maintenance organizations (HMOs) are not under the auspices of insurance-regulating agencies and can choose on their own whether or not to write policies to cover these benefits.

Companies that have experienced difficulty finding an insurance carrier to cover domestic partners in a given state may be able to secure coverage through a carrier in another state. Or, if an insurance provider cannot be located, employers may ask the domestic partner or employee to purchase the insurance individually and accept reimbursement for a portion of the premium cost (Human Rights Campaign n.d.).

Same-Sex versus Opposite-Sex Eligibility

Some companies that provide domestic-partnership benefits offer them to all unmarried partners, and some offer them only to gay and lesbian couples on the grounds that heterosexual employees can marry. This development came as a surprise to many gay and lesbian activists, who were essentially working against marriage bias, regardless of sexual orientation (Mickens 1994).

There have been a few legal challenges to plans that are offered only to same-sex unmarried partners, and these usually have failed (*Foray v. Bell Atlantic*, 80 FEP Cases 65 [DC S. N.Y. 1999]; *Irizarry v. Board of Education of Chicago*, 83 FEP Cases 808 [DC N. Ill. 2000]).

Some employers and employee groups that are trying to achieve domestic-partnership benefits advocate setting up plans that do not distinguish between heterosexual and homosexual partners, often because of the belief that the plans will be viewed as less discriminatory or less "pro-gay." Others, however, believe that if the impetus behind providing such benefits is to assist a group that is otherwise precluded from accessing certain benefits, making a distinction between a class that can marry if they so prefer (heterosexual couples) and a class that cannot marry (homosexual couples), offering benefits to one class but not the other is justified and defensible. So far the courts have agreed.

Taxation

Employer-provided benefits to domestic partners are taxable income to the employee. The IRS (private letter ruling 9717018) determined that domestic partners do not qualify as spouses for purposes of the exclusion from gross income of employer-provided health insurance. The fair market value of the health insurance coverage provided for the nonemployee partner is included in the gross income of the employee partner unless the nonemployee partner qualifies as the employee's dependent.

An individual can qualify as a dependent other than by blood, marriage, or adoption provided that the taxpayer is responsible for more than half of the individual's support. However, if the relationship between the taxpayer and the individual violates local law, the individual cannot be considered a legal dependent. Since many states still have criminal sodomy, fornication, or cohabitation laws, same-sex and heterosexual domestic partners could be violating local law.

COBRA

The Consolidated Omnibus Budget Reconciliation Act of 1995 (COBRA) requires most employers to offer employees the opportunity to pay for continued health coverage on their own in the event that their coverage ends due to events such as divorce or termination. COBRA does not, however, require an employer to extend those rights to domestic partners. Nevertheless, employers may decide to extend COBRA rights to domestic partners with the approval of their insurance carrier or HMO (Human Rights Campaign n.d.).

Backlash

Two phenomena—the growing tendency among employers to reach out to the gay community by offering domestic-partner benefits and including gay and lesbian issues in their diversity programs and a trend of people's being more vocal about their religious beliefs—are likely to continue to clash in the workplace ("Religion and Sexual Orientation" 1999). Three employees of a state corrections facility objected to a mandatory training seminar on gays and lesbians in the workplace, protested by carrying Bibles into the session and reading silently from them, were reprimanded for that behavior, and sued their employer, alleging that its actions violated their rights to free speech and free exercise of religion and their state constitutional rights of freedom of speech and freedom of conscience (*Altman v. Minnesota Department of Corrections,* 80 FEP Cases 1166 [DC Minn. 1999]). A federal judge denied each of the plaintiffs' claims except those alleging denial of their rights to freedom of religion and conscience and ordered the employer to withdraw the reprimands.

Many employers, small and large, have instituted domestic partner benefits with little fanfare, while others—such as IBM, Wells Fargo, Eastman Kodak, and the Coors Company—have garnered positive publicity and are continually cited for being in the vanguard. A small handful of employers have come under public attack for such policies, usually by religious political groups. In 1996, the Southern Baptist Convention threatened to boycott the Walt Disney Co. because of its "gay-friendly" policies, including offering domestic-partner benefits to the same-sex partners of employees. For the most part, media coverage and public reaction to the extension of such benefits have been reasonable because many Americans recognize the basic unfairness of not offering equal pay in terms of benefits to lesbian and gay workers (Pride At Work 1999).

Apple Computer experienced some difficulty when commissioners of Williamson County, Texas, voted to deny Apple a standard $750,000 tax abatement for its proposed $80 million facility because they did not approve of Apple's gay-friendly policies, specifically the equal benefits for unmarried couples. When Apple decided to build elsewhere, Williamson County relented, offering a different incentive package totaling nearly a million dollars (Mickens 1994).

International Rights for Same-Sex Couples

Employment Discrimination

Pursuant to an action of the European Union (Directive 2000/78/EC of 27 November 2000) that added sexual orientation as a prohibited ground of employment discrimination, all member states of the European Union are required to adopt laws, regulations, or administrative provisions to implement the directive by December 2003. A few

European countries (Denmark, Finland, France, Ireland, Slovenia, and Sweden) now have employment laws that prohibit discrimination on the ground of sexual orientation ("The International Lesbian and Gay Association" n.d.).

Right to Marry and Partnership Registries

Denmark and the Netherlands permit same-sex marriages with all the trappings, including adoption and divorce. Norway and Sweden permit same-sex couples to register their partnerships. Outside of Europe, Brazil, Australia, and New Zealand recognize some legal rights for same-sex partnerships ("The International Lesbian and Gay Association" n.d.).

Conclusion

The number of gay people in America often is debated because there have been no definitive studies. Recent surveys indicate it ranges from 2% to 6%. The Voter News Services said 4.2% of voters in 1998 identified themselves in exit polls as gay, lesbian, or bisexual.

An "unmarried partner" box was introduced by the U.S. Bureau of the Census in 1990 but is only now receiving a major push by some gay civil rights groups, which are putting ads in gay-oriented newspapers and magazines and sending e-mail urging gays and lesbians to check this category if they qualify. The National Gay and Lesbian Task Force also is talking to other gay groups about possibly pushing for a sexual orientation question on the 2010 census. Advocates say the government should collect information on gays because the census affects public policy and federal funding for research and community services. They say the data is important as lawmakers consider legislation on hate crimes and gay families.

The 1990 census showed that more than 145,000 households reported themselves as same-sex unmarried partners—81,000 male and 64,000 female. There were about 3 million opposite-sex unmarried-partner households. Gay civil rights groups say that these figures understate the number of same-sex couples living together because many might have marked "spouse" to describe their relationship (Ly 2000).

More employers are recognizing their interest in offering health insurance to same-sex couples since "you can't do a very good job if someone in your life can't get medical care" (BNA 1991). But employers that are considering offering benefits to domestic partners, especially if they are offering the entire array of employee benefits, may want to extend benefits only to couples that cannot legally marry. The marriage and divorce laws help untangle a lot of the legal mess and entitlements, such as rights to pension benefits of "divorced" domestic partners and their underage dependents. A solution to determining what benefits are really needed by domestic partners might be a "cafeteria plan," in which each employee is given a dollar amount and allowed to choose from a menu of possible benefits those that he or she prefers (Mickens 1994).

The real achievement of the rights of same-sex partners, including employment benefits, will come from increasing acceptance by heterosexual Americans. The creation of Pride At Work, a gay and lesbian constituency group within the AFL-CIO, is an important development. However, many heterosexual Americans are very uncomfortable with and disapproving of homosexuals. This is a difficult topic to discuss, even among groups who advocate for civil rights.

Discrimination on the basis of sexual orientation is a basic civil rights and human rights issue. Everyone who believes in equality and justice, homosexual and heterosexual alike, must speak up and help educate their fellow workers, their employers, and their fellow Americans.

Notes

[1] Judge Posner, Chief Judge on the U.S. Court of Appeals for the Seventh Circuit and often associated with the "Chicago school" of economics, presented an intriguing study of the moral, philosophical, political, economic, historical, and psychological issues involved in sexuality generally. His book (Posner 1992) covers copious research, and many of the sources cited are worth pursuing.

[2] *Hopkins v. Baltimore Gas & Electric Co.*, 77 F. 3d 745, 70 FEP Cases 184 (CA 4 1996); *Williamson v. A.G. Edwards and Sons, Inc.*, 876 F. 2d 69, 50 FEP Cases 95 (CA 8 1989), *cert. denied*, 493 U.S. 1089, 52 FEP Cases 96 (1990); *DeCinto v. Westchester County Medical Ctr.*, 807 F. 2d 304, 42 FEP Cases 921 (CA 2 1986), *cert. denied*, 494 U.S. 825, 44 FEP Cases 1672 (1987); *De Santis v. Pacific Tel. and Tel. Co., Inc.*, 608 F. 2d 327, 19 FEP Cases 1493 (CA 9 1979); *Smith v. Liberty Mutual Insurance Co.*, 569 F. 2d 325, 17 FEP Cases 28 (CA 5 1978).

[3] *Macauley v. Massachusetts Commission Against Discrimination*, 21 FEP Cases 927 (Mass. Sup. Jud. Ct. 1979). The court said that as a matter of literal meaning, however, discrimination against homosexuals could be treated as a species of discrimination because of sex. Distinctions based on pregnancy are distinctions based on sex and are "sex-linked." In a somewhat different sense, homosexuality is also sex-linked. However, the court did not think it was free to supply its own reading of the statutory language or its own view of what the policy should be. The uniform interpretation of statutes prohibiting discrimination in employment because of sex has limited the statutes to discrimination between men and women. Discrimination based on sexual orientation has been excluded. *Gay Law Students Assn. v. Pacific Telephone and Telegraph Co.* (19 FEP Cases 1419 [Calif. Sup. Ct. 1979]) found that the ban on sex

discrimination contained in the California Fair Employment Practice Act does not encompass homosexuals.

    [4] *Hopkins v. Baltimore Gas & Electric Co.*, 77 F. 3d 745, 70 FEP Cases 184 (CA 4 1996).

    [5] *Rudow v. New York City Comm'n On Human Rights*, 474 N.Y.S. 2d 1005, 41 FEP Cases 1402 (1984), aff'd, 109 A.D. 2d 1111, 487 N.Y.S. 2d 453 (1st Dep't 1985). Executive order prohibits employment discrimination by any city agency on account of sexual orientation or affectional preference.

    [6] *Romer v. Evans*, 517 U.S. 620, 70 FEP Cases 1180 (1996).

    [7] *Meritor Savings Bank v. Vinson*, 477 U.S. 57, 40 FEP Cases 1822 (1986), cited in *Tanner v. Prima Donna Resorts, Inc.*, 919 F. Supp. 351, 72 FEP Cases 432 (DC Nev. 1996) for the proposition that "Title VII protects all persons, whether male or female, heterosexual or homosexual, from discrimination based on sex"; *Swage v. Inn Philadelphia*, 72 FEP Cases 438 (DC E. Pa. 1996) cites *Pritchett v. Sizeler Real Estate Management Co., Inc.*, 67 FEP Cases 1377 (DC E. La. 1995), which found same-sex harassment actionable because making same-sex harassment never actionable would exempt homosexuals from the workplace laws that govern the conduct of heterosexuals.

    [8] *Baehr v. Lewin*, 74 Haw. 530, 852P. 2d 44 (1993).

References

Bureau of National Affairs. 1991. Recognizing Non-traditional Families. BNA Special Report Series on Work and Family. Washington, DC: Bureau of National Affairs.

Fair Employment Practice Manual. n.d. Washington, DC: Bureau of National Affairs.

Human Rights Campaign. n.d. "How to Achieve Domestic Partner Benefits in Your Workplace." <http://www.hrc.org/worknet/dp>. [March 2000].

"The International Lesbian and Gay Association World Legal Survey—Protection from Discrimination in Employment." n.d. <http://www.ilga.org/Information/legal_survey/Summary.../protection_from_discrimination_i.html>. [December 27, 2000].

Ly, Phuong. 2000. "Be Counted in Census, Groups Urge Gay Live-Ins." *Washington Post*, March 12, p. A14.

Mickens, Ed. 1994. *The 100 Best Companies for Gay Men and Lesbians*. New York: Pocket Books.

Mills, Kim I., and Daryl Herrschaft. 1999. *The State of the Workplace for Lesbian, Gay, Bisexual and Transgendered Americans*. Washington, DC: Human Rights Campaign.

Posner, Richard A. 1992. *Sex and Reason*. Cambridge, MA: Harvard University Press.

Pride At Work. 1999. "Domestic Partnership Benefits & Union Bargaining." <http://www.igc.org/prideatwork/domestic.html>. [March 2000].

"Religion and Sexual Orientation at Work May Produce Combustible Combination." 1999. *Labor Relations Reporter*, September 20, pp. 73–76.

Rosin, Hanna, and Pamela Ferdinand. 2000. "Gays Achieve Breakthrough in Vermont; Legislation Recognizes Same-Sex Civil Unions." *Washington Post*, March 17, p. A1.

Rosin, Hanna, and Richard Morin. 1998. "As Tolerance Grows, Acceptance Remains Elusive." *Washington Post*, December 26, p. A1.

Sanchez, Rene, and William Booth. 2000. "Conservative Mood Shows in Calif. Initiatives." *Washington Post*, March 9, pp. A11–A12.

Tolson, Jay. 2000. "No Wedding? No Ring? No Problem." *U.S. News and World Report*, March 13, p. 48.

ABOUT THE CONTRIBUTORS

Dean Baker is a macroeconomist and codirector of the Center for Economic and Policy Research in Washington, DC. He previously worked as a senior economist at the Economic Policy Institute and an assistant professor at Bucknell University. He received his Ph.D. in economics from the University of Michigan.

A partial list of Baker's publications includes *Social Security: The Phony Crisis* (University of Chicago Press, 1999), co-authored with Mark Weisbrot; "The Costs of the Stock Market Bubble"; "Diverting the Old-Age Crisis: International Projections of Income in the 21st Century"; "Ten Myths about Social Security" (*Atlantic Monthly*); and *Getting Prices Right: The Debate over the Consumer Price Index* (M.E. Sharpe, 1997).

Peter Diamond is an Institute Professor at the Massachusetts Institute of Technology, where he has taught economics since 1966. He received his Ph.D. in Economics from MIT in 1963. He has been president and chair of the Board of the National Academy of Social Insurance, president of the Econometric Society, and vice president of the American Economic Association. He has written widely on public finance, social insurance, and many other economic topics.

In the area of social security, Diamond has been a member of or consultant to numerous congressional and other expert and technical panels. From 1996 to 1998, he chaired the Panel on Privatization of Social Security of the National Academy of Social Insurance. The report of this panel is available from MIT Press.

Sheldon Friedman is a senior economist in the AFL-CIO Department of Public Policy and past president of the IRRA. He began his labor movement career in 1975 as research associate in the UAW Research Department and served as the UAW's research director from 1981 until 1991. He co-edited two previous books, *Restoring the Promise of American Labor Law* and *Organizing to Win*, both published by Cornell Press. He has written widely in the fields of labor economics and industrial relations.

Friedman serves on the Labor Research Advisory Council to the Bureau of Labor Statistics and the national board and economic policy committee of Americans for Democratic Action. He is a member of the Newspaper Guild/CWA and is co-editor of this 2001 IRRA research volume.

Teresa Ghilarducci is associate professor of economics at the University of Notre Dame, where she is the director of the Higgins Labor Research Center. Her books include *Labor's Capital: The Economics and Politics of Private Pensions* and *Portable Pension Plans for Casual Labor Markets: Lessons from the Operating Engineers Central Pension Fund* (with Garth Mangum, Jeff Petersen, and Peter Philips). She has written many articles on pensions, social security, and collective bargaining.

In 1997, the governor of Indiana appointed Ghilarducci to the Board of Trustees of the state's Public Employee Retirement Fund. President Clinton appointed her to the Advisory Board of the Pension Benefit Guaranty Corporation. She holds a Ph.D. in economics from Berkeley.

David C. Jacobs is associate professor of labor, business, and society at the Kogod School of Business at American University. He has served on the faculty at Kansas State University and the University of Michigan–Flint. He is the author of two books, *Collective Bargaining as an Instrument of Social Change* and *Business Lobbies and the Power Structure in America*, and of many articles in academic and professional journals. Jacobs is co-editor of this 2001 IRRA research volume and is writing a monograph on the impact of the Internet on the power of labor.

Helene J. Jorgensen is a labor economist with the Center for Economic and Policy Research and before that was with the AFL-CIO Public Policy Department. She has done research and writing in the areas of labor unions, low-wage workers, discrimination, and contingent work arrangements. In 1999, she authored a 2030 Center report, *When Good Jobs Go Bad*, examining young workers employed by temp agencies.

While at the AFL-CIO, Jorgensen chaired the BLS Labor Research Advisory Council subcommittee on compensation and working conditions. She also serves on the Decennial Advisory Committee to the U.S. Bureau of the Census.

Jorgensen holds a Ph.D. in economics from American University.

Robert E. McGarrah, Jr., is an attorney and, since 1998, a senior policy analyst for the AFL-CIO in Washington, DC, where he concentrates on contingent labor and election reform issues. He formed and directed the first union public policy department at AFSCME in 1982, where he led the efforts on national health insurance and tax reform. He regularly serves on the faculty of the American Law Institute–American Bar Association's health care law and litigation program. He received his J.D. from Villanova University in 1972 and his M.P.H. from Johns Hopkins University in 1999.

Edith Rasell of the Economic Policy Institute is both a physician and an economist. She has written widely on health care financing, social insurance programs, and other related topics. Her work has been published in the *American Economic Review* and the *New England Journal of Medicine*, among other journals. Currently, Rasell directs EPI's Economic Analysis and Research Network, a national association of state-level progressive think tanks. She holds a Ph.D. in economics from American University.

Valerie Rawlston is a research analyst at the National Urban League. She holds an M.S. in economics from the University of North Carolina, where she is completing a Ph.D. in economics.

The primary focus of Rawlston's work at the Urban League has been the implications of Social Security reform for African Americans. She has published two articles: "The Impact of Social Security on Child Poverty" in *The State of Black America 2000* and "Social Security Helps Reduce Child Poverty," co-authored with William Spriggs, in *The National Voter*.

Dallas L. Salisbury is president and CEO of the Employee Benefit Research Institute (EBRI) in Washington, DC. He joined EBRI at its founding in 1978.

Salisbury is a fellow of the National Academy of Human Resources, the recipient of the 1997 Award for Professional Excellence from the Society for Human Resource Management, and the 1998 Keystone Award of "World at Work." He has served on numerous advisory panels and commissions, including the Secretary of Labor's ERISA Advisory Council and the Presidential PBGC Advisory Committee. He has written extensively on economic security topics. His most recent books are *IRA and 401(k) Investing* and *Managing Money in Retirement*, both co-authored with Marc Robinson.

Prior to joining EBRI, Salisbury held positions with the Washington State Legislature, the U.S. Department of Justice, the Pension and Welfare Benefits Administration of the U.S. Department of Labor, and the Pension Benefit Guaranty Corporation. He holds an M.A. in public administration from the Maxwell School at Syracuse University.

Nancy J. Sedmak is managing editor of the Bureau of National Affairs' *Labor Relations Reporter*. She is a past president of the Washington, DC, IRRA chapter, a member of the American Bar Association's Labor and Employment Law Section, and a member of the International Society for Labor Law and Social Security. She is co-author of the fifth and sixth editions of the *Primer on Equal Employment Opportunity* and a contributor to *Labor Arbitration: A Practical Guide for Advocates*.

Sedmak holds a J.D. from Catholic University, an LL.M. in labor law from Georgetown University, and an LL.M. in European Union employment law from the University of Leicester in England.

William Spriggs is director of research and public policy of the National Urban League. He is past president of the National Economics Association and a member of the National Academy of Social Insurance. He edited the National Urban League's *State of Black America 1999*.

Spriggs joined the Urban League following a career in government service and academia, including stints with the Small Business Administration, where he served as senior advisor; the U.S. Department of Commerce, where he served as an economist and special advisor; and the Democratic staff of the Joint Economic Committee of the U.S. Congress, where he served as senior economist. He holds a doctorate in economics from the University of Wisconsin.

Christian E. Weller is a macroeconomist at the Economic Policy Institute (EPI). His research focuses on macroeconomics, financial economics, retirement security issues, and international finance. Before coming to EPI, he was a research fellow at the Center for European Integration Studies at the University of Bonn and worked in the AFL-CIO Public Policy Department. Weller holds a doctorate in economics from the University of Massachusetts.

IRRA Chapters

For contact information on a chapter in your area, visit the IRRA website at www.irra.uiuc.edu.

ALABAMA
Alabama
ALASKA
Alaska (Anchorage)
ARIZONA
Arizona (Phoenix/Tucson)
CALIFORNIA
Gold Rush (Oakland)
Inland Empire (Riverside)
Northern (Sacramento)
Orange County (Anaheim)
San Diego
San Francisco
Southern (Los Angeles)
COLORADO
Rocky Mountain
CONNECTICUT
Connecticut Valley (Hartford)
Southwestern
DISTRICT OF COLUMBIA
Washington, DC
FLORIDA
Central Florida (Tampa/St. Pete)
GEORGIA
Atlanta
HAWAII
Hawaii (Honolulu)
IDAHO
Idaho (Boise)
ILLINOIS
Central
Chicago
LIRA
INDIANA
Delaware County (Muncie)
IOWA
Iowa
MARYLAND
Maryland (Baltimore)
MASSACHUSETTS
Boston
MICHIGAN
Detroit
Mid-Michigan (Lansing)
Southwestern (Kalamazoo)
West (Grand Rapids)
MISSOURI
Gateway (St. Louis)
Greater Kansas City

NEVADA
Southern (Las Vegas)
NEW JERSEY
New Brunswick
NEW YORK
Central New York (Syracuse)
Hudson Valley New York
Long Island
New York Capitol (Albany)
New York City
Western (Buffalo)
OHIO
Central (Columbus)
Greater Cincinnati
Northeast Ohio (Cleveland)
OKLAHOMA
Greater Oklahoma
OREGON
Oregon
PENNSYLVANIA
Central (Harrisburg)
Northeast (Bethlehem)
Northwest (Erie)
Philadelphia
Western (Pittsburgh)
RHODE ISLAND
Greater Rhode Island
SOUTH/NORTH CAROLINA
South Atlantic
TENNESSEE
TERRA
TEXAS
Alamo (San Antonio)
Greater Houston
North (Dallas)
WASHINGTON
Inland Empire (Spokane)
Northwest (Seattle)
WEST VIRGINIA
West Virginia (Morgantown)
WISCONSIN
Wisconsin (Milwaukee)
CANADA
British Columbia (Vancouver)
Hamilton District (Ontario)
FRANCE
Paris

IRRA Organizational Memberships

The IRRA provides a unique forum where representatives of all stake-holders in the employment relationship and their views are welcome.

We invite your organization to become a member of our prestigious, vibrant association. The Industrial Relations Research Association (IRRA) is the professional membership association and learned society of persons interested in the field of industrial relations. Formed more than fifty years ago, the IRRA brings together representatives of labor, management, government, academics, advocates, and neutrals to share ideas and learn about new developments, issues, and practices in the field. Members share their knowledge and insights through IRRA publications, meetings, and IRRA ListServs. In addition, the IRRA provides a network of 60 plus chapters where professionals meet locally to discuss issues and share information.

The purpose of the IRRA is to encourage research and to foster discussion of issues affecting today's workplace and workers. To that end, the IRRA publishes an array of information, including research papers and commentary presented at Association meetings; the acclaimed practitioner-oriented magazine, *Perspectives on Work*; a membership directory; quarterly newsletters; and an annual research volume. Recent research volumes include *The Future of the Safety Net: Social Insurance and Employee Benefits*, Sheldon Friedman and David Jacobs, editors; *Nonstandard Work: The Nature and Challenges of Changing Employment Arrangements*, Françoise Carré, Marianne A. Ferber, Lonnie Golden, and Stephen A. Herzenberg, editors; and *Employment Dispute Resolution and Worker Rights*, Adrienne E. Eaton and Jeffrey Keefe, editors. Other member publications and services include online IR/HR degree programs listings, an online member directory, job announcements, calls and announcements, competitions and awards for students and practicing professionals, and much more.

IRRA is a non-profit, 501(c)(3) organization governed by an elected Executive Board comprised of representatives of the various constituencies within the Association.

Organizational memberships are available on an annual or sustaining basis and include individual memberships for organization designees, a wealth of IRRA research and information, and numerous professional opportunities. Organizational members receive all IRRA publications and services. Your support and participation will help the Association continue its vital mission of shaping the workplace of the future. For more information, contact the IRRA National Office, 504 East Armory Ave., Room 121, Champaign, IL 61820.

IRRA Organizational Members 2001

Thanks for a great year!

Sustaining Members (one-time contribution of $5,000 to $10,000)

- Ford Motor Company
- AFL-CIO
- UAW-Ford National Education, Training and Development Center
- National Association of Manufacturers
- The Alliance for Growth and Development
- United Steelworkers of America
- Boeing Quality Through Training Program
- National Education Association

Annual Members – 2001*

- Communication Workers of America
- George Meany Center for Labor Studies
- Labor Education Institute
- Las Vegas Metro Police Department
- Lucent Technologies
- Massachusetts Institute of Technology
- Michigan State University
- New York Nurses Association
- Pennsylvania State University
- Rollins College
- School of Management and Industrial Relations, Rutgers University
- Society for Human Resource Management
- Texas A & M University
- Institute of Labor & Industrial Relations, University of Illinois at Urbana-Champaign
- Higgins Labor Research Center, University of Notre Dame
- Centre for Industrial Relations, University of Toronto
- Industrial Relations Program, Wayne State University

2001 Annual organizational memberships are available at the following levels:

Annual Benefactor, $5,000 or more — 6 employee members
Annual Supporter, $1,001 to $4,999 — 4 employee members
Annual Organizational, $1,000 — 4 employee members
Annual University, $500-$1,000—2-4 employee members
Annual Small Educational or Non-Profit Institution, $250—2 employee members

Stay On Top of Events with

IRRA ONLINE

www.irra.uiuc.edu

Calls and Announcements
- *Award nominations*
- *Calls for papers*
- *Calls for session proposals*
- *Meetings and seminars*
- *Book proposals*

Jobs & Resumés
- *Current job listings*
- *Free resumé postings*

Quarterly Online Newsletter

IRRA Who's Who – Contact Information
- *Executive Board and Officers*
- *Committees*
- *Interest section convenors*
- *National office staff*

Join IRRA Online

IRRA Events Calendar

IRRA Chapters
- *Chapter profiles*
- *Chapter contacts*
- *Chapter meeting announcements*
- *Chapter awards*
- *Join a chapter*

IRRA Meetings
- *Register online*
- *Badge and packet pickup*
- *Hotel information*
- *Program*
- *Meetings and special events*

IRRA Publications
- *Index for IRRA articles 1992-2001*
- *Index for IRRA authors 1992-2001*
- *IRRA Research Volumes*
- *Perspectives on Work*
- *IRRA Annual Proceedings*
- *IRRA Newsletter Archives*
- *IR/HR Current Degree Program Listings*
- *Instructions to authors*
- *Advertising information*

Subscribe to IRRA ListServs
- *IRRA ListServ*
- *Collective Bargaining Network ListServ*
- *Human Resources Network List-Serv*

Internet Links

COMING IN 2002

- *The IRRA Online Membership Directory–instant access to active members and indexes from the IRRA website. Get the latest member information online only from the IRRA website.*
- *Update your member listing including address and affiliation changes online*
- *More electronic publications from the IRRA*